Music in the Westward Expansion

Music in the Westward Expansion

*Songs of Heart and Place
on the American Frontier*

LAURA DEAN

McFarland & Company, Inc., Publishers
Jefferson, North Carolina

Library of Congress Cataloguing-in-Publication Data

Names: Dean, Laura, 1969– author.
Title: Music in the westward expansion : songs of heart
and place on the American frontier / Laura Dean.
Description: Jefferson, North Carolina : McFarland & Company, Inc., Publishers, 2022.
| Includes bibliographical references and index.
Identifiers: LCCN 2022019727 | ISBN 9781476685229 (paperback : acid free paper) ∞
ISBN 9781476645209 (ebook)
Subjects: LCSH: Music—West (U.S.)—19th century—History
and criticism. | Music—Social aspects—West (U.S.)—History—19th
century. | Pioneers—West (U.S.)—Social life and customs—19th century.
| Oregon National Historic Trail—History—19th century. | BISAC: MUSIC /
History & Criticism | HISTORY / United States / 19th Century
Classification: LCC ML3551.4 .D43 2022 | DDC 780.978/09034—dc23/eng/20220510
LC record available at https://lccn.loc.gov/2022019727

British Library cataloguing data are available

ISBN (print) 978-1-4766-8522-9
ISBN (ebook) 978-1-4766-4520-9

Front cover: Musicians from the Fort Shaw Indian School,
circa 1905 (Montana Historical Society Research Center)

Printed in the United States of America

*McFarland & Company, Inc., Publishers
Box 611, Jefferson, North Carolina 28640
www.mcfarlandpub.com*

Dedicated to my parents, Gail and Richard Dean,
who encouraged my musical journey

Table of Contents

Acknowledgments

Thank you, Gail Dean, my mom, for providing years of lessons and musical experiences and for encouraging a life in music. Thanks, brother Scott Dean, for your love and encouragement. Thank you, sister Rona Williams, for reaching out and for your understanding. Dear Ruby Brown, my daughter, thank you for your love, laughter, and your beautiful violin music. I'd also like to acknowledge my dad and guardian angel, Richard Dean. I miss him every day.

Thank you, Joe Sweeney, my partner in life, for your unwavering support throughout this project. I could not have done this without your enduring patience as you edited the early drafts of the manuscript. Thank you for your love, your insight (and your red pen).

Thank you, Jill Timmons, my dear friend and mentor (Artsmentor, LLC), for seeing the potential in this project, for working with me in the early stages, and for giving me the courage, not to mention the (not so gentle) push to write the book. Thank you to my editor David Alff and to the staff at McFarland for your guidance and assistance with turning the manuscript into a book.

Thank you, Jay Old Mouse, the Northern Cheyenne flute master, for sharing the history of the Northern Cheyenne courtship flute, for your craftsmanship, your music, your infectious humor, and your heart. Rest in peace, my dear music friend. Thank you, Amy Old Mouse, for your hospitality and your friendship.

Thank you, Susan Gibson, for sharing your song-writing story. Thank you, Al Wiseman, for sharing your memories and knowledge of the Métis fiddle tradition. Thank you, Eric Houghton, for sharing your story of *Pioneer Songs*. Thank you, Michael Haynes, for your beautiful artwork. Thank you, Jeremy Agnew, for your photo contributions. Thank you, Ken Robison at the Fort Benton Museum for the research gems. Thank you, Daniel Slosberg, for your input regarding the music of Pierre Cruzatte.

Thank you to the individuals who helped with research and photographs at the Smithsonian Institution, Frick Digital Collections, *True West* Magazine, Brother Van House Museum, National Historic Oregon Trail Interpretive Center, Butte-Silver Bow Public Archives, Butte-Silver Bow Public Library, Idaho State Archives, Library of Congress, Kansas State Historical Society, Montana Historical Society, Oregon Historical Society, History Nebraska, Brigham Young University, Washington State Historical Society, Fort Walla Walla Museum, Whitman College, Wichita State Special Collections, National Portrait Gallery, New York Public Library, New York Metropolitan Museum of Art, and Wyoming State Archives.

Finally, thank you to my dear friends Michelle Josserand and Karrie Crabtree for your longtime friendship and encouragement. Thank you to my earliest music teachers,

Dorothy Allen, Lloyd Reynolds, Jeanette McCormick and also to Tom Mollgaard for an outstanding hands-on music and arts education. Thank you to the wonderful community of Choteau, Montana, my hometown, for providing a nurturing musical atmosphere. Thank you to the C.M. Russell Museum in Great Falls, Montana, for sponsoring a series of "Heart and Place" concert presentations in the Great Falls Public Schools and at the C.M. Russell Museum in 2017. Thank you to my Seattle community of friends, swimming buddies, neighbors, colleagues, and music students who have been following this project from the premier "Heart and Place" concert in 2017.

Preface

*Mr. and Mrs. May—a newly married couple that came into our train
at the junction of the roads—are both musicians: several of our young
men have fine voices, and with Lyde's guitar, and Mr. May's violin we
had an enjoyable musicale away out here in the wilderness.*
—Sarah Raymond Herndon (1865)

On a sunny April morning in 1981, my dad drove me from our house down on Airport Road to the Choteau High School parking lot where I would catch the bus for a multi-school concert band festival which would be held in Conrad, a neighboring community. (Both Conrad and Choteau are rural communities located along the eastern side of the Montana Rocky Mountain Front, wide-open country where the plains dramatically meet the mountains.) Our middle school band had been preparing for months. I loved playing my French horn, and I couldn't wait to get to the festival. When my dad pulled into the parking lot of the school, my friends were waiting on the sidewalk alongside a collection of music stands and instruments. Excited to get on with the day of music, I leaned over, kissed my dad on the cheek, hopped down from the seat of his vintage turquoise Ford pickup and slammed the door shut—the only way to close the door of an old Ford. As my dad slowly pulled away, he casually waved goodbye out of his open window.

That was the last time I saw my dad. While I was in Conrad playing my French horn in the evening concert, he died in a head-on collision on the Augusta Highway, just a few miles outside of Choteau. In my mind's eye, my dad is forever young—32 years old, handsome, and oh, so wonderful, my hero. His sudden death was the worst event of my life and in the life of my family—profoundly tragic. Our small community of Choteau was stunned and deeply saddened. My dad was the football coach, a beloved teacher, husband, and father. School was closed on the day of his memorial service. Students, community members, family, and friends gathered in the auditorium to celebrate his life and to collectively mourn.

How do you go on from such a staggering loss? We were down to three: my mom, my eight-year-old brother, and 12-year-old me. There is nothing to do but to go on with the business of life, one day at a time. My mother single-handedly raised me and my brother while working full time. Knowing how important music is to my heart and soul, she provided access to private piano and vocal lessons and music summer camps, and she arranged for us to attend every performing arts event that came through town. I found refuge in music: listening to music, attending musical events, singing, playing my French horn, playing the piano, and acting in school musicals. Music became my therapy and solace in the face of tragedy. I was working on the first movement of Beethoven's

1

Moonlight Sonata around the time of my dad's accident, which, at the time, expressed the complex emotions I was feeling—anger, sadness, and grief. Music provided comfort in my time of need, just as many of the emigrants in the 1800s found comfort in music in the throes of their physically and emotionally difficult journeys westward. Many of them suffered the loss of family and friends along the way.

Music in the Westward Expansion offers a view of the Oregon Trail through the lens of music, highlights the power of music in difficult times, and encourages the reader to add enriching, meaningful, and healing musical experiences into their personal lives. Most Americans have heard of the Lewis and Clark Expedition, the Oregon Trail, and the Westward Expansion, but few people are aware that an integral component of this movement was music. This book explores a variety of music traditions of the American West during the nineteenth century such as Northern Cheyenne courtship flutes, fiddle music of the Lewis and Clark Expedition, French tunes, dancing fur trappers, hymn-singing missionaries, piano-playing nuns, girls with guitars, wagon-driving balladeers, cowboy crooners, opulent theaters, musical instrument showrooms, Chinese *suona* players, singing farmers, opera enthusiasts, musical miners, and preaching songsters.

Hasn't the story of the Westward Expansion been told enough? This is not the same old story told over again. On the contrary, this is a new take on an old story, and it drills down deeply into the personal experiences of our ancestors, highlighting again and again how music sustained them, inspired them, provided joy, created solace, and in some cases eased diplomatic tensions between disparate groups.

Music in the Westward Expansion represents a model, an archetypal story that offers us a candle in the darkness, a way of creating shared experiences in challenging times. The musical story within the Westward Expansion story offers songs and stories of humanity celebrating diverse cultures, courage, and survival. Above all, this is a rich American story. Whether you are an educator, student, history enthusiast, arts advocate, musician, music therapist, or a curious reader looking for an enlightening story, this book is for you.

The genesis for this book lies in my 25 years as a professional musician and music teacher based in the Pacific Northwest, in addition to my deep personal ties to the region. My familial roots are firmly grounded in Montana, and much of my earliest musical experiences in Choteau, Montana, a rural community of 1,800 people, parallel those of early frontier communities. As a touring artist and educator, I have traveled to many urban and rural settings in the West and experienced firsthand the uplifting role of music. With both a personal connection to the West and a visceral passion for the subject, I initially created *Music of the Westward Expansion: Songs of Heart and Place on the American Frontier* as a solo concert program for Washington, Oregon, and Montana audiences. My early research ignited a desire to learn more about the musical history of the early West and compelled me to write the book, *Music in the Westward Expansion*, in order to share that story with a wider audience.

The narrative highlights musical activities on the Oregon Trail and explores other selected subjects within the rich musical history of the Old West. For example, I've included stories of early explorers in Santa Fe, New Mexico, and also stories of cowboys on the network of cattle trails that originated in Texas. I've narrowed my focus to a select number of topics with the intention of shining a light on how music was an integral part of the Westward Expansion, including what music did for people and what music expressed. This book is not meant to be comprehensive. There are many important and iconic topics which may have underlying music stories but are beyond the scope of this book. Some topics not covered in this book include the Santa Fe Trail, the California Gold Rush, military outposts, the Trail of Tears, the Spanish–American War, the Mormon migration and settlement, and the plight of hundreds of Native American tribes who were displaced from their native lands.

The research for this book included visits to important historical sites and museums in New Mexico, Washington, Idaho, Oregon, and Montana. I also tracked down primary sources, often with the help of archival researchers, in Wyoming, Kansas, Nebraska, Idaho, Utah, and the Library of Congress in Washington, D.C. These primary sources included personal journals, newspaper articles, conversations with experts in various western communities, museum collections, publicly and personally held artifacts, letters, newspaper articles, paintings, photographs, and wax cylinder recordings.

Inspiration for the narrative builds on the research of brilliant writers, scholars, and artists such as Ken Burns, director of the PBS documentary, *The West*, an epic historical account of the entire Westward Expansion. Another important piece of research in the story of the Westward Expansion remains Stephen Ambrose's book, *Undaunted Courage*, which explores the Lewis and Clark Expedition in play-by-play detail. Music is mentioned in both *The West* and *Undaunted Courage* but not as a central theme.

For example, in *Undaunted Courage*, Ambrose points to a journal quote from Meriwether Lewis written on April 28, 1806, about an encounter with the Walla Wallas: "Cruzatte brought out the fiddle and for an hour the men danced, to the delight of the Indians. Then the Indians, some 550 men, women, and children, sung and danced to it."[1]

Another book with an overlapping theme to mine includes *Entertainment in the Old West: Theatre, Music, Circuses, Medicine Shows, Prizefighting, and Other Popular Amusements* by Jeremy Agnew (McFarland, 2011) which highlights a variety of frontier amusements including gambling, gunfights, and brothels. Music is mentioned as one form of entertainment but is not central to the narrative.

Songs and Dances of the Oregon Trail and Early Pioneer Communities by Phillip and Vivian Williams (Voyager Recordings and Publications, 2012) also provided inspiration for my writing. This music book is packed with 60 lead sheets (melodies, lyrics, and chords) along with informative sidebars featuring pioneer journal quotes, games, skits, and historical facts about the Oregon Trail.

I also found inspiration in the book, *Waking the Spirit: A Musician's Journey Healing Body, Mind, and Soul*, by Andrew Schulman (Picador, 2016), an autobiography written by a musician who nearly died from post-surgery complications in 2009. The author credits music—in particular, a recording of Bach's *St. Mathew's Passion*—for saving his life. This life-changing event inspired the author to become a medical musician in a New York City ICU where he plays guitar for critically ill patients. Schulman describes the power of music to soothe patients who feel pain, loneliness, and exhaustion—much like the way music soothed weary pioneers on the Oregon Trail and in their new communities in the West.

Popular culture also provided inspiration for this project. In the after-dinner scene in the Academy Award-winning film *Legends of the Fall*, the youngest Ludlow brother, Samuel, sings a gentle English style ballad, "Twilight and Mist," while his fiancé, Isabel, an educated and cultured woman fresh off the train from the east coast, accompanies him on the Ludlow family piano. His two brothers and their father look on, mesmerized by this poignant musical moment of beauty and tranquility in the wilds of untamed Montana. Though a fictitious story, the *Legends of the Fall* narrative rings true with themes from real life in the West, among them separation from loved ones, death, isolation and cross-cultural tensions.

In 2018, I taught a nineteenth-century Kentucky fiddle tune, "Old Dan Tucker," to a group of Seattle fifth graders. The students could not get enough of skipping around in a circle, swinging their partners, clapping their hands, and singing the humorous lyrics. "Again!" they shouted. "Again!" At the end of the week, when we performed the song for their parents, the audience erupted in applause. "Old Dan Tucker," one of hundreds of folk songs that pioneers carried in their hearts along the Oregon Trail over 150 years ago, and the joy it brings, remains relevant in the twenty-first century.

> Old Dan Tucker was a fine old man
> Washed his face with a fryin' pan
> Combed his hair with a wagon wheel
> And died with a toothache in his heel
>
> So, git outa de way for old Dan Tucker,
> He's come too late to git his supper.
> Supper's over and breakfast cookin',
> Old Dan Tucker standin' lookin'

At every turn, music, dancing, songs, stories, instruments, musicians, and enthusiastic audiences permeate stories of the Westward Expansion. What's more, these stories illuminate the ethnic diversity within the American West. *Music in the Westward Expansion* speaks to the musical legacy of Native Americans, early explorers, cowboys, and pioneers whose stories provide inspirational examples of ways we can sustain ourselves in current times with musical activities. My hope is you, dear reader, will be equally entertained and educated about the music, the instruments, and music's role within the story of the American Westward Expansion. In addition, I hope that you will draw parallels from the nineteenth-century American West to today and the vital importance of music in our twenty-first-century world.

The simple yet profound acts of singing and dancing together, playing instruments, attending musical events, and supporting the arts celebrate the best of humanity, lift us up, and add artistic beauty to our daily lives. Then and now, through music, WE CAN create beauty, experience joy, celebrate humanity, rise above our differences and find common ground in what connects us.

Introduction

Our long journey thus began in sunshine and song.
—Peter H. Burnett, May 22, 1843, from *Recollections
and Opinions of an Old Pioneer*

Most Americans have heard of the Lewis and Clark Expedition, the Oregon Trail, and the Westward Expansion, but few people are aware that music was an integral component of this movement. *Music in the Westward Expansion* views the Oregon Trail and early frontier communities through the lens of music, highlights the power of music in difficult times, and inspires the reader to add simple yet meaningful musical experiences into their own lives.

At the core of the Westward Expansion lies some 400,000 people who uprooted their lives in pursuit of the dream for a better life in the American West. Taking only the bare essentials that would fit into a simple wagon, the pioneers made room for musical instruments right alongside their guns, ammunition, food, and tools. Lured by promises of healthy living, economic prosperity and free land, people readily left behind their homes and loved ones for "the promised land." Emigrants rolled across the Great Plains, forded treacherous rivers, and scrambled over the Rockies in the face of countless hardships. For those early pioneers, music often provided the only spark of light and happiness during what seemed like an endless dusty journey filled with the risk of drowning, disease, and starvation.

Music lies at the **HEART** of this iconic American story and played a central role in sustaining those emigrants on their long journeys. And, regardless of **PLACE,** music remained a connective force among people. On the trail, each group carried both well-established and newly formed musical traditions that would later become an integral part of early frontier communities. That music, as we know from firsthand accounts, played on fiddles, guitars, harmonicas, and other portable instruments, included the sweet melodies of Stephen Foster, art songs, fiddle tunes, folk songs, romantic ballads, and thrilling brass-band marches. Each group wove their own thread of music into the colorful and diverse musical tapestry of the American West.

Throughout their journeys west, travelers drew strength from music as they faced extraordinary physical and mental challenges. Music provided inspiration, entertainment, a sense of community, distraction, worship, healing, and a creative outlet. With music, people celebrated special occasions, remembered home, eased their struggles, and elevated their daily routines. Where words failed, music often offered a gesture of peace and goodwill between diverse cultures. As people settled into early frontier communities, they wasted no time in organizing community dances, community bands, and concerts performed by traveling and local artists. These events provided artistic beauty, buoyed spirits, built community, and provided people with a sense of the life they had left behind.

In a letter to his mother, Mark Twain wrote: "My Dear Mother, the country is fabulously rich in gold, silver, copper, lead, coal, iron, quicksilver, thieves, murderers, desperadoes, lawyers, Christians, Indians, Chinamen, Spaniards, gamblers, Sharpers, coyotes, poets, preachers, and jackass rabbits."[1] In this book, you'll also find that the West included the Northern Cheyenne courtship flute, a "medicine song" exchange between Shoshone Indians and the Lewis and Clark Expedition, a farewell hymn sung by a young missionary (and the first white woman to travel West), a husband and wife duo entertaining fellow travelers with guitar and vocal selections along the Oregon Trail, a cowboy who sang to cattle on his evening rounds, a brass band comprised of gritty miners from Butte, Montana, and a Native American woman who wrote and starred in an opera. Far from a cultural outpost, the West proved a creative incubator for musical expression both on the trail and at trails end. Following is a breakdown of what you will find in each chapter:

"Northern Cheyenne Love Songs" begins with the story of Jay Old Mouse, the designated flute builder for the Northern Cheyenne Indians, and includes an in-depth look at the Northern Cheyenne courtship flute: the legends, the music, and how the instruments are built. This chapter also explores the role of songs within Cheyenne culture.

"The Genesis: The Lewis and Clark Expedition (1804–1806)" explores the many roles music played on the Lewis and Clark Expedition and brims with multiple musical encounters pulled directly from the Lewis and Clark journals. This chapter includes examples of fiddling and dancing by the campfire, music used for celebrations, a Sioux tribe "scalp dance" and a poignant exchange of "medicine songs" between the Corps of Discovery and the Shoshone tribe.

"Trailblazers: Explorers, Mountain Men, and Missionaries" showcases the music and the legacy of the fur trappers, explorers, and missionaries of the early nineteenth century who, collectively, laid down the trail for hundreds of thousands of pioneers who followed in their wagon tracks. This chapter describes the foot-stomping fiddle music at the annual mountain man rendezvous, songs of adventure and discovery from the explorers, and heartfelt hymns of the missionaries.

"Setting the Stage for the Oregon Trail" paints a picture of the mid–nineteenth-century musical life on the east coast, a time when nearly every middle-class family owned some type of instrument, be it a piano, guitar, harp, or violin. Leisure time was often spent making music at home, attending concerts, or going out to the theater. This chapter also explains the struggles of life in the East and the many motivations which propelled the pioneers to embark on the 2,000-mile overland journey to "the promised land."

"Life on the Oregon Trail" describes the three waves of Western migration (1841–1867) when more than 400,000 people rolled west, at first with simple farm wagons, then larger Conestoga wagons, and finally by paddleboat, stagecoaches, and steam engines. The chapter describes the people on the trail, their backgrounds, and what they left behind. Descriptive narratives from handwritten pioneer journals and memoirs lay bare the hardships, risks, and heartaches of life on the trail, which sets the scene for *why* music mattered both on the trail and at trail's end.

"The Music at the Heart of the Oregon Trail Experience" brings to light the story of music on the trail, music being the heart of the experience as well as the thread that bound people together. Selected writings from pioneers describe the songs, dances, musicians, and the instruments of the trail and explain *how* music eased struggles, offered beauty, added comfort, provided solace, and created a link to the world they left behind. The pioneers carried only the clothes on their back and the bare necessities in their wagon, yet many of them experienced a rich musical life in the wilderness.

"We're There! Music on the Homestead and in Early Frontier Communities" shows the tenacity, cultural standards, and urgency the settlers exhibited as they created thriving musical lives in their new frontier communities—their place. This chapter brings to light the many ways pioneers—men, women, and children—incorporated music into their weekly routines, including in church, at barn dances, with music lessons, at community meetings, and in one-room schoolhouses.

"Whoopie Ti Yi Yo: Music and the Real Cowboys in the Old West" explores the important role music played in the daily lives of the cowboys who drove cattle from Texas to points north. This chapter showcases songs and stories that reflect the diversity of the cowboy trail and includes a variety of enduring songs that tell the story of the cowboy era.

"Music in the Settled West: Three Distinct Frontier Communities in 1890" provides a close-up look at the varied musical lives of three distinct frontier communities in the year 1890: Walla Walla, Washington; Portland, Oregon; and Butte, Montana. This chapter explores the population, industry, demographics, musical events, concert venues, music education offerings, and musicians in each of the three communities.

"Western Inspiration: Scholars, Composers, and Musicians" contains an eclectic sample of late nineteenth- and early twentieth-century composers who drew inspiration from the myth and reality of the American West. For example, composers known as "Indianists," including Charles Wakefield Cadman and Arthur Farwell, composed concert music for solo piano and orchestra based on Native American melodies. This chapter also highlights Native American musicians such as Zitkála-Šá (Red Bird) who helped write *The Sundance Opera*.

"The Epilogue" retraces the thread of music from pre–nineteenth-century Native Americans to the present day and reiterates that the inspirational narrative delivered story after story of creativity, community bonding, artistic beauty, solace, and powerful human connections. Drawing parallels to today, the epilogue, with examples from the author's personal experience as a music educator and touring artist, highlights modern-day stories of the power of music to add joy and beauty to daily life. Finally, the epilogue offers a call to action which challenges the reader to seek out meaningful musical experiences in their own life.

"The Appendices" include a representative song list for each chapter, a suggested recordings list, a small collection of lead sheets, and finally, accessible ideas for adding a variety of musical experiences into twenty-first century lives. From joining a ukulele group to playing handbells in church, from hosting a sing-along in the home to attending a local high school band concert, this section offers a long list of experiential musical ideas which appeal to a wide variety of budgets, tastes, and audiences.

This Book Is for

- HISTORY BUFFS interested in an unexplored angle of the Westward Expansion.
- K-12 EDUCATORS searching for a dynamic resource for teaching about the

Westward Expansion. Music, dance, and personal stories serve as enticing entry points into history.

- MUSIC EDUCATORS and MUSICIANS interested in exploring the music and dances of the Westward Expansion. The book serves as inspiration for creating performance programs centered around the Oregon Trail and the American West, as well as underserved composers and works.
- MUSIC THERAPISTS looking for stories that highlight the healing powers of music.
- MUSIC ENTHUSIASTS and ARTS ADVOCATES seeking inspirational stories that shine a light on the multiple benefits of musical activities.
- CURIOUS READERS interested in an intriguing American story who may also find inspiration and ideas for adding rich musical experiences into their own lives.

Music in the Westward Expansion offers an opportunity to take a new look at an old story and drill down deeply into the personal experiences of our forefathers and foremothers, discovering again and again how music sustained them, inspired them, provided joy, and in some cases eased diplomatic tensions between disparate groups. I invite you now to join me on this musical journey.

1

Northern Cheyenne
Love Songs

You must play from the heart, from what's inside.
—Jay Old Mouse

The Northern Cheyenne courtship flute is alive and well and an important part of the Cheyenne people's history, according to Jay Old Mouse, the designated flute maker for the Northern Cheyenne Indians. Jay traces his legacy of flute musicianship and craftsmanship back to the late 1800s. In the old days, the flute was an instrument of love, a kind of Cupid's arrow that was played by young men hoping to woo the woman of their dreams into marriage by impressing her with the magical music of the flute.

While searching for Native American musicians of the West, I stumbled upon an online article featuring Jay Old Mouse and his induction into Montana's Circle of American Masters, an esteemed honor for artists and craftsmen of the Big Sky state.[1] I dug a little deeper on the Web and found some videos of Jay giving Cheyenne flute presentations to groups of elementary school children. I watched a video about Jay titled, "How Cheyenne Men Wooed Their Soulmates with the Courtship Flute."[2] Enthralled with Jay's beautiful playing and the legend of the flute, I knew I had to meet him. Several months and many phone calls later, my husband and I flew from Seattle to Billings, stayed in a hotel and got up early the next morning for the 90-mile drive in our rental car to Jay's home on the Northern Cheyenne Indian Reservation on the outskirts of Busby, Montana, which is located in the southeastern part of Montana. Learning about the rich Cheyenne flute tradition felt like stepping back in time to another world, an older world. Jay says we met through "the moccasin telegram," which is his way of saying our meeting was meant to be.

Jay's flute story is a story within the larger story of the Northern Cheyenne people. Before relocating to the southeastern part of Montana, the Cheyenne originally lived in the area of present-day Minnesota, but they gradually moved west of the Missouri beginning in the early 1800s. As a group, they settled on the high plains where they acquired horses, traded with neighboring tribes, lived in tipis, and hunted buffalo and other game. The Cheyenne maintained a rich cultural life including warrior societies, seasonal traditions, religious ceremonies, storytelling, music and dance. Early in the nineteenth century, the Cheyenne split into two groups—the Northern Cheyenne, who live in Montana, and the Southern Cheyenne, who live in Oklahoma.

The history of the United States government taking over the lands of the Cheyenne, as well as all Native American tribes, is an unforgivable and ugly chapter in the history of the United States. In the Westward Expansion, businessmen grew rich and the United States government grew powerful through the exploitation of the land and natural resources of the West, stopping at nothing in the name of greed, economic gain and political power—even though that land and those resources were never theirs for the taking. Native Americans suffered unimaginable loss as promises and treaties were made and broken. Many native people lost their lives in senseless massacres and embittered battles. Others were brutally treated and captured as prisoners of war, separated from families, displaced from their native lands, and forced onto reservations. The plight and struggle of many Native Americans continue to this day across America. This part of United States history remains a chapter we can never and should never forget. A discussion of this complex subject is beyond my knowledge and beyond the scope of this book. However, I do wish to honor the first musicians of the West by sharing the story of an authentic style of Native American music as told by an authority on the subject.

The morning I met Jay Old Mouse was on a warm August day under a sparkling sun and a big, blue Montana sky. The scene illustrated why Montana is referred to as "Big Sky Country." Western meadowlarks were singing from the fields, and the smell of sweet grass floated on the gentle breeze—a quintessential Montana summer day. Jay and his wife, Amy, were waiting for us when we pulled up the drive to their house, which is located on the outskirts of Busby, Montana. Their home sits at the end of a long driveway off of highway 212, surrounded by grasslands and gently rolling hills. We greeted one another with hugs—like long-lost friends. We went inside, and Jay said, "Welcome to my Indian home. I'm going to call you the music lady."

Jay invited us to sit at his kitchen table where he unpacked a weathered trunk full of vintage photographs. He unrolled beaded leather pouches housing his collection of flutes, some of them dating back to the early 1900s. He picked up one of the flutes, placed his fingers over the sound holes and played slow-moving melodies, quick bird-like-sounding improvisations, and a familiar tune—"Amazing Grace." He says his fingers don't move like they used to, yet he played trills and quick passages effortlessly. Some of his songs were slow with resonant, sustained lower notes connected in long phrases that carry across a big room—or across the prairie. Other tunes gave the impression of a bird leaping from branch to branch with trills, ornaments and quick accented notes. Jay claims the secret ingredient in his playing is that his music flows straight from his heart.

Jay traces his flute lineage back three generations, starting with John Turkey Legs, referred to as Turkey Legs, who lived near Fort Keough (Miles City, Montana) in the late 1800s. Turkey Legs passed the tradition to Grover Wolf Voice, who then passed it to Jay's maternal grandfather, Douglas Glenmore, also known as Black Bear. Black Bear passed the tradition to Jay Old Mouse. Jay's Cheyenne name is Pėhévena'hāne (Good Killer). Jay says that it is important, to this day, that Cheyenne children have a traditional name and that the child should use that name for their entire life when they pray, so the creator will hear their prayers.

Turkey Legs is the oldest known link in Jay's flute lineage. A photo in Jay's collection features Turkey Legs standing near Fort Keogh with a flute in his hand circa 1890. An ethnomusicologist and composer, Thurlow Lieurance, recorded Turkey Legs on the Northern Cheyenne reservation near Lame Deer, Montana, in 1912. That wax cylinder recording is preserved in the Library of Congress. An original flute from Turkey Legs was given to Thurlow Lieurance and is on display in the Thurlow Lieurance music library at Wichita State University.

Incidentally, Thurlow Lieurance composed a solo piano piece titled, "Indian Flute

Call and Love Song," loosely based on the original flute recording played by John Turkey Legs. The piece, like many pieces in the "Indianist" style of composing (which will be discussed in Chapter 10), has some elements of the original recording, such as sustained notes, accents, trills, and warbles or tremolos, but sounds more like early twentieth-century art music than the traditional music of the Northern Cheyenne flute.

Turkey Legs passed the flute tradition to Grover Wolf Voice. In the 1970s, writer, musician, and photographer, Jerry Mader, met and spent time with Grover Wolf at Grover's home in Lame Deer, Montana. Grover was in his 80s at the time when the two met. According to Jerry, Grover Wolf Voice was an imposing figure, standing 6 feet, 5 inches tall with large hands, a gentle handshake, a quick wit, and a captivating personality. He was also a devotee of the peyote tradition, a Native American tradition in which peyote, a small narcotic cactus found in the Southern United States and in Mexico, is ingested to

Grover Wolf Voice holding a Northern Cheyenne courtship flute (courtesy Jay Old Mouse).

bring about healing. According to Mader, though Wolf Voice was plagued with rheumatoid arthritis and chronic pain, his crutches would disappear as he danced with the best of them at powwows.[3]

Wolf Voice, like Jay, also presented the flute tradition to school-aged children in the community with flute demonstrations and storytelling. In his presentations, Grover said that when a young man played the flute for a woman, "if his playing and love were true, the flute's medicine would literally fly out of the instrument as sparks of fire, embers of love, shooting stars in the night."[4] The legacy of the flute weighed heavily on Grover's mind—he wondered if the legacy would continue. However, through the dedication, musicianship and craftsmanship of Jay Old Mouse, indeed, the tradition is alive today.

Douglas Glenmore, also known as Black Bear, is Jay's maternal grandfather. His grandchildren, including Jay, formed a drum group when Jay was in his teens called Black Bear, named after their grandfather. Their grandfather, Black Bear, made all of the drums for the family. Jay remembers, "He'd make our drums and he would talk to us about the seriousness of the songs and the drums. You know he wasn't a ceremonial man, but he knew quite a bit and shared that with all of us grandkids."[5]

Douglas Glenmore (left), also known as Black Bear, and Jay Old Mouse, each holding a Northern Cheyenne courtship flute near Busby, Montana, circa 1990 (courtesy Jay Old Mouse).

Josephine Glenmore, Jay's grandmother, married Douglas Glenmore in 1941. In an interview conducted in 1985, an interviewer, Royal Jackson, asked her, "What is your husband's name?" Josephine said his name was originally David Seminole, but he changed it to Douglas Glenmore in 1955. She went on to tell the story that he changed his name because there were four Josephine Seminoles, and the mail in Lame Deer kept getting them mixed up. According to Josephine, she and Douglas looked in magazines and newspapers and came up with the name Glenmore. She laughed as she explained to the interviewer that later on she learned that "Glenmore" was a brand of whiskey. Josephine did not approve of liquor or drinking at all. She commented to the interviewer, "I would never have settled on that name."[6]

Josephine and Douglas had five children, 15 grandchildren and at least six great-grandchildren.[7] Of all of those grandchildren, Douglas Glenmore, or Black Bear, chose Jay to carry on the courtship flute tradition. Black Bear approached Jay about making a flute when Jay was around 18 years old. Jay says Black Bear chose him because, even at 18, he was levelheaded, had a strong sense of community, stayed out of trouble and was skilled with his hands. At that time, he was into hot rods, hunting, and softball. He wasn't thinking about building flutes. Rather than ask Jay directly if he was interested in carrying on the flute tradition, Black Bear simply asked Jay, "Would you like to build a flute?" It took Jay a year to build his first flute. In that time Black Bear taught him about the flute tradition and passed on the craftsmanship skills. Jay says, "In the time that I was chosen as the flute maker, I led a good life." Jay added, "I've always led a good life, I've never been an alcoholic I never battled alcohol or drugs. I like to show people that I'm a worthy man. I have a house, I have a family, I have a horse, and I raised my boys the best I can."[8]

Jay, an excellent storyteller, commands attention with his mesmerizing voice. In his unhurried manner, he told the story of the courtship flute tradition: When it was time for a young man to find a bride, he would ask the flute maker of the tribe to build a flute so that he could use the powerful love medicine in the flute to woo his wished-for wife. There is a Cheyenne tradition of offering gifts when you request something from someone. The young man would go to the flute maker and offer him gifts such as a horse, a hide, a rifle, a bow and arrow, or other valuable goods. If the flute maker thought the young man was serious about the request, he would agree to build the flute, and the flute would become a part of the young man's life.

Jay Old Mouse playing a Northern Cheyenne courtship flute at his kitchen table in his home, Busby Montana, 2017 (author's photograph).

According to Jay, in the evening when all was peaceful, the young man would sit on a hill above the camp and play music from his heart while thinking of the woman he loved. The woman would follow the music, they would meet, and if it was meant to be, the relationship would grow from there. After winning the heart of the woman, the man would play the flute for many different purposes, including for prayer, for entertainment, for his children, for healing, and for hunting purposes. (The flute can sound like the bugling of an elk, which draws the elk in close to the hunters.)

Jay offered a second courtship flute legend, which has to do with a snake. The legend says that when the young man played the flute to woo his lover, a snake would hear the music, then find the woman and inject her with a love potion which would make her fall in love with the flute player. Jay prefers the first legend to the snake legend.

Jay commented, "There's not a bunch of young men trying to find me and ask to build them a flute to win the heart of a woman. But, if they do come, and if they are serious about it, I think it would help them because the flute still has very powerful medicine."[9]

Cheyenne courtship flutes are built by hand from cedarwood, which is sourced from the hills around Jay's home near Busby. The two pieces of wood that make up the flute are joined with a binding element such as tree sap or glue. The seams connecting the two flute halves are invisible to the eye and perfectly smooth to the touch. The flute is a tube shape, about five hands long, with a small hole in the top end for blowing into. There are six finger holes on the front of the flute which are used for producing a variety of pitches. At the top end on the front of the flute, above the finger holes, are two square holes which direct the airflow into the flute. This part is called the chamber. A small wood carving in the shape of an elk, called a top piece, is tied on with thin pieces of deer hide; it covers one of the square holes of the chamber. The position of the top piece is integral to sound production. The elk, considered the animal of love, represents food, shelter, and clothing. A moon is carved on one side of the elk's body and on the other side the sun. The two symbols represent one complete cycle of day and night.

As the designated flute maker and keeper, whenever he is asked to play, Jay plays—sometimes for hours at a time. He is frequently asked to play for birthday parties, weddings, funerals, local schools, and community gatherings. Whether his flute is used for healing purposes, for educational purposes, or for giving joy, he always "chases the right tune" to fit the occasion. He says the flute does not belong to him; it belongs to the Cheyenne people.

Jay estimates that he has made around 100 flutes, give or take. I purchased one of his flutes, and I was told by Jay's sister that I'm in good company with my purchase. As it turns out, Stephen Ambrose, the author of *Undaunted Courage: Meriwether Lewis, Thomas Jefferson, and the Opening of the American West*, ordered a flute from Jay many years ago. Traditionally, the flute is played only by men, but Jay gave his blessing for me to play and talk about the flute. He has built flutes for other women who are interested in the flute for healing or for educational purposes.

The courtship flute Jay built for me is a rich reddish-brown cedar color with wood grain detail with a lovely carved elk top piece and a multicolored beaded band which wraps around the circumference of the flute, just above the six evenly spaced sound holes. It smells like cedar and is smooth to the touch. Jay taught me where to put my fingers, how to blow, and told me to "play from the heart."[10] I felt both honored and humbled to experience this hands-on lesson on an instrument built by the master himself. In the lesson, Jay taught me about breathing, trilling, and how to shape the melodies for an authentic sound.

Does Jay have a young person in mind to carry on the legacy of the flute making? He said it does weigh on his mind that he'll have to find someone, and hopefully they will take care of the tradition, help people through the music of the flute, and keep the tradition alive for the Cheyenne people.

After our morning of music, we drove over to a restaurant which is across the road from the Little Bighorn Battlefield, where the Cheyenne, Arapaho and the Lakota Sioux battled the United States Seventh Cavalry Regiment led by Lt. Col. George Armstrong Custer in 1876. As we entered the restaurant, workers and patrons warmly greeted Jay. He's a popular man in his community. His kindness, optimism, and sense of humor are infectious.

Jay is a well-known community leader on the Northern Cheyenne Reservation and beyond. In 2014, he performed in Helena at the Montana capitol when he was inducted into Montana's Circle of American Masters, an esteemed honor for artists and craftsmen of the Big Sky state. He has also given flute presentations in Las Cruces, New Mexico, for Native American border patrol officers and in Cheyenne, Wyoming, for Frontier Week.

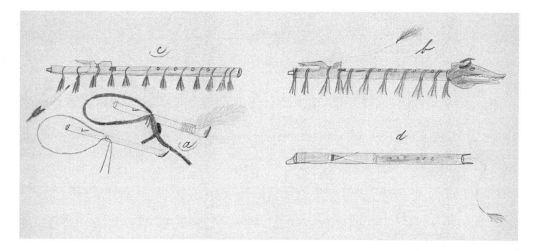

Daniel Little Chief drawing of Cheyenne musical instruments, with descriptive text by Albert Gatschet, 1891. Musical instruments identified as: a) whistle (tapin) of golden eagle's bones; b) whistle in shape of rattlesnake; c) whistle of red cedar; d) whistle of sumac wood (Manuscript 2016-a, National Anthropological Archives, Smithsonian Institution).

Not only is Jay the keeper of the flute tradition and a community leader; he also works for the nearby Colstrip School District as a homeschool liaison between students, faculty, and parents. He announces for rodeos, powwows, athletic events, and delivers important information to members of the reservation over his mobile PA system. Delivering announcements from the cab of his truck, Jay is a modern-day camp crier, a position he has held for decades. When he was a teenager, he took part in a special ceremony which gave him blessings to speak publicly on a microphone. The camp crier position dates back to the old days when the crier gathered tribal members together, kept people calm, and announced vital information. In *Cheyenne Memories*, author John Stands in Timber and Jay's great-grandfather remembered the story of a camp crier in the winter that followed the famed Custer battle:

> It happened that after the camp had been set up, a crier came through the village calling all the men to come together. Brave Wolf said that the crier spoke for Box Elder, a blind medicine man who could predict the future. Box Elder was having the crier announce that they must stay where they were camped, but find good places to hide when the soldiers attacked them, and build breastworks there. "Many, many soldiers are coming," he said, "and many Indians with them. They are on their way to kill all the Cheyennes. But I am going to ask the Great Spirit to prevent them."[11]

With Jay's work as the Northern Cheyenne flute maker, his message to his community and to everyone he comes into contact is this: "I believe that clean and sober is one of my messages, and everybody knows that, but, you know, everybody battles those demons. When I'm out there, whether it be a sporting event, rodeo, or just general information like, 'get out and vote,' or 'go enroll at Dull Knife (college),' or 'stay home and stay safe from COVID-19,' I'm just trying to keep people calm. I've had people come up and tell me that when they hear my voice that it's comforting to them."[12]

While in the finishing stages of completing the manuscript for this book, Jay Dale Old Mouse, Pėhévena'hāne (Good Killer), passed away at the age of 53. In the words of his family, "he began his journey across the Milky Way to *Séáne,* the 'Happy Hunting

Grounds.'"[13] As of now, according to his wife, Amy Old Mouse, the future of the Cheyenne flute tradition is unknown. My hope is someone in the Northern Cheyenne community will take on the flute-building tradition and that the tradition will survive in the hands of a new dedicated caretaker, as it has for hundreds of years.

Another comforting presence in the Cheyenne community was Jay's great-grandfather, John Stands in Timber (1882–1967), who wrote about Cheyenne music, songs and singing and how music played an important role in traditional Cheyenne life. John Stands in Timber told the story about one particular style of song, sung by women, which teased men about their lack of courage.

> A man could not court a girl unless he has proved his courage. That was one reason so many were anxious to win good war records. A girl's mother was with her all the time, and if he walked up to her the mother would talk about him and ask what he had done in battle. In fact, they were all afraid of what people, especially the women, would say if they were cowardly. The women had a song they would sing about a man whose courage had failed him. The song was: "If you are afraid when you charge, turn back. The Desert Women will eat you." It meant the women would talk about him so badly it would have been better to die.[14]

A similar song went: "If you had fought bravely I would have sung for you." John Stands in Timber said, "My grandfather and others used to tell me that hearing the women sing that way made them ready to do anything. It was hard to go into a fight, and they were often afraid, but it was worse to turn back and face the women."[15]

Women sang songs to prepare men for battle, for example, in an account of the Battle of the Little Big Horn. Kate Big Head, also known as Antelope, a Cheyenne woman who was there at the battle, recalled how songs were used on the battlefield. She remembered, "I found a pony and followed the warriors to watch the fighting as I often did since my nephew, Noisy Walking, expected me to watch and sing songs to give him courage." Antelope called these songs "strong-heart songs."[16]

According to Stands in Timber, the Cheyenne military societies included the Swift Foxes or Kit Foxes, the Elks, and the Dog Men, also known as the Dog Soldiers. Each of these societies had their own songs, which the men shared at tribal dances. For example, Stands in Timber mentions a war-bragging song from the Swift Foxes that went, "whenever my friends are afraid, I will be the one to make it easy—for my fighting warriors."[17]

Another war song sung before battle went, "My friends, only stones stay on earth forever. Use your best ability." Yet another song said, "I am afraid of the old man's teeth; I will go either way." This meant it was better to die in battle at a young age than to die of old age. Stands in Timber said, "There were hundreds of songs, and they came to the people in many ways. Sometimes a man made one up, or heard it in a dream or vision. Sometimes he heard it from an animal out in the hills."[18]

The Kit Fox Society had a tradition where the members of the society would gather and dress at a certain tipi. They would dance in front of that tipi four times and move on in a single file to one of the tribal chiefs. They would play hand drums and sing a special song celebrating one of their own warriors who had done a brave deed, John Stands in Timber explained:

> He would come out in the middle then and dance alone, showing what he had done—perhaps taking out a knife he had used to scalp an enemy with, and acting out what had happened. When he was through dancing, he would let out a war whoop and talk out loud, telling everyone just what he has done. The drummers started their song, and all the membership started dancing, making war cries and running to change position when the song was repeated.[19]

George Bird Grinnell, anthropologist, writer, and conservationist, spent time with both the Northern and Southern Cheyenne in the late 1800s. According to Grinnell, a summer evening in a Cheyenne camp was a busy place. People crossed back and forth between lodges, socializing with one another as firelight shone from each individual lodge. Curls of smoke drifted up from the top of each brightly lit lodge. All the while, music accompanied the variety of activities happening in the cool of the evening. For example, there might be a large drum and singers accompanying a social dance. In another part of camp, a doctor might be singing a sacred song of healing accompanied by a hand drum. Gamblers in someone's tipi might be singing quick and lively songs as an accompaniment to their game of chance. And the sound of the "love notes" played on a flute might be heard in the distance. This camp symphony also included the howl of coyotes, the barking of dogs, the neigh of ponies, the excited voices of children, and the musical laughter of women.[20]

Singing was a part of Cheyenne life. There were a variety of songs for social, sacred, and religious occasions, while other songs were simply for entertainment. Songs were often sung as an accompaniment for games, and sometimes songs were sung as expressions of love. Everyone sang, including men, women, and children. The various types of songs included prayer songs sung by doctors and women to help with healing. Mothers and grandmothers sang baby songs or lullabies to children. Mourning songs honored the dead. Morning songs welcomed the day. Religious songs enhanced sacred ceremonies and personal prayers. Grinnell notes: "A certain song, known as the horse song, may be sung over a horse, in order to make him strong, sound, and swift, for a particular occasion."[21]

Wolf songs were said to have come from the wolves who passed the songs on to scouts who were out looking for enemies on the prairie. The young men, or scouts, were called "wolves," and sometimes the songs sounded like the howling of wolves. Wolf songs served many purposes, including comforting the lone scout out on the prairie. Some wolf songs were sung to give strength and courage to warriors riding into battle; others were sung for entertainment in the quiet of the evening. Wolf songs were also sung "by men when they felt depressed, downhearted, lonely, or discouraged."[22]

Wolf songs were also sung to ask for protection from the Great Spirit. Some wolf songs expressing love and longing were sung by both men and women to their sweethearts. These songs often expressed missing a lover, anticipating a meeting with a lover, or celebrating a reunion with a lover. For example, a song for a lone traveler, translated to English, said, "My love, it is I who am singing. Do you hear me?"[23] Another love-themed wolf song went: "My love, come out of the lodge, I am searching for you."[24] A woman's song addressed to her lover, *Tá mă vă in,*' is translated as "put your arms around me, I am not looking."[25]

Several Cheyenne songs have been preserved in the work of ethnomusicologist, Natalie Curtis. In the late 1800s, Natalie, a trained classical pianist, traveled west and became fascinated with Native American music and culture. She made a home in New Mexico and tirelessly traveled throughout the West from tribe to tribe, by train and sometimes by horseback, in order to capture what she believed was a vanishing culture of music and songs. She sat and listened to the songs and stories of elders, chiefs, and medicine men, and she transcribed those Native American songs and stories with a simple pen and paper, note for note and word for word. She transcribed over 200 songs and stories from 20 different Native American tribes. Hiamovi (High Chief or High Wolf) of

the Cheyenne accompanied Natalie from camp to camp, introduced her to tribal leaders, and explained the purpose of her visit. Hiamovi's presence and support made her
work possible.

Her transcriptions are compiled in her book: *The Indians' Book: Authentic Native
American Legends, Lore and Music,* first published in 1907 and is still available today.
This book includes songs and stories from different Native American tribes, including
the Cheyenne. In the words of Hiamovi, or High Chief, "The Indian wise-speakers in
this book are the best men of their tribes. Only what is true is in this book."

Chief Honihi-Wotoma (Wolf-Robe) sang and talked about one of the oldest Cheyenne melodies: *Hohiotsitsi No-otz,* translated as *Morning Song.* According to Wolf-Robe,
"the song is sung by old men, often from the summit of the hills at dawn." Below are the
Cheyenne words and the English translation as transcribed by Natalie Curtis.[26]

> **Hohiotsitsi No-otz *Morning Song***
> *Ehani nah-hiwatama.* He, our father
> *Napave vihnivo.* He hath shown his mercy unto me.
> In peace I walk the straight road.

Other Cheyenne songs found in *The Indians' Book* include: "*Ohwiwi No-otz*" ("Song
of the Offering/Sundance Song"); "*Aotzi No-otz*" ("Victory Song"); "*Nai No-otz*" ("Healing Song"); "*Meshivotzi-No-otz*" ("Lullaby"); and "*Wawahi No-otz*" ("Swinging Song").
The variety of songs found in the book speaks to the many roles of singing and the variety of songs within the Cheyenne people.

The Indians' Book includes a song about the courtship flute with the Winnebago
People of present-day Nebraska. "*Wunk-Hi Na-Wan,*" ("Love-Song") was sung and told
by Winnebago women. Natalie transcribed the story:

> In the summer of the olden time there might often be heard at eventide the call of flutes. It
> was the young upon the hill-side piping love-songs. Everyone may know a love-song when he
> hears it, for the flute-tones are long and languorous, and are filled with a soft tremor. When a
> maiden heard the flute-music of her lover without, she always found it necessary to leave the
> tipi to draw water or to visit some neighbor.
>
> In this song the maid asks leave of her mother to go to see her uncle, but the music tells that
> it is really her lover to whom she is going. The old people were not often deceived when the
> flute-music sounded.[27]

> **Wunk-Hi Na-Wan *Love-Song***
> Na-ni, dega-go Mother, let me go to my uncle!
> E-dja wa-de-kjela!

There are many myths and legends about how the flute came to Native Americans.
Many have to do with birds, others feature elk, and some tell the story of animals taking the form of humans in order to teach a young man about the construction and the
implementation of the flute.

A Cheyenne legend about the flute's origin goes something like this: Many years
ago, before the white men came, the flute was given to the Cheyenne people by the Great
Spirit. The legend goes, a young Indian boy was lost and alone in the forest; the Great
Spirit looked down and saw that the boy was alone and decided to give him a gift. The
Great Spirit sent a small bird to sit on a hollow branch of an old tree, and it began peck-
ing holes in the branch. The Indian boy was sitting below the tree, and as the wind blew,
he could hear beautiful sounds coming from the branch of the tree; each hole of the

branch produced a different sound. The boy realized this was a gift from the Great Spirit. He climbed the tree and gently removed the flute from high in the tree and blew into it, imitating the wind blowing across the branch, and was able to produce a beautiful sound. He brought the branch to his people and told them about the wonderful gift given by the Great Spirit.[28]

Ed Wapp, Jr. (1943–2016), a Comanche musician, scholar and educator, wrote this poem honoring the Native American flute from the perspective of the flute:

> I was one part of a red cedar standing high on the mountain.
> I was taken by a young man, whittled, and given a sweet voice.
> I became the night voice of the young man speaking to his sweetheart,
> Singing his tender thoughts.[29]

Another flute legend comes from the Sioux: A long time ago a young man went out from his camp to hunt an elk because his people were hungry. He followed the tracks until he finally came upon the elk. Though he was a skilled hunter, he was not able to reach the elk with his bow and arrow. The young man was determined, so he kept following the elk until nightfall when he stopped to sleep. As he went to sleep, he heard a sad, ghost-like song that at the same time was beautiful and hopeful. He fell asleep with this song in his ears and began to dream. In his dream a redheaded woodpecker was singing the very same song he had heard before falling asleep. The woodpecker said, "Follow me and I will teach you."

When the hunter awoke, he saw a woodpecker on the branch of a tree, and once more, he heard the song, and he wished to find the singer. The woodpecker led him through the woods and landed on a branch of a cedar tree. The woodpecker tapped away at the branch. As a gust of wind came up, the young hunter heard the song again and realized the song was coming from the branch; it was whistling through the holes that the woodpecker had carved. The hunter asked to take the branch home.

Once home, the hunter tried and tried to make a sound from the branch, but no sound came out. He decided to fast and pray, hoping that he would receive a vision which would tell him how to make the branch sing. On the fourth night of fasting, in a dream, the woodpecker again appeared, turned himself into a man and instructed the hunter how to make the branch into an instrument that would sing. When the hunter awoke from his dream, he found a cedar tree and crafted an instrument with a hollowed-out middle and sound holes from one of the cedarwood branches, just as the woodpecker had shown him. He played his flute by softly blowing into the mouthpiece and fingering the holes. The people of the village were astounded with this beautiful music. The hunter ended up wooing the daughter of a great chief with his flute, who became his wife, and the hunter himself became a great chief.

Other young men soon began to whittle bird-shaped flutes from the branches of cedarwood so they could create their own love music. The tradition and beautiful music traveled from tribe to tribe thanks to a young elk hunter, a woodpecker, a cedar tree, and the wind.[30]

The Sioux courtship flute, similar to the Northern Cheyenne and the Winnebago courtship flute, functioned as an instrument of love. Young men played the flute hoping to win the heart of a woman. The woman would hear the love music drifting through the camp and would sneak out of her parents' home in the still of the night, following the sound of the flute to meet the man playing the beautiful music. The Sioux flute is also made of cedarwood, like the Northern Cheyenne flute. The difference is the flute of the

Sioux is carved into the shape of a bird with a long neck and a head with an open beak, which is where the sound comes out.

Each Native American tribe wove their own songs, instruments, and stories into the fabric of the West. Aaron Carapella, of the Cherokee Nation, is a scholar and cartographer who estimates that between the years 1590 and 1850 (pre-reservation period) there were roughly 590 tribal nations, tribes, sub-tribes, and bands living in the area we call the United States.[31] Major tribes of the Northern Plains, living where the Westward Movement would sweep across over the course of the nineteenth century, included the Assiniboine, Crow, Blackfeet, Plains Cree, Arikara, Hidatsa, Plains Chippewa, Mandan, Lakota, Arapaho, Nez Percé, Cayuse, Walla Walla, Umatilla, Chinook, and Cheyenne. While there are some common musical elements among the tribes, such as courtship flutes, songs, drums, and rattles, each of these tribes has its own culture, language, religion, ceremonies, and musical traditions.

The original people were in the West for some 10,000 years before the launch of the Westward Expansion, and more than likely, music has been part of the Western landscape for as long. At an ancient buffalo hunting ground near Casper, Wyoming, archeologists discovered a flute made from an antler thought to be 6,000 years old.[32] Throughout the ages, native people have used music for religious purposes, for celebration, for healing, and for love.

Not only in the West, but globally, flutes are part of our collective history as human beings. Evidence of this lies in ancient artifacts and cave paintings. The oldest musical instruments ever found, in hillside caves in southwestern Germany, are flutes made from bird bones and mammoth ivory. These flutes are thought to be between 42,000 and 43,000 years old.[33] In the Southwest United States, ancient petroglyphs of Kokopelli, the humpback flute-playing deity, are etched into abandoned pueblos and rock faces, including Mortendad Cave near Los Alamos, New Mexico. The oldest known wooden flutes in the United States, thought to be constructed between 620–670 BC, were found in 1931 in the Prayer Rock District of northeastern Arizona. The cave where they were found by a team of archeologists headed by Earl Halstead Morris was dubbed "the Broken Flute Cave." The flutes are now housed at the Arizona State Archives.[34]

The previous images of crayon drawings (pg. 15), created in 1891 by Wuxpais, Daniel Little Chief, a Cheyenne man who lived at the Pine Ridge Agency in South Dakota, provide a picture of the Cheyenne courtship flute of long ago. The explanations of the instruments, as told to Daniel Little Chief, were written down by Albert Gatschet:

Musical Instruments (as described by Little Chief to Albert Gatschet)
(*tapínun'hts*)
a. A whistle, *tapín*, made of golden eagle's bones, ornamented by a feather, also of the golden eagle; the two whistles are tied to a string 6–8 inches long, which serves to hang them around the neck.
b. Whistle in the shape of a rattlesnake, with a feather from the golden eagle. The snake has horns on account of having been seen with horns in a dream. Buckskin fringes hang around it. The whistle consists of red cedar wood, over which a rattlesnake skin is stretched, the rattle having been removed. The whistle is two or more feet long and is pierced with four to six holes.
c. Same kind of whistle also made of red cedar, but without the snakeskin. A feather from the golden eagle is hanging down from it. About 2 inches long, six holes.
d. Same kind of whistle or clarinet, made of sumach (sumac) wood, about two feet long, feather as above.[35]

No one knows exactly how long the Cheyenne have been playing the courtship flute. What matters is that the story of Jay Old Mouse and the flute reminds us that the Cheyenne, along with other Native American peoples, played the first music and were the first musicians in the West. Music within Native American cultures served many roles, including courtship, healing, entertaining, storytelling, meditating, praying, hunting, war preparations, celebrating, and soothing. Native American music remains an important and inspiring thread within the musical tapestry of the West and a cornerstone within the history of music in the United States.

The following chapters of this book illustrate that music played a profound role within every group that hit the trail in the time of the Westward Expansion. Moreover, every group had some type of musical interaction with Native Americans, including the Lewis and Clark Expedition, fur trappers, missionaries, pioneers on the Oregon Trail, cowboys on the open range, and townsfolk in early frontier communities. In the early twentieth century, composers such as Charles Wakefield Cadman and Arthur Farwell used Native American melodies in their compositions. Composers, musicians, and audiences continue to find inspiration in music inspired by the larger-than-life personalities and the romance of the American West.

Once, only Indians lived in this land. Then came strangers from across the Great Water. No land had they; we gave them our land. No food had they; we gave them of our corn. The strangers are [have] become many and they fill all the country. They dig gold—from my mountains; they build houses—of the trees of my forests; they rear cities—of my stones and rocks; they make fine garments—from the hides and wool of animals that eat my grass. None of the things that make their riches did they bring with them from beyond the Great water; all comes from my land, the land the Great Mystery gave unto the Indian–*Hiamovi* (High Chief) (Chief among the Cheyennes and the Dakotas).[36]

2

The Genesis

The Lewis and Clark Expedition (1804–1806)

In the evening Cruzatte gave us some music on the violin
and the men passed the evening in dancing singing
&c and were extreemly cheerfull.
—Meriwether Lewis

The Lewis and Clark Expedition of 1804–1806 launched the nineteenth-century Westward Expansion of the United States and remains one of the greatest adventure stories in American history. Launched by President Thomas Jefferson, and under the leadership of Captains Meriwether Lewis and William Clark, the Corps of Discovery explored land acquired in the Louisiana Purchase of 1803, collected flora and fauna, developed trade relations with Native Indians, and charted unknown territory. The Corps paddled up the Missouri River, crossed the treacherous Rocky Mountains by horseback, and paddled down the Snake and Columbia Rivers to the roaring Pacific Ocean. After wintering at Fort Clatsop on the Pacific Coast, the Corps reversed their route and journeyed back to the start. Over the course of two years, ten months, and four days, the expedition covered some 8,000 miles round trip.

While faced with formidable obstacles such as raging currents, disease, swarms of insects, snakes, grizzly bear attacks, subzero weather conditions, and starvation, the Corps of Discovery prevailed. In the Lewis and Clark story, we find stunning examples of teamwork, scientific discoveries, the kindness of strangers, courage, diplomacy, leadership, cross-cultural exchanges, powerful examples of women's leadership in life-and-death situations—AND MUSIC! In fact, music played a paramount role in the success of the expedition.

The captivating Lewis and Clark story has been told time and time again; this time, let us travel the well-worn Lewis and Clark trail with music as the focal point. The Lewis and Clark journals kept by men of the expedition serve as a guide to shining a light on the role of music along the trail. Over 100 of the journal entries involve musical references and events.* The men of the expedition literally fiddled, danced and sang their way across the continent throughout their epic adventure. What's more, the Corps also witnessed and often participated in music and dance traditions of indigenous peoples along the way.

The Corps included two fiddlers: Pierre Cruzatte and George Gibson. Cruzatte, the most often mentioned of the fiddlers, a seasoned boatman and trader of the lower

---

*The journal entries from the *Journals of the Lewis and Clark Expedition* have been preserved in their original form without spelling or grammatical corrections.

Missouri, was the son of a French father and an Omaha Indian mother. He spoke French, Omaha, and was fluent in sign language, the *Lingua Franca* of the Western frontier.[1] Cruzatte served as a navigator, boat captain, diplomat, and negotiator with Native Americans along the way. In the journal entries, Pierre Cruzatte shows up under multiple names, such as "Peter," "the Old Man," and "the one-eyed Frenchman." Picture a one-eyed, weathered, wiry man with a French accent and an eye patch expertly guiding the keelboat through the swift eddies of the Missouri. In the evening, by the campfire, he tucks a fiddle into the crook of his arm and plays a fireside concert of favorite dance tunes that he has learned by ear through the years. His delighted fellow travelers clap, stomp, dance and sing along to the music. Cruzatte often played the violin for Native Americans on the journey. The journal accounts indicate that on multiple occasions, the Indians were curious about the instrument and enjoyed the fiddle music and the dancing that went along with it.

George Gibson, the second fiddler, was hired as a sign language interpreter as well as a hunter. William Clark wrote about the duo on October 19, 1805. The Corps, traveling westbound, set up camp on the banks of the Columbia River. Curious Yakimas and Wanapams lined the river bank in order to catch a glimpse of the men of the Corps.

Pierre Cruzatte   *George Gibson*

Pierre Cruzatte and George Gibson by Michael Haynes (courtesy Michael Haynes).

Eager to make a favorable impression on the Indians, Captains Lewis and Clark offered their guests tobacco and music: "Indians Came from the different Lodges, and a number of them brought wood which they gave us, we Smoked with all of them, and two of our Party Peter Crusat & Gibson played on the *violin* which delighted them greatly."[2]

Meriwether Lewis commented on Cruzatte's fiddle playing in a journal entry on June 25, 1805: "The party that returned this evening to the lower camp reached it in time to take one canoe on the plain and prepare their baggage for an early start in the morning after which such as were able to shake a foot amused themselves in dancing on the green to the music of the violin which Cruzatte plays extreemly well."[3]

Music served multiple purposes throughout the journey. In one role, music built a bond between members of the Corps while elevating their daily routine and building moral. A typical day for the Corps included paddling upriver, offloading supplies, setting up camp, hunting for game, cooking over a campfire, sewing clothes and moccasins, repairing equipment, breaking down camp, and packing the canoes. On March 30, 1805, William Clark commented on the evening music in camp: "all the party in high Spirits they pass but fiew nights without amuseing themselves danceing possessing perfect harmony and good understanding towards each other."[4]

In another role, music (usually accompanied by whiskey) provided a festive atmosphere on special occasions. For example, on Meriwether Lewis's 30th birthday, August 18, 1804, William Clark noted, "the evening was Closed with an extra Gill of Whiskey & a Dance untill 11 oClock."[5]

Music played a diplomatic role between the Native Americans and the men in the Corps. You might even say the Corps of Discovery was a traveling song and dance ensemble. Along the expedition, the Corps encountered some 50 Native Indian tribes; among those included were the Mandan, Sioux, Assiniboine, Piegan, Shoshone, Nez Percé, Flat Head, Crow, Blackfeet, Chinook, and the Clatsop. The captains would often order the fiddle to be played as a peace and goodwill offering or as a diversion. On Sunday, June 8, 1806, John Ordway journaled that the men of the Corps danced to fiddle music for the Nez Percé: "our party exercised themselves running and playing games called base in the evening danced after the fiddle as the Indians were anxious to See them."[6]

As a sign of friendship, Indian tribal leaders routinely invited the men of the expedition to either watch or participate in dancing alongside tribal members. After witnessing a Sioux dance on September 26, 1804, John Ordway wrote about the musical encounter which included drums, rattles, singing, and a drum being thrown into the fire. (The phrase "&. C." often shows up in the journals, meaning—etc.)

in the evening the 2 Captains myself and a nomber more of the party went to their village to See them dance. they had a fire in the center of their lodge. the Band formed a line which were the men. the Squaws formed on each Side of the fire & danced and Sang as the drumm and other ratles &.C. were playing. they danced to the center untill they met, then the rattles Shook and the houp was Given. then the Squaws all fell back to their places. when the [other?] mens music Seaced the womens voice Sounded one part of the tune delightful. then the other Music would commence again, our Captains Gave them some Tobacco to Smoke during the dance. one of the warries thought he had not received a Small peace of the last tobacco they had he Got mad and broke one of their drumms, hove 2 in the fire and left the line. Some of the rest took them out, they then took a Buffaloe Robe & held up in their hands and beat on it and continued on their dance till late in night.—The chiefs came on & Slept with us in a friendly manner—[7]

Regarding the instruments on the expedition, the words "fiddle" and "violin" are used interchangeably in the journals. There is no physical difference between a fiddle and a violin. Traditionally, the word "violin" is often associated with formal affairs, art music, and elegant balls. Someone trained as a violinist usually reads music notation and may learn pieces from a written score. A "fiddle," on the other hand, is often associated with informal occasions, folk tunes, and "country style" dancing. Fiddle tunes are frequently passed down, generation to generation, through the aural tradition. Sarah Olds, violinist, historian and educator, commented, "The fact that either violin survived the trip is astonishing, especially considering the sheer physical danger the instruments would have been in during the travel between 620 separate camps during the 863-day journey."[8]

Despite the limited space on the keelboat, the captains made room for the two violins, which, no doubt, took up precious cargo room along with weapons, ammunition, food, camping gear, medical supplies, tools, spare parts, whiskey, and gifts for the Indians they would be meeting along the way. According to Lewis's supplies records, those gifts included musical instruments—half a dozen Jew's harps. A Jew's harp, or jaw-harp, according to the Harvard Dictionary of Music, is "a primitive instrument consisting of an elastic strip of metal, one end of which is attached to a small horseshoe-shaped frame of metal or wood."[9]

Along with the Jew's harps and fiddle, the journals also mention four tin blowing trumpets which were probably meant for communication from boat to boat and boat to shore. However, the trumpets may have played a cameo role in musical ensembles. On January 1, 1805, Ordway wrote: "carried with us a fiddle & a Tambereen & a Sounden horn. as we arived at the entrence of the vil. we fired one round then the music played. loaded again. then marched to the center of the vil, fired again. then commenced dancing. a frenchman danced on his head."[10]

The instrument collection, along with the violins, more than likely included makeshift percussion instruments crafted from sticks, pots, pans, spoons, animal bones, and hides. Patrick Gass documented an interaction with the Sioux on August 30, 1804:

Captain Lewis gave the visitors the supplies to make a drum including a deer skin and a half of a keg. A foggy morning, and heavy dew. At nine o'clock the Indians came over the river. Four of them, who were musicians, went backwards and forwards, through and round our camp, singing and making a

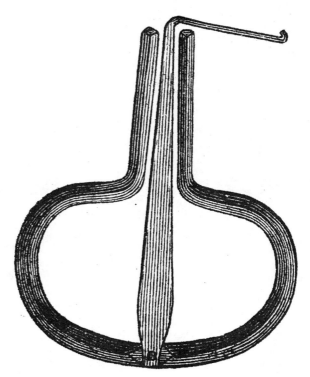

Nineteenth-century Jew's Harp (iStock/ilbusca).

noise. After that ceremony was over they all sat in council. Captain Lewis and Captain Clarke made five of them chiefs and gave them some small presents. At dark Captain Lewis gave them a grained deer skin to stretch over a half keg for a drum. When that was ready they all assembled round some fires made for the purpose: two of them beat on the drum, and some of the rest had little bags of undressed skins dried, with beads or small pebbles in them, with which they made a noise. These are their instruments of musick. Ten or twelve acted as musicians, while twenty or thirty young men and boys engaged in the dance, which was continued during the night.[11]

Along with the instruments already mentioned, let's not forget every man carried an instrument with him—his own singing voice! Joseph Mussulman, Lewis and Clark scholar and music professor, wrote, "Singing, like dancing was considered a manly pastime. One measure of a man's social status was his ability to remember a goodly number of tunes to perform them with a fitting sense of style, and to summon an impressive variety of songs for a given situation."[12]

This discussion of instruments and singing songs along the trail beg the questions: What tunes were played on those fiddles? What music did the men dance to? What songs did they sing? While we have many detailed journal entries about impromptu dance performances and musical encounters, not one entry mentions the title of a fiddle tune or a song. No mention! What a pity, or as the fiddler Cruzatte may have exclaimed, *Quel Dommage*! With no written record of the repertoire, we can only speculate about the musical selections of the Lewis and Clark Expedition. Joseph Mussulman suggested, "We can narrow the field somewhat by remembering that the criteria Captains Meriwether Lewis and William Clark established for the recruits favored rugged outdoorsmen rather than 'gentlemen's sons,' so it is probably safe to assume that most if not all of the men preferred popular music."[13]

Mussulman points to popular music of the time as possible trail tunes, including patriotic songs such as "Yankee Doodle" and an American Revolution marching song, "Chester." Other popular songs of the era include "Oh Dear What Can the Matter Be" and "The Rose Tree."

The Rose Tree

A rose tree in full bearing,
Had flowers very fair to see,
One rose beyond comparing,
Whose beauty attracted me;
But eager for to win it,
Lovely, blooming, fresh, and gay,
I found a canker in it,
And threw it very far away.

How fine this morning early,
Lovely Sunshine clear and bright,
So late I lov'd you dearly,
But now I've lost each fond delight;
The clouds seem big with showers,
The sunny beams no more are seen,
Farewell ye happy hours,
Your falsehood has changed the scene.[14]

If any in the Corps found inspiration in the protestant revivalist movement of the 1790s, it is possible that popular hymns of the day may have made their way into camp. Popular hymns of the day included "Kedron" and "Go Down Moses."

Nine of the men hailed from Kentucky where traditional Appalachian ballads with Scots-English and Irish origins were popular. Examples of ballads in this genre include "Matty Groves," "Barbara Allen," "The Cuckoo" and "Pretty Saro."

"Pretty Saro"

Down in some lone valley in a lonesome place
Where the wild birds do whistle, and their notes do increase
Farewell pretty Saro, I bid you adieu
But I'll dream of pretty Saro wherever I go

My love she won't have me, so I understand
She wants a free holder who owns house and land
I cannot maintain her with silver and gold
Nor buy all the fine things that a big house can hold

If I were a merchant and could write a fine hand
I'd write my love a letter that she'd understand
I'd write it by the river where the waters o'er-flow
And I'll dream of pretty Saro wherever I go[15]

Yes, the men were rugged frontiersmen, but perhaps one or more of the men had a "high brow" upbringing and held fast to memories of a mother or maybe an uncle with a penchant for art music. In that case, the first American art song, written in 1759, composed by Francis Hopkinson (text by Thomas Parnell), "My Days Have Been So Wondrous Free," may have fit the bill with lyrics that speak of nature and water.

"My Days Have Been So Wondrous Free"

My days have been so wondrous free,
The little birds that fly
With careless ease from tree to tree,
Were but as bless'd as I.
Ask gliding waters, if a tear
Of mine increas'd their stream?
Or ask the flying gales, if e'er
I lent one sigh to them?[16]

Regarding the intersection of music and dance on the trail, Robert Hunt of the Lewis and Clark Trail Association suggests that dancing may have been a free form style of dance accompanied by jigs and hornpipes on the violin, which are two types of dance tunes. It is possible the men engaged in "Big Circle Dancing," a formal style of dance with patterns in which half of the men would have played the women's part. Some possible dance tunes of the trail still floating around to this day include "Fisher's Hornpipe," "Devil's Dream," "Whiskey Before Breakfast," and "Boil the Cabbage." Hunt suggests, being half French, Cruzatte may have included French favorites such as "Jolie Blonde," "Old French Hornpipe," and "La Belle Catherine."[17]

With some knowledge of the instruments of the trail along with some speculation regarding the songs and tunes that were played, let us turn our attention to a series of musical events as they unfolded over the course of the expedition. The following selected journal entries, presented in chronological order, illustrate the important role of music and dancing throughout the Lewis and Clark Expedition.

In the few days leading up to the launch of the expedition, Joseph Whitehouse wrote about dancing with French ladies, on Friday, May 18, 1804: "This morning very pleasant, part of this day we were employ'd, procuring necessary's for our Voyage; in the

Evening we were amused at a Ball, which was attended by a number of the French ladies, who were remarkably fond of dancing."[18]

The journey officially began on May 21, 1804, when the Corps of Discovery departed from St. Charles, Missouri. The party included 45 men, some of whom were hired boatmen who would not be along for the entire length of the trip. The expedition consisted of hearty, unmarried, rugged men who could survive the rigors of life in the unknown frontier. On good days, the crew averaged 12 to 15 miles while paddling up the Missouri; other days were a bust due to windy conditions, as was the case on June 11, 1804. Clark noted that the men spent a day doing chores, hunting and enjoying some dancing and singing "as the wind blew all this day from N, W. which was imedeately a head we Could not Stur, but took the advantage of the Delay and Dried our wet articles examined provisons and Cleaned arms, my Cold is yet verry bad—the river begining to fall our hunters killed two Deer, G Drewry killed 2 Bear in the Prareie to day, men verry lively Danceing & Singing &c."[19]

On August 16, 1804, John Ordway commented that the party celebrated with music after a successful fishing excursion yielding over 700 fish: "pleasant morning. the party in high Spirits fiddleing & danceing last night."[20]

On August 20, 1804, the party suffered the only death of a Corps member on the entire journey when Charles Floyd died from apparent appendicitis near what is now Sioux City, Iowa. Details of the death and funeral service were told by John Ordway: "He was layed out in the most decent manner possable. we proceded on to the first hills on N.S. where we halted and dug a Grave on the top of a round knob & buried the desed with the honours of war. the funeral Serrymony performed &c—we named this hill Sgt. Floyd's Bluff."[21]

While the journal entry regarding Floyd's funeral does not mention music, one can't help but wonder if the men sang at the gravesite, perhaps a hymn of the era such as "Come the Fount of Every Blessing," composed by Robert Robinson in 1758.

> Come, thou Fount of every blessing,
> tune my heart to sing thy grace;
> streams of mercy, never ceasing,
> call for songs of loudest praise.
> Teach me some melodious sonnet,
> sung by flaming tongues above.
>
> Praise the mount I'm fixed upon it
> mount of God's redeeming love.
>
> Here I find my greatest treasure;
> hither by thy help I've come;
> and I hope, by thy good pleasure,
> safely to arrive at home.
> Jesus sought me when a stranger,
> wandering from the fold of God;
> he, to rescue me from danger,
> bought me with his precious blood.[22]

After Floyd's death, the men forged on—paddling upriver against the mighty current of the Missouri, and in a few days, made their first encounter with the Sioux. In a sign of friendship, the Corps invited the Sioux to their camp. The Corps were treated to songs and dances accompanied by a drum and other small instruments. Ordway wrote about the experience on August 30, 1805:

after dark we Made a large fire for the Indians to have a war dance, all the young men prepared themselves for the dance. Some of them painted themselves in curious manner Some of the Boys had their faces & foreheads all painted white &C a drum was prepared, the Band began to play on their little Instruments, & the drum beat & they Sang. the young men commenced dancing around the fire. it always began with a houp & hollow & ended with the Same, and in the intervales, one of the warries at a time would rise with his weapen & Speak of what he had done in his day, & what warlike actions he had done &.c.[23]

On September 24, 1804, Clark recounted another experience with the Sioux which included a dinner of dog meat, buffalo meat and potatoes followed by smoking, singing, drumming, and dancing. The dance the men witnessed on this night was a scalp dance, which was a type of a victory celebration:

The great Chief then rose in great State and Spoke to the Same purpos and with Solemnity took up the pipe of peace and pointed it to the heavens, the 4 quartrs and the earth, he made Some divistation [dissertation?], & presented the Sten [stem] to us to Smoke, after Smokeing & a Short Harrang to his people we were requested to take the meat, and the Flesh of the Dog gavin us to eat—We Smoked untill Dark, at which time all was cleared away & a large fire made in the Center, Several men with Tamborens highly Decorated with Der & Cabra Hoofs to make them rattle, assembled and began to Sing & Beat—The women Came forward highly decerated with the Scalps & Trofies of war of their fathes Husbands & relations, and Danced the war Dance, which they done with great chearfulness untill 12 oClock, when we informed the Chief we intended return on bord.[24]

Ordway described another evening of music and dance on September 26, 1804: "in the evening the 2 Captains myself and a nomber more of the party went to their village to See them dance. they had a fire in the center of their lodge. the Band formed a line which were the men. the Squaws formed on each Side of the fire & danced and Sang as the drumm and other ratles &.C. were playing. they danced to the center untill they met, then the rattles Shook and the houp was Given. then the Squaws all fell back to their places. when the [other?] mens music Seaced the womens voice Sounded one part of the tune delightful."[25]

After leaving the Sioux, the expedition spent the fall of 1804 paddling upstream and camping along the Missouri headed toward the Mandan and Hidatsa villages located in present-day North Dakota. Stephen Ambrose, author of *Undaunted Courage,* explained that the Mandan villages were the center of trade for the Northern Plains Indians, including the Crow, Assiniboine, Cheyenne, Kiowa, and Arapaho, along with whites from U.S. and Canadian fur-trading operations.[26] Here the Corps established Fort Mandan and spent a brutally cold but peaceful winter with the Mandan and Hidatsa people.

Christmas and New Year passed with a great deal of celebration among the men of the Corps and the Indians. Music was a terrific diversion for the men, and perhaps all that dancing in the cozy lodges kept them warm in the subzero temperatures of the winter. On December 25, 1804, Whitehouse wrote: "This morning being Christmass, the day was announced by the discharge of our Swivels, and one Round from our small arms of the whole company.... The Men then prepared one of the Rooms, and commenced dancing, we having with us Two Violins & plenty of Musicians in our party."[27]

During their winter stay at Fort Mandan, the Corps first met the invaluable member, Sacajawea. Sacajawea, of Shoshone descent and the daughter of a Shoshone chief, was captured by the Hidatsa Indians and torn from her family when she was around 12 years old. Her name is spelled many different ways, including Sacagawea, Sakakawea, and Sacajawea. In his journal, Clark once referred to her as "Janey."

In the Shoshone language, Sacajawea means "Bird Woman." After her capture by the Hidatsas, she was "purchased" by Toussaint Charbonneau, a French Canadian fur trader who claimed her as one of his "wives." Together they had a baby, Jean Baptiste, who would become known by William Clark as "Pomp" and "Pompy."

Lewis and Clark at Three-Forks by Edgar Samuel Paxson, Mural at the Montana State Capitol, oil on canvas, 1912 (courtesy Montana Historical Society).

Sacajawea and Charbonneau were both recruited by the Corps as interpreters. Sacajawea, 16 years old, with an infant just over a month old when she joined the expedition, not only proved her competence as an interpreter but also as a wilderness guide. Her diplomatic skills became an important asset in meeting native tribes along the way, including negotiating with the Shoshone for the acquisition of the horses needed for crossing the Bitterroot Mountains located in the panhandle of present-day Idaho and Western Montana. Sacajawea's skills, keen knowledge, and quick thinking proved invaluable as the expedition made their way west. When a pirogue capsized on May 14, 1805, it was Sacajawea who jumped into the raging river to recover important scientific equipment and journals.

The journalists made no mention of Sacajawea participating in dances or singing. However, I imagine she sang lullabies to her baby, like most mothers do. Although Sacajawea was Shoshone by birth, she was living among the Hidatsa when her baby was born. She may have chosen a Hidatsa lullaby to soothe her baby. Or perhaps she sang songs in her first language: Shoshone. Beverly Crum, Shoshone singer and scholar, wrote that many Shoshone songs have to do with nature and were passed down from generation to generation. One such song, "Sai Paa Hupia," or "Boat and Water Song," is a round dance. Traditionally, round dances begin in the evening and continue until daybreak. Different singers take turns singing throughout the night.[28] (A round dance is a type of social dance.)

"Sai Paa Hupia"

Sai paa weyaa, Sai paa weyaa, Sai paa weyaa, Sai paa weyaa.
Piaa toyaakatete mantu, Toyaatu mantu, Tewekkwintoote.
Piaa toyaakatete mantu, Toyaatu mantu, Tewekkwintoote.

"Boat and Water Song"

Water carries the boat, Water carries the boat, Water carries the boat, Water carries the boat.
Towards the big mountain range, Towards the mountains, Swirling.
Towards the big mountain range, Towards the mountains, Swirling.[29]

And there is also the possibility that Toussaint Charbonneau sang a French lullaby to his little son, Jean Baptiste. "Au clair De la Lune" dates back to the eighteenth century.

Au clair de la lune,
Mon ami Pierrot,
Prête-moi ta plume
Pour écrire un mot.
Ma chandelle est morte,
Je n'ai plus de feu.
Ouvre-moi ta porte
Pour l'amour de Dieu.

By the light of the moon,
My friend Pierrot,
Lend me your quill
To write a word.
My candle is dead,
I have no light left.
Open your door for me
For the love of God.

After wintering with the Mandan and Hidatsas, the Corps continued on their quest toward the Pacific. On April 7, 1805, 31 men, one woman (Sacajawea), one baby (Jean Baptiste, also known as Pomp), and Clark's dog (Seaman) worked their way up the Missouri River into unchartered territory. The days were long, the going was tough, and the men worked hard paddling the boats as well as hunting and transporting the kill to the camp. In celebration of finding a favorable spot for an encampment, Clark ordered music and whiskey to lift the haggard spirits of the Corps. His journal entry from April 26, 1805, reads:

> I walked down and joined the party at their encampment on the point of land fromed by the junction of the rivers; found them all in good health, and much pleased at having arrived at this long wished for spot, and in order to add in some measure to the general pleasure which seemed to pervade our little community, we ordered a dram to be issued to each person; this soon produced the fiddle, and they spent the evening with much hilarity, singing & dancing, and seemed as perfectly to forget their past toils, as they appeared regardless of those to come.[30]

The Corps spent the Fourth of July 1805, at White Bear Island after the completion of the month-long portage around the Great Falls in present-day Great Falls, Montana. The portage was one of the most physically demanding events of the entire journey. The men enjoyed a feast of bacon, beans, suet dumplings and buffalo meat followed by fiddle music and dancing. Lewis recounted the celebration in his journal for that day: "our work being at an end this evening, we gave the men a drink of sperits, it being the last of our stock, and some of them appeared a little sensible of it's effects the fiddle was plyed and they danced very merrily untill 9 in the evening when a heavy shower of rain put an end to that part of the amusement tho' they continued their mirth with songs and festive jokes and were extreemly merry untill late at night."[31]

On August 13, 1805, the party met the Shoshone Indians. In an amazing twist of fate, Sacajawea recognized that the chief, Cameahwait, was her long-lost brother whom she remembered from her childhood. A tearful reunion ensued between brother and sister. No doubt this familial bond strengthened relations between the Corps and the Shoshone.

At this point in the journey, the men desperately needed horses from the Shoshone for traveling over the steep, treacherous Rocky Mountains. After a horse deal was negotiated, Clark employed the use of music in order to lighten the mood, as he was worried about the horse negotiation falling through. Here, Clark ordered the fiddle to be played. You could say music sealed the deal! Clark's journal entry from April 26, 1805, reads:

> I directed the fiddle to be played and the party danced very merrily much to the amusement and gratification of the natives, though I must confess that the state of my own mind at this moment did not well accord with the prevailing mirth as I somewhat feared that the caprice of the indians might suddenly induce them to withhold their horses from us without which my hopes of prosicuting my voyage to advantage was lost; however I determined to keep the indians in a good humour if possible, and to loose no time in obtaining the necessary number of horses.[32]

In September of 1805, after crossing the Rocky Mountains in snowy conditions and bitter temperatures, the members of the Corps were nearly starving when they encountered the Nez Percé near what is known today as the Weippe Prairie in Idaho. The Nez Percé, who had never seen white men before, fed the Corps salmon and roots, which made the men critically ill. It's not surprising that there was no mention of music, dancing, or celebration, as the entire group was suffering from dysentery. With the men in such a weakened state, the Nez Percé could have easily killed the members and taken all of their supplies and trade goods, which would have secured a position as the richest tribe west of the Mississippi. It was a Nez Percé woman, Watkuweis, who saved the lives of all the members of the Corps. Stephen Ambrose explained:

> According to their oral-history tradition, when they first met Clark and his six hunters— who had also gorged themselves on roots and fish and gotten dysentery- they considered killing them for their weapons. They were dissuaded by a woman named Watkuweis (meaning "Returned from a Far Country.") She had been captured by Blackfeet some six or seven years earlier, taken into Canada, and sold to a white trader. She lived with him, among other traders, for several years before somehow finding her way home. The traders had treated her far better than the Blackfeet had done, so when Clark arrived she told the warriors, "these are the people who helped me do them no hurt."[33]

Watkuweis and Sacajawea serve as examples of influential Indian women. Each in her own way saved the expedition from failure. Ambrose wrote, "The expedition owed more to Indian women than either captain ever acknowledged. And the United States owed more to the Nez Percé for their restraint than it ever acknowledged."[34]

While in the company of the Nez Percé, Chief Twisted Hair proved a valuable ally. He not only taught the men how to construct canoes by burning out large tree trunks but also agreed to take care of the horses until the men returned after their trek to the Pacific Coast. On October 5, 1805, the expedition departed from the Nez Percé camp and made their way down the Clear Water River to the Snake River to the Columbia and ultimately to the Pacific Ocean. On October 16, when the expedition had reached the Columbia River, William Clark wrote: "a Chief came from their Camp which was about ¼ of a mile up the Columbia river at the head of about 200 men Singing and beeting on their drums Stick and keeping time to the musik, they formed a half circle around us and Sung for Some time, we gave them all Smoke, and Spoke to their Chiefs as well as we could by Signs informing them of our friendly disposition to all nations."[35]

As the members of the Corps neared the Pacific Ocean, tempers flared as the men grew agitated with theft committed by the local Indians. Clark reminded his men to behave peacefully in order to insure a friendly reception in the future. What better way to affect diplomacy than through music? Whitehouse wrote about a performance featuring the dancing of York accompanied by Cruzatte's fiddle. The Indians were fascinated with York's black skin and thought he possessed powerful medicine. York, Captain Clark's slave, although an integral member of the Corps, was never paid for his service. Clark's journal entry from October 26, 1805, reads:

> we gave to each Chief a Meadel of the Small Size a red Silk handkerchief, arm band, Knife
> & a piece of Paint, and acknowledged them as chiefs; as we thought it necessary at this time
> to treat those people verry friendly & ingratiate our Selves with them, to insure us a kind &
> friendly reception on our return, we gave Small presents to Several, and half a Deer to them
> to eate. we had also a fire made for those people to Sit around in the middle of our Camp,
> and Peter Crusat played on the violin, which pleased those nativs exceedingly. the two Chiefs
> and several men deturmined to delay all night (yorked Danced for the Inds).[36]

In November of 1805, Clark declared: *Ocian in view! O! the Joy.*[37] The Corps had traveled over 4,000 miles from the beginning of the expedition. Journal accounts of Fort Clatsop, where the Corps wintered, indicate a miserable, cold and wet winter with very little game to hunt. There were few celebrations and little mention of music with the exception of songs sung on Christmas Day. Clark wrote on December 25, 1805: "at day light this morning we we[re] awoke by the discharge of the fire arm of all our party & a Selute, Shoute and a Song which the whole party joined in under our windows, after which they retired to their rooms were Chearfull all the morning."[38]

On March 3, 1806, the party departed from Fort Clatsop for the return trip to St. Louis, this time they paddled up the Columbia. In the face of strong currents, troublesome portages, food shortages, thievery from curious Indians along the route and the looming Rocky Mountain crossing, the fiddle provided a welcome relief for weary spirits. On April 16, 1806, Clark reported: "I Set out late and arrived at Sunset and informed. the natives that in the morning I would trade with them. he gave me onions to eate which had been Sweated. Peter played the violin and the men danced."[39]

As the Corps made their way upriver, music played on. For example, Lewis reported a fiddle and dance event on April 23, 1806: "we Caused the fiddle to be played and Some of the men danced. after them the nativs danced. they dance different from any Indians I have Seen. they dance with their Sholders together and pass from Side to Side, defferent parties passing each other, from 2 to 7. and 4 parties danceing at the Same time and Concluding the dance by passing promiscuisly throu & between each other."[40]

On the return trip, a profound story of music and friendship between the Corps and the Walulas (Walla Wallas) is mentioned in the journals. Chief Yellepit of the Walulas threw a big party in honor of the Corps of Discovery and asked the neighboring Yakimas to come. On this festive occasion, Chief Yellepit asked the men of the Corps to trade medicine songs with his people. When a medicine song is given away, there is a powerful medicine gifted to the recipient of that song. This was not only an exchange of songs but an exchange of friendship. The men of the Corps obliged by singing two songs, and the Indians sang one. More than any other story of music in the journals, this one invites the question—What songs did the men choose? What did the medicine songs of the Walla Walla sound like? Sadly, we'll never know! On April 28, 1806, Ordway wrote:

> we played the fiddle and danced a while the head chief told our officers that they Should be lonesome when we left them and they wished to hear once of our meddicine Songs and try to learn it and wished us to learn one of theirs and it would make them glad. So our men Sang 2 Songs which appeared to take great affect on them. they tryed to learn Singing with us with a low voice. the head chief then made a Speech & it was repeated by a warrier that all might hear. then all the Savages men women and children of any Size danced forming a circle round a fire & jumping up nearly as other Indians, & keep time verry well they wished our men to dance with them So we danced among them and they were much pleased, and Said that they would dance day and night untill we return.[41]

Joseph Mussulman, Lewis and Clark scholar and music professor, suggested that "Come Ye Sinners, Poor and Needy," an enduring hymn written by Joseph Hart in 1759, might have been one of the medicine songs that the Corps chose.[42]

"Come Ye Sinners, Poor and Needy"
Come ye sinners, poor and needy,
Weak and wounded, sick and sore,
Jesus ready stands to save you,
Filled with pity, love and power.
He is able, He is able,
He is willing, doubt no more,
He is able, He is able,
He is willing, doubt no more.

In May of 1806, the Corps arrived at Camp Chopunnish in present-day Idaho, home to the Nez Percé. Under the advice of Chief Twisted Hair, the party stayed at the camp for a few months until the snow melted enough for a safe passage eastbound over the Rocky Mountains.

The last entries regarding a fiddle were written on June 8, 1806. Lewis wrote: "after dark we had the violin played and danced for the amusement of ourselves and the Indians." Clark's journal entry from the same day reads: "after dark the fiddle was played and the party amused themselves in dancing."[43]

After this event, the violins were never mentioned again. Perhaps there was an accident with instruments, maybe they were stolen or left behind, or perhaps the strings snapped or the fiddlers ran out of rosin for the bows. Any number of things could have happened. Perhaps the violins were simply packed away on the boat, and all attention was focused on racing back to St. Louis. However, Cruzatte, the primary fiddle player, is mentioned again before the journey is over. On August 11, 1806, Cruzatte, possibly because of his poor eyesight, accidentally shot Lewis in the behind. Luckily, Lewis, although he undoubtedly suffered a great deal of pain and must have had to lie down in the boat on his side, was not fatally injured.

On their return visit to the Mandan village, the Corps said goodbye to Sacajawea, Charbonneau, and the baby, Jean Baptiste. On August 17, 1806, Lewis wrote: "we also took our leave of T. Chabono, his Snake Indian wife and their Son Child who had accompanied us on our rout to the Pacific ocean in the Capacity of interpreter and interpretes."[44] Indeed, Sacajawea interpreted as well as guided the men through a foreign wilderness, negotiated with Indian leaders, taught the men of the expedition how to forage for food, saved valuable journals and instruments from a watery end when a boat capsized, and the list of her contributions goes on. Toussaint Charbonneau, Sacajawea's husband, was paid for his service to the Corps, but Sacajawea didn't receive a penny. She was an unpaid, working teenage mother. Her son, John Baptiste, and her daughter, Lizette, born a few years after the expedition, were both adopted and raised by William Clark, who also financed their education in St. Louis, Missouri. Jean Baptiste (Pomp) later returned to the West as a wilderness guide and fur trapper.

After saying their goodbyes at the Mandan village, the men of the expedition once again took to the water. Headed for St. Louis in the keelboat, the Corps raced downstream on the mighty Missouri River. Clark's journal from September 14, 1806, mentions a song-filled evening: "received a dram and Sung Songs until 11 o Clock at night in the greatest harmony."[45] This entry marks the last mention of any type of music on the voyage. The Corps arrived in St. Louis on September 23, 1806, where people lined the banks of the river, cheering on the men and their victorious expedition. On the final day of the voyage, in a letter to President Thomas Jefferson, Captain Meriwether Lewis wrote: "It is with pleasure that I anounce to you the safe arrival of myself and party.... In obedience to your orders we have penitrated the Continent of North America to the Pacific Ocean, and sufficiently explored the interior of the country to affirm with confidence that we have discovered the most practicable rout which dose exist across the continent by means of the navigable branches of the Missouri and Columbia Rivers."[46]

On October 9, 1806, the *Palladium Newspaper* of Frankfort, Kentucky, reported: "We congratulate the public at large and the particular friend of Messrs. Lewis and Clark and their enterprising companions, on the happy termination of an expedition, which will, doubtless, be productive of incalculable commercial advantages to the Western Country, at no very distant period."

In summary, music accompanied the Corps along the 8,000 miles of the Lewis and Clark Expedition and served in a variety of roles from the start of the expedition through to the end. While we will never know the names of the tunes and the songs that were played, we do know that the music of the trail included fiddle tunes, vocal music, percussion instruments, bugles and Native American drumming. Along the way, music facilitated friendship, peace and diplomacy between members of the Corps and Native Indian tribes. In the spirit of cross-cultural exchange and to impress the Indians, members of the Corps performed for the Native Americans along the trail, and in turn, Native Americans invited the Corps into their world of ceremonies and celebrations, which often included music and dancing.

All the while, music served multiple roles, including celebration, entertainment, comfort, distraction, inspiration, communication, encouragement, worship, creativity, and healing. While the story of Lewis and Clark ends here, the larger story of the Westward Expansion begins. Prompted by the successful Lewis and Clark Expedition, the likes of explorers, mountain men, missionaries, pioneers, minors, railroaders, merchants, teachers, preachers, performers, artists, tradesmen, emigrants, cowboys, and fortune seekers followed in the steps of Lewis and Clark over the course of the nineteenth century. Each group carried their own music traditions as they pursued a foothold in the West.

3

Trailblazers

Explorers, Mountain Men, and Missionaries

Mirth, songs, dancing, shouting, trading, running, jumping,
singing, racing, target-shooting, yarns, frolic, with all sorts
of extravagances that white men or Indians could invent,
were freely indulged in. —James Beckwourth

The success of the Lewis and Clark Expedition launched the next wave of nine-teenth-century westbound groups which included explorers, fur trappers (also known as mountain men), and missionaries. Each of these disparate groups wove their own songs, experiences, and observations into the musical tapestry of the West. Explorers set out to survey the regions of the West, to establish U.S. authority, and to build trade relation-ships with indigenous people. Fur trappers paddled up the Missouri River and crossed into the interior of the Rocky Mountains in pursuit of beavers, prized for their lucrative pelts. Zealous missionaries headed west eager to convert Indians to Christianity.

Members of each of these groups kept journals and shared personal accounts of their adventures. These written and oral histories bring to light an array of musical tra-ditions that were present in the early nineteenth-century West—from Spanish fandan-gos in New Mexico to French Canadian boating songs along the Missouri to the "Dog Dance" of the Kanza tribe in present-day Kansas.

In 1805, before Lewis and Clark and the Corps of Discovery had completed their expedition, General James Wilkinson assigned explorer Zebulon Pike and his crew of 20 men to explore the northern frontier, to find the source of the Missis-sippi River, and to establish the United States' trade presence in the region. Pike kept a journal of the expedition which included entries about music—according to Pike's accounts, the expedition members included musicians who played violins and other unknown instruments. On September 10, 1805, Pike wrote about a Sioux dance that he witnessed during his northbound journey: "Men and women danced indiscrimi-nately. They were all dressed in the gayest manner; each had in their hand a small skin of some description: they frequently run up, pointed their skin, and give a puff with their breath; when the person blown at, whether man or woman, would fall, and appear to be almost lifeless, or in great agony; but would recover slowly, rise, and join in the dance. This they called their great medicine, or as I understood the word, the dance of religion."[1]

Pike wrote about music onboard the boat on September 16, 1805, while sailing from St. Louis to St. Paul on the Mississippi: "Mr. Frazer embarked in my boat. At first the breeze was very gentle, and we sailed with our violins and other instruments playing;

but the sky afterward became cloudy, and the wind blew quite a gale. My boat plowed the swells, sometimes almost bows under."[2]

On September 6, 1806, as Pike and his men were preparing for their return trip to St. Louis, Pike wrote: "All hearts and hands were employed in preparing for our departure. In the evening the men cleared out their room, danced to the violin, and sang songs until eleven o'clock."[3]

Similar to the journal accounts of the Lewis and Clark Expedition, Pike failed to mention exactly which songs his men sang and danced to. This leaves the repertoire list up to speculation. Zebulon Pike was a U.S. Army man, so perhaps the men sang popular military tunes of the day such as "He Who His Country's Liv'ry Wears" or "When a Woman Hears the Sound of the Drum and Fife." Both songs, written by Victor Pelissier, accompanied a popular patriotic play—*Glory of Columbia*—produced in 1803 at the Park Theatre in New York. Pelissier's variety of compositions, which included operas, musical farces, odes, patriotic songs and orchestral accompaniments, represented the style of music popular in the United States in the early 1800s—the years that marked the beginning of the Westward Expansion.

If patriotic songs weren't the favored repertoire of the Pike expedition, perhaps the men sang, fiddled, and danced to rousing French Canadian boating songs such as "*Dans mon chemin.*" Or the men may have sung favorite Scottish and English ballads such as "Ye Banks and Braes o'Bonnie Doon," "The Lass with the Delicate Air," "The Wayworn Traveler," or the wildly popular song from the turn of the nineteenth century, "Crazy Jane," about a woman who goes insane and aimlessly wanders the streets because of her unfaithful lover's transgressions.

> Why, fair maid, in ev'ry feature,
> Are such signs of fear express'd?
> Can a wandering wretched creature,
> With such terrors fill thy breast?
> Do my frenzied looks alarm thee?
> Trust me, sweet, thy fears are vain;
> Not for kingdoms would I harm thee;
> Shun not then poor Crazy Jane.
>
> Dost thou weep to see my anguish?
> Mark me, and avoid my woe,
> When men flatter, sigh and languish,
> Think them false—I found them so.
> For I lov'd—Oh, so sincerely,
> None could ever love again
> But the youth I lov'd so dearly,
> Stole the wits of Crazy Jane[4]

The purpose of Pike's second expedition, launched in 1806, was to explore the south and west area of the Louisiana Purchase in present-day Colorado, find the headwaters of the Arkansas and Red Rivers and to negotiate treaties with Indian tribes. While the expedition never found the headwaters of the rivers, Pike and his men measured the altitude of the 14,000 ft. peak, which is now called Pike's Peak in central Colorado. After surviving a brutal Rocky Mountain winter, on their way back to St. Louis the expedition found themselves in Spanish Territory. Pike and his men were captured by Spanish authorities and summoned by the governor of Santa Fe. After several months in Santa Fe, the men were escorted across Texas and released at Natchitoches, Louisiana.

While in the custody of the Spanish, Pike and his men, although they were detainees in a foreign country, nevertheless enjoyed parties and elaborate dinners complete with music and dancing. Pike's accounts of his time in New Mexico, written upon his return, include descriptions of the musical traditions he encountered around the area of Santa Fe. According to Pike, dancing, music, and gambling were the primary amusements of the people living there. Pike reported that the people danced the fandango, a lively dance of Spanish origin. Pike wrote the dance was "danced by one man and two women who beat time to the music, which is soft and voluptuous, but sometimes changing to a lively gay air, whilst the dancers occasionally exhibit the most indelicate gestures."[5]

Pike also saw people dancing the minuet, which was originally a French dance. According to Pike, "The minuet is still danced by the superior class only; the music made use of is the guitar, violin, and singers, who in the first described dance [the fandango] accompany the music with their hands and voices, having always some words adapted to the music, which are generally of such a tendency as would in the United States occasion every lady to leave the room."[6]

Pike described music in the public square: "At every town of consequence is a public walk, where the ladies and gentlemen meet and sing songs, which are always on the subject of love, or the social board. The females have fine voices, and sing in French, Italian, and Spanish, the whole company joining in the chorus." Pike went on to describe music in private homes and how "the ladies play on the guitar, and generally accompany it with their voices. They either sit down on the carpet cross-legged, or loll on a sofa. To sit upright in a chair appeared to put them to great inconvenience."[7] Another example of music in the home occurred during a dinner with Father Rubi in the village of St. Philip's located in New Mexico. Pike wrote that his company was entertained with music played on bass drums, French horns, violins, and cymbals.[8]

A Pretty Girl in the West by Mary Hallock Foote, United States, 1889 (?) (Library of Congress).

One of the most infamous mountain men and explorers, Kit Carson, traveled and worked in many areas of the West, including Oregon, the Sierra Nevada Mountains, and the Rocky Mountains. His many occupations included trapper, hunter, scout, soldier, rancher, and Indian fighter. In Kit Carson's autobiography, dictated to Dewitt C. Peters, Carson described a variety of musical experiences during his time in the West. In 1826, when Kit Carson first arrived in New Mexico, at the age of 16, Mexico had already gained independence from Spain (in 1821). Like other explorers, Carson marveled at the vibrant musical life in New Mexico. Carson's vivid descriptions speak to the diversity of cultures and languages that were present in early nineteenth-century Santa Fe. According to these early musical descriptions, the music of the region included a mixture of Spanish, Mexican, and indigenous influences.

> The music consists of a high-strung violin and a species of guitar. This is perambulated about the town. The players perform light dancing tunes and accompany the music with their voices, making up the words as they go along. This music is learned entirely by ear and is transmitted from one generation to another through the means of these fandangos. The vocal music is anything but harmonious to the ear, but some of the airs, when played on the instruments, are rather pleasing, and one, on hearing them, finds himself often humming them afterwards. The powers of music are nowhere better illustrated than among these people. Their ready ear quickly catches a new tune, and it is not uncommon to hear, in a Mexican town, a *señorita* giving vent to a negro melody or a favorite polka which she has heard some American sing or whistle. At Santa Fé there are several noted players on the violin and harp who cannot read a word of music, yet they can play on their respective instruments with taste and skill.[9]

As many of the early explorers witnessed, the area of Santa Fe was a hot spot of diverse musical activity including a variety of instruments, dances, languages, and styles of music. Yet another traveler, Josiah Gregg, explorer, trader and author of *Commerce on the Prairies*, observed that dancing, accompanied by music, served as the primary amusement in the Southwest. Gregg wrote that the term "fandango" refers not only to a certain dance but to a social dance gathering, much like a "ball." He explained that "balls" were "very frequent, for nothing is more general throughout the country than dancing. From the gravest priest to the buffoon—from the richest nabob to the beggar—from the governor to the ranchero—from the soberest matron to the flippant belle—from the grandest *señora* to the *concinera* [cook]—all partake of this exhilarating amusement."[10]

Gregg wrote that the "musical instruments used at the *bailes* and *fandango*s are usually the fiddle and *bandolin,* or *guitarra*, accompanied in some villages by the *tombé* or little Indian drum. The musicians occasionally acquire considerable proficiency in the use of these instruments. But what most oddly greets, and really outrages most Protestant ears, is the accompaniment of divine service with the very same instruments, and often the same tunes."[11]

> Some of the explorers mentioned *fandangos*, and a closer investigation of the music style reveals that *fandango* was popular throughout Europe, New Mexico, and the United States in the late eighteenth century and into the early nineteenth century. The *fandango* is "a Spanish dance in moderate to quick triple time danced by a couple to the accompaniment of castanets."[12] Several European composers of the late eighteenth century composed fandangos, for example: "*Fandango, R.* 146" for piano by Spanish composer Padre Antonio Soler, "*Fandango with Variations*" for piano, by Portuguese composer, João Bomtempo; and "*Fandango Variado*" for solo guitar, by Spanish composer, Dionisio Aguado. The composer mentioned earlier

in this chapter, Victor Pelissier, composed a *fandango* in 1802 that was danced at the New York Theatre for the pantomime, *Bil Blas*.[13] [A pantomime, which originated in England, was a light-hearted theatrical production accompanied by music.]

Trajes Mexicanos, un Fandango (**Mexican dresses/costumes**), **lithograph by C. Castro and C. Campillo, 1869 (New York Public Library).**

Along with *fandango*s, more than likely, the music of Santa Fe included *sone*s, a style of music that combined Mexican, Spanish, African, and Indigenous influences. Another song style, the *jarabe*, intended for dancing, emerged around 1800.[14] The *jarabe* was a type of romantic and sensual courtship dance between a man and a woman, and the steps were considered sexually suggestive, even though the men and the women didn't touch each other during the dance. A modern version of the *jarabe*, with roots stretching back to the original *jarabe* style is the well-known Mexican folk dance, "*jarabé Tapatio*" (The Mexican hat dance), composed by Jesus González Rubio in 1924. To this day, "*jarabé Tapatio*" is often referred to as the national dance of Mexico.[15]

Another style of music of the West included the songs of the French Canadian *voyageurs*, known for their singing. Explorers and fur trappers depended on these masters of the water to transport them up the Missouri River and into the rugged waterways of the plains and the Rocky Mountains of the Western frontier. Explorer Benjamin Bonneville commented on the music of the Canadian voyageurs. "They wielded their paddes [paddles] with the wonted dexterity, and for the first time made the mountains echo with their favourite boat songs."[16] Apparently the voyageurs also sang during portages, Bonneville commented: "It is at these places called 'portages' that the Canadian *voyageur* exhibits his most valuable qualities, carrying heavy burdens, and toiling to and fro, on land and in the water, over rocks and precipices, among brakes and brambles, not only without a murmer, but with the greatest cheerfulness and alacrity, joking and laughing and singing scraps of old French ditties."[17]

John Bradbury, a naturalist who explored the interior of the American West in the years 1809–1811, explained in his journals how the Canadian oarsmen kept up a steady pace while singing songs in a call-and-response style: "We slept on board the boat, and in the morning of the 14th took our departure from St. Charles, the French Canadians measuring the strokes of their oars by songs, which were generally responsive betwixt the oarsmen at the bow and those at the stem: sometimes the steersman sung and was chorused by the men." Below are the French lyrics and English translation as written by John Bradbury in his book, *Travels in the Interior of America in the Years 1809, 1810, and 1811.*

I
Derrière chêz nous, il ya un etang?
Ye, ye ment.
Trois canards s'en vont baignans,
Tous du lông de la rivière,
Legèrement ma bergère,
Legèrement ye ment.

II
Trois canards s'en vont baignans,
Ye, ye ment.
Le fils du roi s'en va chassant,
Tous du lông de la rivière,
Legèrement ma bergère,
Legèrement, ye ment.

III
Le fils du roi s'ezi va chassant,
Ye, ye ment.
Avec son grand fusil d'argent,
Tous du lông de la rivière,
Légèrement ma bergère,
Légérement, ye ment.

I
Behind our house there is a pond,
Fal lal de ra.
There came three ducks to swim thereon:
All along the river clear,
Lightly my shepherdess dear,
Lightly, fal de ra.

II
There came three ducks to swim thereon,
Fal lal de ra.
The prince to chase them he did run
All along the river clear,
Lightly my shepherdess dear,
Lightly, fal de ra.

III
The prince to chase them he did run,
Fal lal de ra.
And he had his great silver gun
All along the river clear,
Lightly my shepherdess dear,
Lightly, fal de ra.[18]

Voyageurs by Charles M. Russell, 1898, oil on board in grisaille (courtesy Minneapolis Institute of Art, gift of James J. Hill, III, Maude Hill Schroll, and Louis W. Hill, Jr., 81.108.1).

While on the upper Missouri, Bradbury and his men encountered a war party of Arikara, Mandan and Gros Ventre. The chiefs of the party invited Bradbury to camp near them on the banks of the Missouri River. In the evening, Bradbury and his men observed a type of singing that went on late into the night. He described a pleasing song sung with vocables (syllables such as ha, hi-ye, le, and hey-a) which are liberally used in many traditional Native American songs.

> The singing now commenced and continued at intervals until past midnight. The song is very rude, and it does not appear that they combine the expression of ideas and music, the whole of their singing consisting in the repetition of the word ha six or seven times in one tone, after which they rise or fall a third, fourth, or fifth, and the same in quick time. I observed that their voices were in perfect unison, and although, according to our ideas of music, there was neither harmony nor melody, yet the effect was pleasing, as there was evidently system, all the changes of tone being as exactly conformable in point of time, as if only one voice had been heard. Whenever their performance ceased, the termination was extremely abrupt, by pronouncing the word how in a quick and elevated tone.[19]

The Stephen Long Expedition of 1820 was another expedition sent out to explore the Western frontier. While on an exploration in the western part of present-day Kansas, the Long Expedition encountered the Kansa people, also referred to as Kanza or Konza. Edwin James, a botanist and geologist on the expedition, wrote about the music and dance of the Konza:

> The Indians collected around the fire in the centre of the lodge, yelling incessantly; at length their howlings assumed something of a measured tone, and they began to accompany their

voices with a sort of drum and rattles. After singing for some time, one who appeared to be their leader, struck the post over the fire with his lance, and they all began to dance, keeping very exact time with the music. Each warrior had, besides his arms, and rattles made of strings of' deer's hoop, some part of the intestines of an animal inflated, and enclosing a few small stones, which produced a sound like pebbles in a gourd shell. After dancing round the fire for some time, without appearing to notice the strangers, they departed, raising the same wolfish howl, with which they had entered; but their music and their yelling continued to be heard about the village during the night.

This ceremony, called the dog, dance, was performed by the Konzas for the entertainment of their guests. Mr. Seymour took an opportunity to sketch.[20]

Following the era of explorers such as Meriwether Lewis, William Clark, Zebulon Pike, John Bradbury, and Stephen Long came the fur trappers, also known as the mountain men. The height of the trapping era lasted from 1822 to 1840. The movement was spurred on by major fur companies, including the American Fur Company and the Rocky Mountain Fur Company of the United States, along with the Hudson Bay Company and Northwest Company of Canada. Mountain men, hired by the fur companies, worked in small groups or alone throughout the rugged Rocky Mountain region of the West. Mountain men lived in constant danger of mother nature, grizzly bears, and sometimes attacks by native tribes. In particular, trappers went after the pelts of North American beavers. The demand for beaver pelts was driven by well-heeled city dwellers in the east coast of the United States and Europeans who craved the latest fashion trend of the time—beaver hats.

The interior of the hut of a Mandan chief by Karl Bodmer and N. Desmadryl, between 1839 and 1842. According to the Library of Congress: "Swiss-born Karl Bodmer accompanied Prince Maximilian zu Wied-Newied on his travels to the United States from 1832 to 1834. They visited Mandan leader Dippäuch in his home at Mih-Tutta-Hand-Kusch from December 1833 to April 1834, carefully depicting life on the North American plains" (Library of Congress).

When they weren't trapping animals in the wilderness, mountain men would wait out the season in forts or winter camps such as Bent's Fort near present-day La Junta, Colorado. George Bird Grinnell, anthropologist and naturalist, explained that besides trading, the forts and trading posts were hubs of social activities which included music:

> On holidays, such as Christmas and the Fourth of July, balls were often held at the fort, in which the travelers present, the trappers, employees, Indians, Indian women and Mexican women all took part. Employed about the post there was always a Frenchman or two who could play the violin and guitar. On one occasion Frank P. Blair, then twenty-three years old, afterward a general in the Union army, vice-presidential candidate, and United States senator, played the banjo all night at a ball at the fort.[21]

According to David Dary, historian and writer, the mountain men would trap in the fall and the spring. In the late spring, the fur trappers, or mountain men, fully loaded with beaver pelts, would sell the pelts to fur buyers. Trappers met up with tradesmen in "beaver country" where they sold their bounty of furs and filled up with supplies for another year of trapping. This meeting of mountain men, fur traders, suppliers, Indians, explorers and sometimes preachers and missionaries became known as the annual rendezvous, which, according to David Dary, was a "fair, vacation, fiesta, and reunion all rolled into one."[22] Activities of the rendezvous included drinking, storytelling, gambling, foot races, wrestling, arm wrestling, shooting competitions and, of course, music and dance.

Mountain man Bill Hamilton described the many cultures represented at the rendezvous along with a list of activities: "Besides the trappers there were at the rendezvous many Indians-Shoshones, Utes, and a few lodges of Navajos—who came to exchange their pelts for whatever they stood in need of. The days were given to horse-racing, foot-racing, shooting-matches; and in the evening were heard the music of voice and drum and the sound of dancing."[23]

Hamilton also wrote about a dance of the Shoshone in the evening at the rendezvous: "at night the young folks would keep the village awake until midnight with their singing and dancing. They enjoyed life for all its worth, giving no heed to the morrow."[24]

James Pierson Beckwourth was born into slavery in Virginia to an African American mother and an English father. He obtained emancipation as a young adult and moved to St. Louis where he worked as a blacksmith apprentice before making his way west in 1822. Through the years he worked as a trapper, explorer, frontier guide and businessman. Among his many adventures, he claimed he became a beloved chief of the Crow tribe in present-day Montana. A natural storyteller and larger-than-life figure, he dictated his life story to Thomas D. Booner, who molded Beckwourth's narrative into a book, *The Life and Adventures of James P. Beckwourth, Mountaineer, Scout, and Pioneer, and Chief of the Crow Nation of Indians,* which was published in 1856. This may be the first account of life in the West as told by an African American. His story included several detailed descriptions of musical events that he either witnessed or participated in. On one occasion, he painted a picture of an annual rendezvous:

> The absent parties began to arrive, one after the other, at the rendezvous. Shortly after, General Ashley and Mr. Sublet came in, accompanied with three hundred pack mules, well laden with goods and all things necessary for the mountaineers and the Indian trade. It may well be supposed that the arrival of such a vast amount of luxuries from the East did not pass off without a general celebration. Mirth, songs, dancing, shouting, trading, running, jumping, singing, racing, target-shooting, yarns, frolic, with all sorts of extravagances that white men

or Indians could invent, were freely indulged in. The unpacking of the medicine water contributed not a little to the heightening of our festivities.[25]

After his days as a fur trapper, Beckwourth lived with the Crow Indians where he often fought against enemy tribes. This particular war story mentions music. The Crow brutally attacked a group of Black Feet Indians who were passing through the area. Beckwourth tells the story: "When we arrived within sight of our foes we found them all very merry; they were singing the Wolf Song, or Song of the Spies, they having no suspicion that they were so near to the Crow Village. We went cautiously up to the forts, which were but a few yards apart; and while they were yet singing, we pointed our guns, and, at a signal given by me, all fired. The whole party were slain; their notes were cut short in death."[26]

In another account, Beckwourth remembered participating in a scalp dance. "That night the scalp dance was performed, which I took part in, as great as any man as any. I sung the Crow song, to the special admiration of the fair sex."[27] Beckwourth also described the dance and drumming style of the Crow Indians: "All the dancing is performed in the open air, with the solid ground for a floor. It consists of jumping up and down, intermixed with violent gestures and stamping; they keep time with a drum or tambourine, composed of antelope-skin stretched over a hoop, the whole party singing during the performance."[28]

Moving on from Beckwourth, yet closely linked to the history of the fur trappers, are the Métis people of mixed European and indigenous ancestry who are mostly concentrated in Canada and the Northern part of the United States today. The Métis, to this day, maintain a deep-rooted fiddle-playing and step-dancing tradition which dates back to the fur-trapping era. In the film *Medicine Fiddle*, Michael Loukinen explained, "Reflecting both European and Native influence, this hybrid fiddling and dancing culture moved West with the fur trade from Ontario across the Northern United States and Canada."[29] The fiddle tradition is a way for Métis to keep their culture alive and also a way for people to remember their loved ones who have passed away.

Al Wiseman, of the Métis tribe, lives in Choteau, Montana, where I grew up. When I spoke to him in 2017, he was 80 years old. I asked him how the Métis became interested in the fiddle. He said French, Irish and Schottische fur trappers from Canada introduced the fiddle in the West. "Once the Métis got a hold of the fiddle, they were off, they had a God given talent." The fiddle was played in private homes where the music would go all night into the morning. At dinnertime, the musicians played the "Supper Waltz"; then they took a break and soon picked up their instruments and got back to work. People brought sandwiches, and there was always a coffeepot on the stove—no electricity in the early days. The lead fiddler accompanied by a guitarist or another fiddler would play the chords, keeping time, which was called "bumping" or "bucking." Al Wiseman added, "If no other musicians were available to accompany, the fiddler would keep time with their feet."[30]

Al Wiseman spoke to Kirsten Inbody, a Montana journalist, about the profound role of the fiddle in the Métis culture. "It wasn't an easy life up there (on the South Fork of the Teton River near Choteau, Montana), but two things held them together—great faith in the Lord and the fiddle." He commented further, "They called the mountains and open spaces their church. Fiddling dances were about every Saturday night."[31]

Al Wiseman told me one more story about the healing power of music. One of Al's friends, a Métis fiddler by the name of Marvin Fatty Morin, had a debilitating stroke.

Following the stroke, Morin wasn't able to remember his own name, and the doctors told him he would never be able to play the fiddle again. Morin told the doctor, "to hell with it, I'll play again," and he did play again. Wiseman explained how Morin, who played from memory, would sometimes have to ask his wife how to start a tune; she would strike up a chord, and he would play.

Al Wiseman lent me a personal cassette tape featuring Morin playing Métis fiddle tunes accompanied by another fiddler. The tape was recorded after Morin's stroke. On the tape, Morin commented that he plays all of the tunes by instinct. His repertoire included "Ragtime Annie," "Maiden's Prayer," "du reine hornpipe," "Goodnight Waltz," "Maple Sugar," and many others.[32] Morin's love for the music, his mastery of the fiddle and his command of the repertoire shined through in every irresistible tune on the cassette tape. Wiseman explained, "it's always been said Métis music was played straight from the heart."[33]

The Métis fiddle repertoire included jigs, reels, waltzes, two-steps, and schottisches. The music was passed down through the generations via the oral tradition. It was mostly men who played the fiddle. The position of lead fiddle player was a coveted spot, and some fiddlers did not give up their position easily; consequently, the older fiddlers were reluctant to teach the songs to the younger fiddle players.

Some of Al Wiseman's favorite Métis fiddle tunes include "Leather Britches," and "Red River Jig." "Red River Jig," by the way, is the Métis national anthem. Al Wiseman reminded me that Pierre Cruzatte, the fiddle player of the Lewis and Clark Expedition, was Métis. Indeed, Cruzatte was of Omaha Indian and French descent.

On March 26, 1922, the *Missoulian* published a story by Will Caves about music in the fur-trapping era. According to the *Missoulian* article, Alexander Ross led an expedition through what Ross referred to as "The Valley of Troubles," still known today as Ross' Hole in southwest Montana, near the Idaho border. The party was made up of "two Americans, 17 Canadians, five half-breeds, 31 Indian children 25 Indian women, and 64 children: with 32 horses."[34] The company toiled through snow and freezing temperatures; they were hungry, wet, and cold and not making much progress on their journey; morale was low. Alexander Ross devised a plan to lift the party members' spirits. According to the *Missoulian* article:

It occurred to Alexander Ross that if by some means he could manage to restore cheerfulness to the

Marcus Whitman sketch, artist unknown (courtesy Whitman College and Northwest Archives).

company he then eventually would succeed in his enterprise. In the company was a fiddler, a genius, who contrived a crude but apparently quite satisfactory violin and bow, while another had a drum. Ross announced that they would have a "show" that evening. There was a large tent, in and about which gathered the entire party. With fiddle and drum for an orchestra, different members were each prevailed upon to add his little to the entertainment: a song, a dance, a story, or a recitation. Probably many of the efforts were ludicrous. At all event they were productive of much merriment and were continued well into the night. The morning found the gloom entirely dispelled, and with everyone in good humor, the men went back to the gigantic task in earnest, to the end that there were no more unnecessary delays.[35]

Towards the end of the fur era, mountain men and tradesmen guided missionaries who went west to convert indigenous people to Christianity, or in the words of the missionaries, to civilize "the heathens." One of the earliest missionary parties to go west included the Presbyterian missionaries Marcus Whitman and his wife, Narcissa Prentiss Whitman, along with Henry H. Spalding and his wife, Eliza Hart Spalding. In

Narcissa Whitman sketch, artist unknown (courtesy Whitman College and Northwest Archives).

1836, the party traveled by a simple wagon and horseback from New York on a grueling 3,000-mile journey across the continent to Oregon Country. Narcissa and Eliza often rode their horses, and when they did, they rode side saddle, in the style of a "proper lady." Narcissa and Eliza were the first white women to make the journey west.

Narcissa Prentiss married Marcus Whitman on the evening before their departure to the West in March of 1836. She was 27; he was 33. The closing hymn was "Yes, My Native Land." Narcissa sang out in her beautiful soprano voice, which she was known for. Family and friends cried into their handkerchiefs; perhaps the guests sensed they would never see Narcissa again.

> Bear me on, thou restless ocean
> Let the winds my canvass swell;
> Heaves my heart with warm emotion,
> While I go far hence to dwell,
> Glad I bid thee, glad I bid thee- Native land, Farewell, Farewell.

Missionaries such as the Spaldings and the Whitmans wrote letters home about the beauty, the open space and the healthy living available in the West. Religion was the bedrock of American culture in the nineteenth century, and people identified with the missionaries. On June 3, 1836, while on her journey West, Narcissa wrote in her journal: "I wish I could describe to you how we live so that you can realize it. Our manner of living is far preferable to any in the States. I never was so contented and happy before neither have I enjoyed such health for years."[36] Narcissa wrote about friendly encounters with Native Americans. For example, when she first encountered the Pawnee, she commented that she and Eliza were visited throughout the day and night by curious Pawnee who would peek in the tent and grin in astonishment at the sight of the two white women.

Inspired by personal letters and journal accounts of the missionaries, people in the East envisioned themselves crossing the plains and starting a new life just as the missionaries had done. Narcissa Whitman wrote a letter to Reverend and Mrs. Leverett Hull from Vancouver (in present-day Washington state) on October 25, 1836. Narcissa gives praise for her new home: "The means of sustenance and comfort we find here, so much beyond our expectations when we left home, calls the most sincere praise and gratitude to God from ourselves and our beloved friend at home."[37] In the same letter she pleads with her friends to join her: "You see that we are situated alone and need help immediately. We want a minister with us. Will any of the dear Christian friends at home hear us and help us in this great work?"[38]

This kind of plea affected the attitudes and actions of east coast residents such as Sarah Raymond Herndon who found inspiration in the actions of the missionaries. On her overland journey of 1865, Sarah wrote in her journal: "When devoted men and women leave home, friends, and enjoyments of life to go to some far heathen land, obeying the command: 'Go, preach my Gospel, to every creature,' we look on and applaud and desire to emulate them."[39]

The Whitmans first arrived at Fort Vancouver in 1836. Narcissa Whitman was charming and with a beautiful voice, according to a former pupil, Dr. William Fraser, who wrote about his time with the Whitmans and the Spaldings at Fort Vancouver: "In the autumn we were cheered by the society for Doctor Whitman and his worthy partner, not forgetting Mr. and Mrs. Spalding. By these good people the vocal powers of the young and the school children were developed and improved. Poor Mrs. Whitman was prima donna. I still remember a hymn learnt from her: 'Watchman, Tell Us of the Night.'"[40]

"Watchman Tell Us of the Night"

Watchman, tell us of the night,
what its signs of promise are.
Traveler, what a wondrous sight:
see that glory-beaming star.
Watchman, does its beauteous ray
news of joy or hope foretell?
Traveler, yes; it brings the day,
promised day of Israel.

Watchman, tell us of the night;
higher yet that star ascends.
Traveler, blessedness and light,
peace and truth its course portends.
Watchman, will its beams alone
gild the spot that gave them birth?
Traveler, ages are its own;
see, it bursts o'er all the earth.

Watchman, tell us of the night,
for the morning seems to dawn.
Traveler, shadows take their flight;
doubt and terror are withdrawn.
Watchman, you may go your way;
hasten to your quiet home.
Traveler, we rejoice today,
for Emmanuel has come!

On September 13, 1836, Narcissa wrote: "This morning visited the school to hear the children sing. It consists of about fifty-one children who have French fathers and Indian mothers."[41] Eliza Spalding and Narcissa Whitman stayed at Fort Vancouver for eight weeks while their husbands looked for mission sites. At the request of Doctor McLoughlin, who was in charge of the fort and the school, Narcissa taught songs to the children. On September 30, 1836, "I sing about an hour every evening with the children, teaching them new tunes, at the request of Doctor McLoughlin."[42]

Myra Eells visited the Whitmans' home at *Wailatpu* (the place of Rye Grass) near the homes of the Cayuse and the Walla Walla Indians in what is now Eastern Washington. She commented about a meeting led by Marcus and Narcissa for about 40 to 50 Indians of all ages who were gathered together on the shady side of the house for a reading lesson. At the end of the lesson, according to Myra Eells, "a hymn in the Nez Percé language, learned by rote from their teachers, was then sung, and the exercises closed with prayer by Dr. Whitman in the same tongue."[43]

Neither the Nez Percé nor the Cayuse converted to the Christian faith during the Whitmans' time with them at the mission. However, there is a record that the Nez Percé enjoyed prayers and also singing the hymns taught to them by Narcissa Whitman. Jefferson Farnham explored the West in the early nineteenth century and witnessed the Whitmans at work with the Nez Percé and Cayuse. He also wrote of Narcissa's boundless energy, "Mrs. Whitman is an indefatigable instructress. The children read in monosyllables from a primer lately published at the Clear Water station. After reading, they repeated a number of hymns in the Nez Percé, composed by Mr. Smith, of the Spokane station. These were afterwards sung. They learn music readily."[44]

According to Mr. B.F. Nichols, who was at the mission from October 1844 to February 1845, Dr. Whitman was also involved in teaching hymns at the mission: "While attending school at the mission I often heard the Doctor preach. He held regular church services on Sunday and had prayer meeting every Wednesday night. I have heard him preach to the Indians in their native tongue, and lead them in the singing of hymns in their own language which he had himself composed. He seemed to take great interest in his mission work, more than any man I ever saw."[45]

The Whitmans had a daughter named Alice. Narcissa wrote about her darling daughter in a letter to Mr. Lyman P. Judson dated September 28, 1838: "Dear child, you know not how tenderly we love her. She loves to sing so well, especially Nez Percé hymns, that her mother finds great comfort in her & most all of her talk is about Jesus Christ & the Savior as she has learned to lisp his blessed name."[46]

A crushing tragedy struck the Whitmans when two-year-old Alice died in a drowning near the family's home. After their daughter's death, the Whitmans fostered three children of mixed European and Indian descent; they also took in seven siblings who had been orphaned on the Oregon Trail. The Whitmans eventually gave up trying to

Whitman Mission sketch, artist unknown (courtesy Whitman College and Northwest Archives).

Christianize the Indians and turned their attention to helping emigrants on the Oregon Trail by offering their mission outside of Walla Walla as a way station.

With thousands of emigrants passing through the Walla Walla area, tensions between pioneers and the Cayuse reached a climax in 1847. A devastating case of measles wiped out an estimated half of the Cayuse tribe who lived near the Whitman Mission. Many of the Indians blamed the Whitmans for the measles outbreak, and the Cayuse revolted, killing the Whitmans and 11 others in what came to be known as the Whitman massacre. Cassandra Tate, a Whitman historian, wrote, "The attack accelerated efforts to extend federal authority over the present-day states of Washington, Idaho, and Oregon and parts of Montana and Wyoming. It also helped make Narcissa—the only woman to be killed—a symbol of the cultural clashes that played out between whites and Indians throughout the West."[47]

Regarding the hymns of the Nez Percé, in 1897, Juliet L. Axtell, a missionary woman in present-day Idaho, compiled a book of hymns taught to the Nez Percé by early missionaries. Levi W. Jonas, native Nez Percé and the superintendent of the First Indian Presbyterian Church in Kamiah, Idaho, translated the hymns into the Nez Percé language. Juliet Axtell mentioned that some of the hymns were contributed by Henry Spalding, who had traveled west with the Whitmans. "Awake and Sing the Song," written in 1784 by William Hammond, is one of the hymns represented in the hymnal. To this day, some of the hymns taught to the Nez Percé by the Spaldings and the Whitmans over 200 years ago are still sung at worship services, for instance, at the First Indian Presbyterian Church in Kamiah, Idaho, which is the first Indian Presbyterian church, built in 1871. The church has ties going back to Chief Twisted Hair, who met Lewis and Clark in 1805. The son of Nez Percé Chief Twisted Hair, Hallalhotsoot, nicknamed Chief Lawyer, born

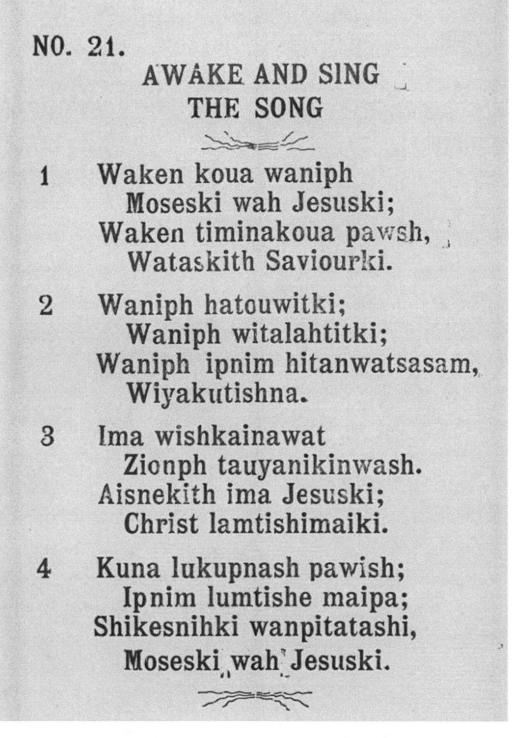

NO. 21.

AWAKE AND SING THE SONG

1 Waken koua waniph
Moseski wah Jesuski;
Waken timinakoua pawsh,
Wataskith Saviourki.

2 Waniph hatouwitki;
Waniph witalahtitki;
Waniph ipnim hitanwatsasam,
Wiyakutishna.

3 Ima wishkainawat
Zionph tauyanikinwash.
Aisnekith ima Jesuski;
Christ lamtishimaiki.

4 Kuna lukupnash pawish;
Ipnim lumtishe maipa;
Shikesnihki wanpitatashi,
Moseski wah Jesuski.

"Awake and Sing the Song" printed in the Nez Percé language from Juliet L. Axtell's *Gospel Hymns in the Nez Perce Language* (N.P., 1897) held at Washington State University Libraries' Manuscripts, Archives, and Special Collections (courtesy WSU Libraries).

circa 1800, was the founder of the church and had worked with both the Spaldings and the Whitmans as a guide and teacher.

On the heels of Lewis and Clark, the explorers, fur trappers, and missionaries contributed to the rich musical traditions of the American West. Explorers such as Zebulon Pike witnessed and wrote about the musical traditions of Spanish and Mexican people who had been living in the New Mexico region before the 1600s. Through their words, we know that music, accompanied by dance, was the number one diversion for people living in New Mexico. Mountain men such as Bill Hamilton danced and sang to fiddle music at the annual rendezvous, an event where Native Indians, French, English, and United Statesmen gathered together for trade, celebration, and social connection in the Rocky Mountain wilderness. James Beckwourth, an African American frontiersman, made his way west and witnessed the annual rendezvous and the music traditions of the Blackfeet, Cheyenne, and Crow firsthand. The Métis fiddle culture, still alive today, is a result of the mix of indigenous and European cultures dating back to the fur-trading era. Missionaries such as the Whitmans and the Spaldings used music as a tool for their missionary work as they taught Christian hymns to the Nez Percé.

For all of these groups of various ethnicities, educational backgrounds, and motivations who made their way west, the music they carried in their hearts undoubtedly provided comfort in their place in the rugged frontier, helped them connect with each other, and reminded them of the lives they left behind in the East. The music and dance traditions these groups heard and witnessed as they traveled throughout the West served as a reminder that they were by no means the first musicians or audiences in the West. Music of Native Americans, each tribe with their own music and dance traditions, filled the Western landscape long before the early explorers, trappers and missionaries arrived on the scene. Furthermore, the language and songs of the West, along with indigenous languages, included French, Spanish, Italian and English. The next group of people called to the West would be emigrants on the Oregon Trail who would literally follow in the wagon tracks of early explorers, fur traders, mountain men, and missionaries.

4

Setting the Stage for the Oregon Trail

American Musical Life and Oregon Fever (circa 1830–1850)

The Oregon fever rages here. Since the visit of an agent
from Missouri, on his way to Washington City, sundry meetings
have been held and projects formed for emigration to that newly
found El Dorado: but whether any of our citizens will be so foolish
as to leave a comfortable home for a wilderness, remains to be seen.
—New York Daily Tribune, February 23, 1843

While the missionaries Narcissa Whitman and Eliza Spalding taught hymns to the Nez Percé in the wilds of Oregon Country, grizzled fur trappers, Native Americans, and fur tradesmen tapped their toes and danced to fiddle tunes at the annual summer Rocky Mountain Rendezvous. And in the East, music played multiple roles in the day-to-day lives of Americans. In a broad-brush stroke, this chapter explores the vibrant home and community musical life of nineteenth-century Americans and presents some of the reasons why so many Easterners found themselves in the grip of "Oregon Fever."

Throughout the nineteenth century, music in the United States flourished in private homes, churches, urban centers and rural communities. In this era, a time before radio, television, and the internet, music was the main form of entertainment. Regardless of socioeconomic status, race, or geographical background, participation in some type of regular musical activity was the norm for many people living in the United States. Music teachers found plentiful opportunities for teaching students in both private and public settings. Instrumental and sheet music retailers, door-to-door instrument salesmen, and music publishers fed the appetites of music hungry Americans. Eager audiences regularly attended public performances, including symphony orchestras, theater productions, operas, instrumental and vocal recitals, and ballets. Mid-nineteenth-century Americans enthusiastically welcomed opportunities for singing together—be it around the home piano, in community meetings, at church, in school, or in organized choral societies.

Participation in "singing schools," which focused on reading music notation and singing a cappella in groups, was a particularly popular organized musical activity that swept across the nation in the mid-nineteenth century. "Singing schools" were not really schools; rather, they were well-attended three-week workshops taught by itinerant singing instructors who traveled from town to town. *The Sacred Harp,* an instructional singing book published in 1844, introduced shape note notation—a method for singing instructors to teach four-part harmony to large groups of singers in a short amount of time.

The importance of music in the nineteenth-century United States was evident within the publishing industry. Women's periodicals such as *Godey's Magazine and Lady's Book* regularly included sheet music along with articles on fashion, knitting patterns, housekeeping tips, and short stories. *Godey's Magazine* often included reviews of the latest sheet music releases, and these reviews provide us insight into the popular music of the day. The style of songs and pieces, often referred to as parlor or salon music, included sentimental ballads, variations on popular songs, lighthearted dance tunes, and were of moderate difficulty—aimed at the skills of the amateur musician. This type of repertoire satisfied the musical needs of musicians who sang and played in their home environments for their own enjoyment or for the entertainment of visiting guests. Below is the music review as it appeared in *Godey's Magazine and Lady's Book*, Volume 38, 1839:

> "My Mother I Obey!" Words by Charles P. Shiras. Music by Henry Kieber. a comical and pretty song.
> "New Mary Blane Waltz," by Matthias Keller. This favorite version is dedicated to the lady herself whose name it bears.
> "The Maiden Polka," by E. Lenschow. This fine folk polka is dedicated to the Junior Bachelors' Association and is a companion to the favorite "Bachelor Polka."
> "Bouquet of Melodies. No 2," by Edward Pique. Mr. P. has arranged for the guitar a selection of popular melodies and is publishing them in numbers.

Another periodical, the *Lady's Musical Library*, for the amateur musician, featured an array of sheet music in a variety of styles such as waltzes, marches, popular songs of the day, and traditional folk songs. The sheet music was arranged for guitar, solo piano, four-hand piano, and voice with piano accompaniment. And yet another publication, the *Musical Visitor*, a monthly journal marketed to amateur as well as professional musicians, featured articles about composers, concert reviews, singing tips, music history, and current sheet music, along with a wide range of topics from child-rearing tips to political commentary to obituaries.

Newspaper articles of the time spoke of the prevalence of music in the home and of the importance of music within family life. In 1810 the *Philadelphia Mirror of Taste and Dramatic Censor* reported: "Almost every home included between the Delaware and the Schuylkill has its piano or harpsichord. Almost every young lady can make a noise upon some instrument or other … we take it for granted that we are a very musical people."

On July 7, 1843, the *Holly Springs Gazette,* printed in Holly Springs, Mississippi, published an article about the importance of music in a family. Below are the main points as they appeared in the paper:

1. Music is a talent which every child has in a greater or lesser amount; a talent to be watched and cultivated.

2. The early culture of musical talent in children, is a point of far higher importance than has yet been appreciated by parents.

3. The encouragements of the profession of teaching music is an important duty of parents and head of family.

4. The cultivation of both vocal and instrumental music is both desirable and wise. Give your Daughter a piano or a guitar and your son a flute along with private instruction on their instruments.

5. Music in families is a means of domestic cheerfulness. A musical family, in spite of perplexities and trials, will be a cheerful family. You can have the sunshine of cheerfulness in your house, in the most rainy, cheerless, wintry day which ever was, if you have music. (This last point seems particularly apropos of those families who would soon find extreme trials and tribulations on the Oregon Trail.)

Many of the families that took to the Oregon Trail came from educated, middle-class backgrounds and would have been the kind of people that read the journals and periodicals that were mentioned above. Thanks to the industrial revolution many people in the middle class and upper-middle class found themselves with ample free time on their hands for indulging in musical activities and held a keen desire to better themselves through the arts. At the turn of the nineteenth century, almost every middle- and upper-class family owned some type of musical instrument. An instrument in the home, such as a flute, harp, piano, melodion (a type of small organ), harpsichord, or guitar signaled a sophisticated, educated, and refined family.

The ability to play an instrument was a highly desired skill for young ladies of marriage age. In the nineteenth century, it was expected by family and society that women should marry. Young women's education, daily activities, and social interactions were aimed at attracting a desirable husband who would provide a home, a stable income, and all of the necessities of life. As part of their education, young ladies often learned how to play the piano or harpsichord, the harp, the guitar, and they also learned to sing. For the most part, young women did not play the violin at this time; it was thought of as a masculine and an inappropriate instrument for a young lady.

Guitar playing and singing often went hand in hand. Ladies sang songs and accompanied themselves on the guitar or they provided accompaniment to others. Many examples of paintings and drawings of the era showcased women playing guitars in parlor settings. The earliest guitars were imported from Europe and made their way into American parlors in the early 1800s. These early guitars, often referred to as parlor guitars, were small instruments with nylon strings which were played by fingerpicking the strings with the thumb and three fingers. The style of guitars created a warm and gentle sound conducive to small spaces—perfect for the parlor in early American homes. Sheet music of the early 1800s included pieces written in standard music notation—the chords and strumming patterns were written out on the staff rather than written in the modern style of using chord symbols.

A renowned woman guitarist and composer of the time was Delores Bevares de Goñi, who immigrated to the United States from Spain in 1840. Her guitar concerts were wild successes in New York, Richmond, Washington, D.C., and Philadelphia. She was so popular, in fact, that in 1843, C.F. Martin Sr., of Martin guitars, built Delores de Goñi a special guitar from Rosewood sourced from Guatemala, called the "de Goñi," that featured an × bracing design which created a superb tone. The guitar also featured heart-shaped pearl tuning pegs.[1]

On November 7, 1840, the *Morning Herald* of New York reprinted a concert review from the *London Morning Post*, which celebrated Madame de Goñi's musicianship and explained the desired sound and expression of the nineteenth-century guitar.

Madame de Goñi is a performer of the highest order upon that most difficult instrument, the guitar, which in her hands, becomes the medium of transferring to the senses of her pleased auditors, a correct notion of the romantic and most charming music with which lovers of

Woman playing an upright piano, published between 1817–1824. This image was an advertisement for George E. Blake, a Philadelphia piano-forte maker (Library of Congress).

Spain are traditionally connected. We recognized with much pleasure that no attempt was made at a display of outrageous execution, which is altogether opposed to the nature and construction of the instrument. The guitar is only pleasing when it becomes the interpreter of sentiment, or the support of the voice, for which latter its illimitable powers of modulation peculiarly adapt it, appears to be fully aware of this, for her performances on the instrument were marked throughout by her confining herself to the legitimate application; but this application was characterized by a tone deep in pathos, such as, we believe, a woman only can feel and express. The lady played three airs of her own composition, which were very beautifully written as well as executed.

Madame de Goñi later became Mrs. Knoop when she married her second husband, George Knoop, a cellist she met and performed with in the United States. Her compositions, all written for the guitar, include, "L'Ahambra Waltz," "The Flowers of Andalusia," "Rosignol Polka," "Carnival of Venice," and "The Adieu."

Madame De Goni (Maria Dolores Esturias y Navarres) by A.G. Powers, oil on canvas, New Orleans, 1840 (courtesy Frick Art Reference Library).

When Americans traveled west on the Oregon Trail, they took the minimal amount of belongings that would fit into their wagons. For the most part, pianos and other heavy, cumbersome keyboard instruments, such as pump organs and harpsichords, were given away or sold. However, guitars made the trip, and mostly women are mentioned as the guitarists in journals, while men are mentioned as singers and violinists. Chapter 6, "The Music at the Heart of the Oregon Trail Experience," digs into the instruments on the trail.

Male musicians of the early nineteenth century typically played the flute, string instruments such as violin and violoncello (cello), the piano, and later on, in the mid-nineteenth century, band instruments such as the cornet and saxhorn (a brass instrument). For men, music provided a way of interacting in social situations. A man who could read music and play the piano could cozy up next to a lady on the piano bench for some lively four-hand music. If he wasn't a pianist, but he could read music, then he could stand by to turn pages for a lady playing a solo piece. Musical interactions represented an acceptable way for young men and women to interact.

And what kind of music did people play in their parlors? Published music of the nineteenth century included a wide variety of genres. For example: opera themes such as Bellini's "Norma"; folk songs such as "Come All Ye Fair and Tender Girls"; patriotic tunes such as "A Yankee Ship and a Yankee Crew"; and favorite hymns such as "Wondrous Love" were all mixed together and served up as an American musical stew for the delight of both musicians and audiences. Music was a participatory event—when it came time to gather around the piano for sing-alongs, everyone participated.

Between the years 1820–1860, those interested in playing the ever-popular piano may have turned to music from early American composers such as Louis Moreau Gottschalk, William Mason, and Anthony Philip Heinrich, who was known as "The Beethoven of America." Gottschalk, a New Orleans-born virtuosic performer, utilized both Latin American and Creole influences in his compositions. This time period coincided with the Romantic Period in music. Typical music of the time, especially keyboard

Louis Moreau Gottschalk. Artist: Major Sarony and Knapp, circa 1860. Lithograph with tinstone on paper (National Portrait Gallery, Smithsonian Institution).

and vocal music, included programmatic pieces—music that expressed scenes in nature, journeys, moods, or places. Rondos, dances, and sets of variations were also popular.

"Woodman, Spare That Tree," written in 1837 with words by George Pope Morris and music by Henry Russell, is considered to be the first environmental protest song. Marion Dix Sullivan composed over 20 songs, including "The Blue Juniata," written in 1844 and named for a river in Pennsylvania. "The Blue Juniata" stands out as the first popular music hit written by a woman.

The fact that the women Marion Dix and Delores di Goñi were successful with their music was an anomaly of the nineteenth century. While women were expected to know how to play the piano, guitar, harp, or other instruments, the idea of a woman performing in a public venue beyond the parlor or the idea of a woman composing music for commercial sales were both ostentatious notions at the time. Women such as Marion Dix and Madame di Goñi were the exceptions to the rule. Other exceptions to the male-dominated publishing industry include several parlor songs in sheet music form that were written by women, such as "I've Got the Blues Today" by Miss Sarah Graham, "The Ella Waltz" for piano by Miss Emily Wandell, and "Sentimental Polka" for piano by Adele Hohnstock.

Oftentimes, a composition was written by a woman, but the composer's name was incomplete or the piece was attributed to "Anonymous." For example, Young Lady of Georgia wrote "No More, Song" for solo piano. A Lady of Virginia wrote "Lady Mine," also for solo piano. "Bounteous Beauty [from] White Lady," a vocal solo with piano accompaniment, was attributed to the composer named: An Amateur.

One woman, Eliza Cook, wrote the lyrics to what may be considered a protest song about the unjust practice of hunting Native Americans and stealing their land: "Oh Why Does the White Man Follow My Path: Song of the Indian Hunter," with music by William Dempster, was published in 1846.

> Oh! why does the white man follow my path,
> Like the hound on the tiger's track?
> Does the blush on my dark cheek waken he wrath?
> Doe he covet the bow on my back?
> He has rivers and seas, where the billows and breeze
> Bear riches for him alone;
> And the sons of the wood never plunge in the flood
> Which the white man calls his own.
> Why then should he come to the streams where none
> But the red-skin dare to swim?
> Why, why should he wrong the hunter-one,
> Who never did harm to him?
> The Father above thought fit to give
> To the white man corn and wine;
> There are golden fields, where they may live,
> But the forest shades are mine.
> The eagle hath its place of rest,
> The wild horse where to dwell;
> And the Spirit that gave the bird its nest,
> Made me a home as well.
> Then back, go back from the red man's track,
> For the hunter's eyes grow dim,
> To find that the white man wrongs the one
> Who never did harm to him.

Is seems that east coast residents were fascinated with Native Americans and their culture, and this fascination was reflected in some of the sheet music of the time. In addition to the song mentioned above, the Library of Congress digital collection includes other songs with Native American themes such as "The Indian's Prayer" (1846) for voice and piano, "The Indian's Dream" (1848) for voice and piano, and "The Indian's Song of Peace" (1851) for voice and piano.

Other songs with a westward-looking theme spoke of the open space, the freedom, and the adventure to be had in the West such as "Westward Ho!" (1839), "Oh Fly to the Prairie" (1839), "Prairie Song" (1850), "My Home's on the Prairie Lea" (1850), "Prairie Waltz" (1850), and "To the West" (1854). Judging from the composition dates of these other westward migration-themed songs, it seems people started catching "Oregon fever" as early as the 1830s, and that fever was still burning hot into the 1850s. Letters and personal accounts of the early missionaries and fur trappers spoke of the lush farm land, clean living, and economic opportunities to be found in the West. These alluring stories enticed thousands of emigrants to pack up and leave a life of familiarity for a new adventure in the West.

The polka represented yet another style of mid-nineteenth-century music. In 1844, the same year that Miriam Dix composed "The Blue Juniata," the polka, originally from Bohemia, was all the rage in Europe and America, and "Polkamania" filled the air. "Everyone who could devise a tune, from amateur to Johann Strauss, composed polkas."[2] Polka sheet music burst onto the American music scene, including "The Favorite American Polka," "The Esmerelda Polka," and "The Polka Song." Other popular songs in the year 1844 included "Miss Lucy Neale" by James Sanford, "Open Thy Lattice, Love" by Stephen Foster, and "Spring Song, No. 6, Op. 5" by Felix Mendelssohn from the collection, "*Sechs Lieder ohne Worte*" (Songs Without Words).

The Public-School Singing Book published in Lancaster, Pennsylvania (1848), features lyrics to over 150 songs. This musical time capsule paints a musical picture of the type of songs that were important at the time. The type of songs in the songbook included sacred songs such as "Prayer," "The Blissful Hope," and "Trust in the Lord." Patriotic songs included "My County Tis of Thee," "The Star-Spangled Banner," and "Hail Columbia." Nature songs included "The Sweet Birds Are Winging," "From His Humble Grassy Bed," and "Don't Kill the Birds."

> Don't kill the birds, the little birds,
> That sing about your door;
> Soon as the joyous spring has come,
> And chilling storms are 'er,
> The little birds, how sweet they sing!
> O let them joy live,
> And never seek to take the life
> Which you can never give.[3]

Several songs in the book were inspirational: "There's Much Good Cheer," "Try Again," "Never Look Sad," and "We Will Rise." Many songs celebrated temperance: "Temperance," "The Drink for Me," "Temperance Call," and "Temperance Ode."

"Temperance Ode"

> Sparkling and bright in its liquid light
> Is the water in our glasses,
> 'Twill give you health, 'twill give you wealth,

> Ye lads and rosy lasses
> O then resign your ruby wine,
> Each smiling son and daughter,
> For there's nothing so good for the youthful blood,
> Or sweet as sparkling water.

Music publishers advertised their newest sheet music offerings in newspaper and journal advertisements from the Northern to the Southern United States. All types of sheet music were fair game for the home or parlor musician. Sheet music included arrangements for solo instruments as well as duos for a combination of instruments such as voice and piano, voice and guitar, guitar and piano, flute and piano, and violin and piano. Songs that idealized love and family life were particularly popular, such as this example of a love-tinged ballad:

"Ah! May the Red Rose Live Always"
—written by Stephen Foster (1850)

> To smile upon earth and sky!
> Why should the beautiful ever weep?
> Why should the beautiful die?
> Lending a charm to every ray
> That falls on her cheeks of light,
> Giving the zephyr kiss for kiss,
> And nursing the dew-drop bright
> Ah! may the red rose live alway.

Stephen Foster (1826–1864) was America's first songwriter. His carefully crafted compositions still hold up today with their memorable melodies and tender lyrics idealizing love, compassion, and simple home life. Songs such as "Beautiful Dreamer," "Gentle Lena Clare," and "I Dream of Jeanie with the Light Brown Hair" wistfully speak of lost loves. "Old Folks at Home" and "My Old Kentucky Home" idealized home and family life. "Hard Times Come Again No More" spoke to the struggles of the marginalized and the poor.

His works included enduring melodies of love, courtship, home and family life. In the journals of the emigrants on the Oregon Trail, Foster's songs are mentioned time and time again. His music cut across all classes and endured through the twentieth century until today. Sadly, Stephen Foster led a tragic life. Though he was a talented and well-known composer, he was plagued by alcoholism. People said he could write a song in the morning, sell it in the afternoon, and spend all of the earnings on alcohol by the end of the same night. He died alone at the age of 38 with just a few cents to his name.

Foster's lively tunes and clever lyrics such as "Camptown Races," "Ring de Banjo," and "Oh Susanna" were used in the popular stage idiom of the day—minstrel shows. The banjo, originally brought to America by African slaves, increased in popularity in the 1830s and 1840s with the inception of minstrel shows, which featured performance troupes caricaturing Black performers. "NOTE: The acts of minstrels, who typically performed in blackface, featured exaggerated and inaccurate representations of Black People in songs, dances, and comic dialogue. The popularity of minstrel shows in their heyday played a significant role in promoting negative racial stereotypes. Professional minstrel shows had fallen out of favor and effectively disappeared by the mid–20th century."[4]

One of the most popular performers of the nineteenth century was William Henry Lane, known as "Master Juba," an African American performer who "developed a unique style of using his body as a musical instrument, blending African-derived syncopated rhythms with movements of the Irish jig and reel. Lane's melding of these vernacular dance forms is recognizable today as the foundations of the ever-evolving style of American tap dance."[5] Not only a dancer, he also sang and was a tambourine virtuoso. At first, he performed in minstrel shows, and even though he was a Black man, he was required to wear blackface. At the time, white audiences would not tolerate a Black man on stage. However, in time, because of his tremendous talent, he performed without blackface for audiences all over the United States and in England.

Justin Holland was another important African American musical figure of the mid-nineteenth century. Born as a free man in Norfolk, Virginia, in 1817, he studied music at Oberlin College in Cleveland, Ohio, and went on to become a classical virtuosic guitarist, composer, teacher and social activist. He arranged over 300 works for the guitar and composed 30 original pieces.[6] His contributions to nineteenth-century guitar literature include "La Prima Donna Waltz," "Still I love Thee," and "Holland's Comprehensive Method for Guitar."

Other popular music of the era idealized home and family life. "Home, Sweet Home," with a sweet and easy-to-sing melody, was originally written for an opera in 1823 by John Howard Payne and John Duff Brown. The song remained popular throughout the nineteenth century and was mentioned as a favorite on the Oregon Trail.

"Home, Sweet Home"

Home! Home!
Sweet, sweet home!
There's no place like home
There's no place like home

'Mid pleasures and palaces
Though I may roam
Be it ever so humble
There's no place like home

A charm from the sky
Seems to hallow us there
Which seek thro' the world
Is ne'er met with elsewhere

To thee, I'll return
Overburdened with care
The heart's dearest solace
Will smile on me there
No more from that cottage
A gain I will roam
Be it ever so humble
There's no place like home

Both well-heeled Americans living in urban centers and Americans who were not as wealthy from rural areas enjoyed meaningful musical experiences that strengthened community bonds. Religion greatly influenced music traditions in both Anglo and African American communities where singing typically accompanied religious services and church gatherings. Favorite songs such as "Amazing Grace," "Rock of Ages," and "Jesus, Lover of My Soul" were sung in churches throughout the South and are still sung today.

Enslaved African Americans sang spirituals to pass time while toiling in the field, to express hope of freedom, and to worship. Spirituals were sung in a call-and-response format with the leader improvising a line and the group answering with the chorus in unison. Many spirituals expressed suffering—"Sometimes I Feel Like a Motherless Child" and "Nobody Knows the Trouble I've Seen." Others, such as "Rock O' My Soul" and "Fare Ye Well" expressed joy.[7] African American spirituals, which evolved into gospel music, were carried west by former slaves, Black cowboys, and African American cavalrymen who all played a part in the story of the Westward Expansion, which added another thread to the rich musical tapestry of the American West.

The Shakers, a protestant group, lived communally in villages and extolled the virtues of pacifism and productivity; moreover, they were against slavery. "Simple Gifts," a Shaker song, written in 1843 by Elder Joseph Bracket, represents another religious song that was popular in the 1800s and remains popular to this day. Randy Folger, a historian at a Shaker Village in Kentucky, said, "The man who wrote this ['Simple Gifts'] claimed it came to him by divine inspiration, and I truly believe that might be the case. This may be the perfect piece of music. I've sung it close to 15,000 times over the years, and I never get tired of it."[8]

> Tis the gift to be simple, 'tis the gift to be free,
> 'Tis the gift to come down where we ought to be,
> And when we find ourselves in the place just right,
> 'Twill be in the valley of love and delight.
> When true simplicity is gain'd
> To bow and to bend we shan't be asham'd,
> To turn, turn will be our delight
> 'Till by turning, turning we come round right.

While spirituals expressed sorrow and joy, and "Simple Gifts" expressed the grace and beauty of a simple lifestyle, another form of music in the nineteenth century protested alcohol and slavery. Leading this movement was the Hutchinson Family, a musical sibling quartet representative of the style of music popular with Americans in the mid-nineteenth century. In four-part harmony the quartet sang uplifting songs that echoed their political views as abolitionists—against slavery, and reformists—against alcohol consumption. The original group included one sister, Abby, and her three brothers: Judson, John, and Asa. From 1842–1849, the Hutchinsons toured the United States and Great Britain, performing popular songs of the day. Their singing was "simple, sweet, and full of mountain melody."[9] One of their most popular songs was "The Old Granite State."

While the Hutchinson Family played to packed houses in a fledgling nation, the first large wagon train of some 875 emigrants left from Independence, Missouri, on May 22, 1843. At the time, the westernmost states in the nation included Missouri, Kansas and Arkansas, and the biggest cities were New York, Philadelphia, Boston, Charleston, and New Orleans. Articles and advertisements from regional newspapers from the year 1843 shine a light on the diverse musical life of the United States in the year 1843.

In the *New York Herald*, on December 27, 1843, Mr. G. Weiss and Mr. F. Grambs announced that their cotillion band was available to play fashionable music for private parties and soirees.

In Brattleboro, Vermont, July 28, 1843, the Woodbury and Burdett Music Store advertised a new assortment of popular music including "Songs, Duets, Waltzes, Horn pipes, Marches, Quicksteps, and Overtures arranged for the piano forte along with a collection adapted for the flute, violin, and violoncello."

In Alexandria, Virginia, the *Alexandria Gazette* ran a series of advertisements throughout the spring and summer of 1843 for salesman and music instructor, William Pratt, who, by the looks of it, was a busy music educator and music entrepreneur

The Hutchinson Family: Adoniram Judson Joseph, John Wallace, Asa, and Abigail Jemima.
Artist: G. and W. Endicott Lithography, 1843. (National Portrait Gallery, Smithsonian
Institution).

of his time. Mr. Pratt offered music lessons in singing (both sacred and secular), as well as lessons on the piano, guitar, organ, harp, violin, violoncello, and the flute. It seems Mr. Pratt was also in the business of selling and lending pianos, as an advertisement on November 16, 1843, in the *Alexandria Gazette* announced that Mr. Pratt provided the piano for the concert of vocal and instrumental music by Mr. W.V. Wallace.

The *Radical*, of Bowling Green, Missouri, of September 2, 1843, printed an article titled, "Music in Children," which highlighted the benefits of music for children and illustrated the paramount importance of music in nineteenth-century society. The benefits outlined in the article reflect the effect that music would have on emigrants as they crossed the plains and headed for the West. According to the article, music "softens temper, sweetens the disposition, and tunes the heart in unison with all the better feelings of their nature. It creates domestic cheerfulness in the family circle, produces a concord of feeling in the village school, and needs to be universally practiced to fill the world with harmony."

On May 27, 1843, the *Baton Rouge Gazette* ran an advertisement known as a musical card: "H.W. Jolly, Professor of Music, respectfully, informs the ladies and gentlemen of Baton Rouge, that he is prepared to give instructions in music on the Piano or Violin, upon most reasonable terms, and at any time that may suit the convenience of this pupils." Pupils interested in lessons were to apply at his residence, which was opposite the courthouse next to the office of J.J. Burk, Esq. Mr. Jolly mentioned at the end of his advertisement that he also provided music for parties.

On November 3, 1843, the *Ottawa Free Trader* (of Ottawa, Illinois) ran an advertisement for an unusual concert that was held at the courthouse. For one night, Mr. Friend, a celebrated ventriloquist and falsetto vocalist, would be presenting a show sure to astonish and amuse the audience. Tickets were 25 cents.

On November 6, 1843, the *Daily Madisonian* of Washington, D.C., announced an upcoming vocal performance by Henry Russell where Mr. Russell would sing a variety of pieces, including "A Life in the West," "Brave Old Oak," "Fine Old English Gentleman," and "Soliloquy on the Immortality of the Soul," among other favorite songs. Henry Russell was a beloved English-born pianist, composer and performer.

The New York Philharmonic Society of New York, which later became the New York Philharmonic, launched their first season on December 7, 1842. In the second concert of the 1842–1843 season, the evening kicked off with *Eroica*, Beethoven's 3rd symphony, which was originally named *Bonaparte* for Napoleon, whom Beethoven admired. However, when Napoleon declared himself an emperor in 1804, Beethoven lost respect for Napoleon and changed the name of the symphony to *Eroica*. The program for the evening of February 18, 1843, commenced at 8 p.m. and included the following pieces, listed here as they appeared in the original program:

Part I conducted by U.C. Hill.
Sinfonia, No. 3, by Beethoven.
Aria, "*Vieu dilletto e in Ciel la Luna,*" *from Puritani*, by Bellini. Sung by Madame Otto.
Celebrated "Elegie," played by A. Boucher on the violincello, by B. Romberg.

Part II conducted by C.M. Alpers.
Overture to William Tell, by Rossini.
Aria, with Chorus, "*Inflamatus,*" (Stabat Mater), by Rossini, featuring Madame Otto.

Romanza e Rondo Alla Spagniola from Concerto in A flat, by I.N. Hummel,
performed by H.C. Timm.
Overture to Der Freischutz, by C.M. von Weber.[10]

While many Americans experienced a rich and varied musical life, the 1830s ushered in a restless desire for something better, something new—something out West. A feeling of wanderlust pervaded the nineteenth-century American psyche. Despite the nostalgic feelings of family and home expressed in the song, "Home, Sweet Home," and other popular music of the day, folks contemplated giving up their homes, lifestyles, church communities, and the lives they knew in order to follow their dream for a new life in the West. Many would act on that dream and join the great Western migration.

Several factors contributed to the rise of "Oregon Fever." The financial crisis of 1837 resulted in unemployment or low wages for those who held jobs in urban areas. In the rural landscapes of Ohio, Illinois, Kentucky, and Tennessee, epic flooding had wiped out farms. On April 17, 1843, the *Boston Musical Visitor* printed an article about the employment shortage in Boston: "Hundreds of young men and girls, boys and workmen, are at the present time in this city out of employment." The article goes on to say, "There seems to be a floating mass of persons seeking employ, many of whom come to our large cities in vain."

In addition to unemployment, the largest cities, including New York, Boston, and St. Louis, were overcrowded. Diseases—yellow fever, malaria, typhoid, tuberculosis, and cholera hung in the air. Poor sanitation, unregulated food production, and unsavory activities in big cities such as gambling, prostitution, and drinking made people yearn for a cleaner, healthier way of living. A change in the family structure of the nineteenth century also contributed to the growing desire to go West. For the first time in U.S. history, adult children could move away from home to earn a living on their own in their chosen field, as well as marry whomever they wanted.

Why go west? Enticed by stories from explorers, missionaries, and fur trappers, Americans believed accounts of what the West had to offer such as healthy living conditions, wide-open spaces, fertile farm ground, economic opportunity, free land, and the opportunity to raise a family in "paradise." The possibility of striking it rich in the gold fields attracted fortune seekers. The ruggedness and the wide-open spaces available out west appealed to adventurers. Many thought of the West as the last resort, because, for them, there was no employment and no prospects in the East. One woman explained her motivation for going West: "We had nothing to lose and we might gain a fortune."[11]

Government enticements promised employment for those who settled in the West, no matter what their occupation. For example, on December 14, 1850, the *Weekly National Intelligencer*, published in Washington, D.C., ran a letter from Samuel R. Thursten, delegate to Oregon, "To the People of the United States." In the letter he announced free land in Oregon Country—320 acres if single and 640 acres if married:

> I would wish it to be well understood that this land is among the richest land in the world; that it is nowhere surpassed in productiveness, and in all kinds of grains nowhere has its equal. The climate of Oregon is nowhere equaled for its healthfulness; and, as health is one of the greatest inducements in going to any country, I would wish to be fully understood when I say emphatically that there is not a region of country on the North American continent, not excepting New England, so widely famed for its health.

Mr. Thursten's letter was meant to entice potential emigrants with promises of healthy water, abundant fish and game, forests, prairies, fertile farmlands and a uniform climate. He listed abundant natural resources, including coal, iron, salt, granite, and "probably mines of gold." He promised: "In Oregon you will find ready employment at from five to fifteen dollars per day, according to your trade." He said five years in Oregon will be more profitable than 20 years of living east of the Rocky Mountains. In closing, Mr. Thursten informed people about the three ways to get to Oregon Country: Round Cape Horn (sailing around the southern tip of South America); The Isthmus Route (a complicated route involving a boat to Panama from the east coast, then travel across the Panama Isthmus on foot or by rickety canoe, then another boat to San Francisco); and his preferred route— The Overland Route by wagon—which would take an estimated six months and $500 (for buying a wagon, livestock, and provisions). Mr. Thursten enthusiastically wrote that the Overland Route was the fastest and most economical way to get to Oregon.

Enticements such as this letter from Mr. Thursten, along with the belief it was an American duty to settle the West, known as Manifest Destiny, launched people toward Oregon Country. Moreover, the pervasive frontier mentality meant that some people believed they were above the land and above all living creatures. People with the frontier mindset might have thought: we'll just keep moving west, we'll keep exploiting resources, and the land is ours for the taking. Many Americans had already moved to Ohio, Kentucky, and western Virginia as they became dissatisfied with the living conditions and economic opportunities in the East. Moving west made sense to them. They had already moved before, and they would move again.

As the first group of optimistic emigrants rolled out of Elm Grove, Missouri, in 1843, they left behind many things, among them home, family, friends, AND a rich musical life. The varied roles music played in the East included: a measure of social status and education, an activity at social gatherings, courtship, entertainment, worship, celebration, marking national events, self-expression, and activism. Musical traditions included singing together in community gatherings, churches, and private homes. Many people played instruments for entertainment, including pianos, violins, violoncellos (cellos), harps, flutes, guitars, and banjos. Groups of people readily gathered around to hear their friends and family play instruments and to participate in sing-alongs. Nineteenth-century Americans enjoyed going out for musical entertainment, including intimate recitals for solo or small groups of instruments, listening to musical groups such as the Hutchinson Family, and attending minstrel shows, operas, and symphonic concerts. Nineteenth-century rural America held a strong singing tradition grounded in hymns, spirituals, and gospel music.

The music of the time included a mixture of hymns, folk songs from Europe, and dance tunes such as waltzes and polkas. Concert programs regularly included a mixture of patriotic songs, art songs, opera themes, hymns, spirituals, and concert music. Compositions from well-known European composers such as Amadeus Mozart, Ludwig van Beethoven, Felix Mendelssohn, and Frederic Chopin intermingled popular music of the day made popular through the sale of sheet music by composers such as Stephen Foster and Henry Russell.

As the nineteenth century progressed into the 1850s, when westward migration was at its peak, a popular performer named Jenny Lind, often called the "Swedish Nightingale," toured America from 1850 to 1852. Louis Gottschalk, New Orleans pianist and composer, dazzled audiences with his elaborate piano compositions combining Cuban, French, and American influences. Brass bands became a favorite form of entertainment and a musical tradition that was carried out west by emigrants, military regiments, and even in the mining camps, as we'll explore later in the book.

An understanding of the music sung and played in nineteenth-century homes, churches, and community gatherings lends an insight into what music may have been played and sung on the Oregon Trail and in early frontier settlements. The next chapter takes a look at life on the Oregon Trail, including a look at the people, the route, day-to-day trail life, and the many reasons why music would become so important to people as they said goodbye to the life they knew and headed toward an unknown life in the West.

"I will go West!" composed after the westward migration was well underway, speaks to the reasons for going west, explains what the traveler hopes to find there, and also mentions the train as the mode of transportation for migrating. The transcontinental railroad was completed in 1869, toward the end of the Western migration. Below are the lyrics pulled from the original sheet music held at the Library of Congress; the melody to the song can be found in the back of the book.

"I Will Go West"

Oh! Times are tough amazing rough,
Expenses are alarming,
I will go West, it's far the best,
Try my luck at farming.

For the idea of staying here
To just earn your gruel,
Makes me feel sad and sometimes mad
'Tis so awful cruel.

Goods are so high, I heave a sigh,
At the cost of living,
My loving wife, she sees the strife
And has a spell of crying.

Now there's my boys, my chiefest joys,
To have them in the City,
Amid the harm, gives me alarm
And I ache with pity.

And there's my girls, with auburn curls
May be slaves to fashion,
And lay such stress, on how to dress,
Becomes a ruling passion.

Now it's no use, I've stood abuse.
I'll take all with dear Mary,
Settle down in a country town,
Farm it on a prairie.

My barns replete with corn and wheat,
Lots of milk and butter,
T'would be a shame, to here complain
Or a murmer utter.

Now we'll start with cheerful heart
Nor fear our journey hinders,
For we don't care, a single hair
For smoke or flying cinders.

One end of car we'll shout, hurrah,
Farewell friend and neighbor,
We're going where, there's bread to spare
Easy time of labor.[12]

5

Life on the Oregon Trail

Traveled 14 miles over the worse road ever that was ever made,
up and down, very steep, rough, and rocky hills, through mud
holes, twisting and winding round steps, logs and fallen trees.
—Amelia Stewart Knight 1853 (Amelia gave birth to her eighth
child on the trail before crossing into Oregon)

The largest mass migration in U.S. history took place on the Oregon Trail between 1840 and 1869. During this span, an estimated 300,000–400,000 people traveled as far as 2,000 miles from the eastern United States to Oregon Country. This chapter puts music aside for the moment and explores the route, the people, and the hardships of the trail. Please note: As in the previous chapters, all of the journal entries are left unedited, as they appeared in the original emigrant journals.

As mentioned in the previous chapter, the first large emigrant party departed from Elm Grove, Missouri, in May of 1843 with 875 people, approximately 120 wagons, and 1,000 head of livestock. Three main waves of Western migration followed. In the first wave, from 1841 to 1850, some 250,000 people made the trip west in simple farm wagons. In the second wave, from 1851 to 1855, people traveled by the large Conestoga wagons that many people visualize when thinking of the Oregon Trail. The third wave of migration, from 1856 to 1867, included passage by wagon, stagecoach, and steamboat (up the Missouri River). The first transcontinental railroad was completed in 1869. The train offered a faster, more convenient, and somewhat safer means of travel in contrast to traveling on the grueling Overland Trail by wagon, horseback, or by foot.

The main Overland Trail and all of the smaller trails and shortcuts breaking off of the main trail were collectively referred to as the Oregon Trail, whether the final destination was Oregon or not. Over the years, the width of the trail grew to several miles in some places in order to accommodate the thousands of people, wagons, and livestock bound for points west. Writer David Dary explained, "The Oregon Trail probably should be called the 'Oregon-California-Utah-Colorado-Nevada-Montana-and-Other-Points-West Trail.'"[1] Oregon Territory, established by the United States Congress in 1848, included what we know today as Oregon, Idaho, Washington, and western Montana.

The Oregon Trail began at "jumping off" points, the most popular being Independence, Missouri. However, Westport Landing, St. Joseph, Omaha, and Council Bluffs were also jumping off points. These departure points served as stations for emigrants to purchase wagons, livestock, food, and other supplies for their overland journey. Jumping off points also served as places for emigrants to organize into wagon trains for the overland crossing. Writer and adventurer Francis Parkman first traveled west in 1846.

His travel writings, *Sketches of Prairie and Rocky Mountain Life,* were originally published in 1847 as individual articles in *Knickerbocker Magazine.* He wrote that the jumping off point—Independence, Missouri—was a bustling, crowded place where thousands of emigrants held group meetings, voted on leadership, and established rules for individual overland groups (called parties). He wrote this about Independence:

> A multitude of shops had sprung up to furnish the emigrants and Santa Fe traders with necessaries for their journey; and there was an incessant hammering and banging from a dozen black-smith's sheds, where the heavy wagons were being repaired and the horses and oxen shod. The streets were thronged with men, horses, and mules. While I was in the town, a train of emigrant wagons from Illinois passed through, to join the camp on the prairie, and stopped in the principal street. A multitude of healthy children's faces were peeping out from under the covers of the wagons.[2]

From Independence, Missouri, the trail crossed the northeast corner of Kansas, followed the Platte River across Nebraska into present-day Wyoming, and then crossed over the Rocky Mountains via the South Pass. At Fort Hall, in present-day Idaho, the California Trail split from the main trail and continued through Utah, Nevada, and California. The main trail continued across Idaho, over the Blue Mountains, along the Columbia River, and ultimately, to Oregon City. Several smaller branches veered off of the main trail such as the Mormon Trail, which broke off at Fort Bridger and passed into present-day Idaho and Utah. The Bozeman Trail broke off from the Oregon Trail in present-day Wyoming and led to the gold fields of Montana. The Santa Fe Trail, a completely different route than the Oregon Trail, originated in Independence, Missouri, but took a Southern Route through present-day Missouri, Kansas, Oklahoma, Colorado and New Mexico.

Travelers on the trail were called emigrants. Regarding the word "emigrants," Susan Butruille, writer and historian, points out: "At the National Trails Museum, you learn an important distinction. While the people were traveling to their destination to settle, they were emigrants (or immigrants, depending on whether they thought of themselves as going or coming). Once they settled, they were pioneers."[3]

Along the route, there were several well-known landmarks that were frequently mentioned in emigrant journals. The first of these included Fort Kearny, a U.S. military post in present-day Kansas, known as the "Gateway to the Plains." From there, emigrants traveled to Ash Hollow, considered the entry point to the North Platt River Valley, which was a favorite camping site because of an abundance of wood, water and grass. Next, Scott's Bluff near Chimney Rock served as a major landmark, marking one-third of the distance to the end of the Oregon Trail.

After Scott's Bluff, travelers rolled along to Fort Laramie in present-day Wyoming. Henry Brown wrote, "We arrived at Fort Laramie about June 15th 1847, and remained one day, where we witnessed the first War Dance. There were about 5,000 Sioux Indians who were forming an expedition against their hereditary enemy the Pawnee nation."[4] At U.S. forts dotting the trail, such as Fort Laramie and Fort Bridger in present-day Wyoming and Fort Hall in present-day Idaho, work-weary emigrants could resupply with necessities as well as post letters to family and friends back home in the East.

Independence Rock, located south of present-day Casper, Wyoming, originally a location for the fur trappers and traders' annual rendezvous, served as another well-known landmark where as many as 5,000 emigrants inscribed their names. In 1843, William T. Newby wrote: "We reached the Independant Rock about 10 o clock & lay buy for

Map of the Oregon Trail, Marge Mayes, 1992 (National Historic Trail Interpretive Center, and Bureau of Land Management).

the day. This rock is a bout 200 feet high & is a bout 14 hundred yards a round it. Thare is a number of names ingraved on the rock. My name is engraved a bout 50 feet high in plane vu of the road."[5] On June 10, 1850, James Abby wrote: "Left our encampment this morning at three o'clock, and after an hour's travel came to the Independence Rock. This is the greatest curiosity I have seen on the route. It is composed of pure granite, covers at its base about one hundred acres, and is two hundred and fifty feet in height.—Several thousand names are engraved and painted on this rock."[6]

The next important landmark on the trail, and for some, the most significant point on the trail, was the broad and gradual ascent to South Pass in present-day Wyoming. The South Pass marked the point where the emigrants crossed over the Continental Divide and into Oregon Territory. After the South Pass, emigrants passed through Fort Bridger, a major supply stop and the point where the Mormon Trail veered off of the main Overland Trail. From there, the main trail passed through present-day Idaho and into present-day Washington state where the trail passed by the Whitman Mission, through the Blue Mountains, and eventually to The Dalles on the east side of the Cascade Range.

At The Dalles, some emigrants floated down the Columbia River on rustic ferries (big logs strapped together to create a type of platform) to the end of the trail at Portland, Oregon. Alternately, emigrants avoided the treacherous Columbia River stretch by taking the Overland Route which stretched from The Dalles to the end of the trail on Barlow Road which ended in Oregon City near Portland, Oregon.

Emigrants usually began their overland journeys in March, after the threat of snow had passed. The journey typically took about six months to travel from Missouri to

Oregon country. From the stories of those who had been to the West—explorers, fur trappers, missionaries, and other emigrants who had made the journey—Oregon Trail travelers knew that their survival depended on crossing the steep and dangerous Rocky Mountain passes before the harsh winter weather set in.

Emigrants traveled in groups known as parties, with 25 or more wagons moving along the trail together. A typical day began with a bugle call signaling that it was time to pack up and get moving. Many people walked alongside the wagons, and some rode horses. At midday, the parties stopped for "nooning," which meant lunch and rest for both the emigrants and the livestock. In the evening, the parties set up camp, ate, tended to the animals, relaxed around the fire with stories, music, and dancing, and fell into bed, exhausted from the long day on the road. Most parties took a day off during the week, often the Sabbath. On this day they often rested, washed clothes and bedding, cleaned out the wagon, hunted, and gave the hardworking animals a rest.

Cooking and baking took place over open fires fueled by buffalo chips. The Rev. Evans Parrish wrote: "Wood has been very scarce for several days past, though we found enough 'buffalo chips,' as they call them, meaning dried dung. They burn finely, make a hot fire and a good light."[7]

As the years passed and thousands and thousands of emigrants traveled on the Oregon Trail, the way became littered with abandoned belongings, broken-down wagons, dead livestock, and grave markers. Emigrants reported that parts of the trail reeked with the smell of death and decay. James Abby, who traveled the trail in 1850, wrote, "We find many articles strewed along the road, such as log chains, ox-yokes, horse-collars, cooking stoves, etc., which the emigrants have been compelled to throw away to lighten their wagons."[8] Near the well-known landmark on the trail, Chimney Rock, William Birdsall Lorton wrote on June 22, 1849: "Iron bars, fine stoves, boxes of soap, carpets, locks, nails, and boxes lay by the way thrown out."[9] Amelia Stewart Knight wrote on May 2, 1853, "Pleasant evening; have been cooking, and packing things away for an early

Early Pioneer Western Wagon Trains, 1872 (iStock.com/bauhaus1000).

start in the morning. Threw away several jars, some wooden buckets, and all our pickles. Too unhandy to carry."[10]

A common misconception about the Oregon Trail is that the Indians were enemies of the emigrants. In fact, there were very few Indian attacks. On the contrary, in many cases Indians helped make the journey easier for the emigrants. For example, many of the emigrants bartered with the Indians for food. Calvin Geer, who traveled on the Oregon Trail in 1847, wrote, "I don't remember where we crossed the Snake River the first time, but I remember we came to Salmon Falls and there were lots of Indians there fishing and we got some salmon from them. They had lots of dried salmon and would come up to us and say 'me one shirt, you two salmon swap' and cross their hands."[11]

Indians helped emigrants cross dangerous rivers and in some cases saved lives. Alexander Blevins, who made the overland crossing in 1843, wrote about a near-death drowning experience of a young boy named Moses who was saved by helpful Indians:

> To cross the Crow they dug out canoes of black walnut and lashed them together to form a raft. On this the wagons were put and ferried over. The Zachery family when near the western bank had the misfortune to have the raft sink, immersing the whole family as well as their provisions and all in the water. There were crowds of peaceable Indians on the shore who boldly plunged into the water to their rescue. A little boy about six years old was sitting on an ox-yoke which, being light, floated off with him. The river ran very rapid at this place and the little fellow perched on his frail raft hung on without a cry of fear. Several savages fleet offoot ran down the bank, and after getting a few rods ahead of the boy, went out and brought the young Moses ashore.[12]

William Smedley told the tale of how Indians retrieved some horses that had run away. "Horses being lost, were detained till noon. A friendly Indian went in search of and found them for us. On inquiring his charge for the service, he replied, holding up six fingers, 'Six pony, six dollar.'"[13]

Answering the need for a "how-to" guidebook for those embarking on the overland journey on the Oregon Trail, J. Quinn Thornton wrote the book, *Oregon and California in 1848*, published by Harper and Brothers, New York. Mr. Thornton was among the first waves of settlers who moved West in the 1840s. He suggested emigrants "procure strong, well-ironed, light wagons, made of thoroughly seasoned timber. Each wagon ought to have at least four yokes of strong, healthy, well-broken oxen, with long straight legs." Along with the oxen, Thornton suggested that people should also bring along as many young cows as possible. He said one day of rest per week was essential for both the livestock and the travelers. He warned against taking cutoffs and also against taking too many belongings. Thornton's list of necessary supplies for each adult traveler included:

100 pounds flour
100 pounds butter crackers
100 pounds bacon sides—no hams
50 pounds dried beef
50 pounds of kiln dried corn-meal
20 pounds rice
25 pounds beans
1 light rifle and powder
1 butcher knife
1 small tomahawk—with the nerve to use it not rashly, but effectively when
   necessary.

Thornton suggested, "Green goggles should be provided, to protect the eyes from the otherwise almost intolerable dust. I advise each person to take at least two pair, that the loss of one may be supplied in the event of accidental breaking."[14]

Most of the emigrants heading west on the Oregon Trail whittled down their stash of personal belongings to the bare necessities that would fit into a wagon. With limited space, they could not take much, especially "luxury items" such as family heirlooms and furniture. However, many travelers did choose to take portable instruments, including violins, harmonicas, button accordions, rocking melodeons, guitars, banjos, flutes, and keyed bugles. Perhaps the emigrants thought of instruments as essential to the trip. (More about these instruments, the musicians, and the music in the next chapter.)

Who were these people headed west? The majority of people heading west in the years 1840–1850 included farm people from Indiana, Illinois, Iowa, Ohio, Kentucky, Tennessee and Missouri. These people were working people from middle-class backgrounds.[15] People wishing to travel required enough means to get on the road and a complete wagon setup including oxen, a wagon, and spare parts. It was told that people needed approximately $600–$1,000 in order to outfit themselves for the crossing. The journey was too long and arduous for many older people and too expensive for many low-wage earners. Most of the upper class were happy to stay in the East where they were not affected by the economic downturn, unsanitary living conditions, and unemployment. The wealthy had large estates and numerous servants as well as their own sources for food production. They lived in a bubble, so to speak, away from the overcrowded cities and unsavory living conditions.

Many of the emigrants were farmers looking for a new start in the "land of milk and honey." These were people used to physically demanding labor who possessed the resilience and stamina for life on the trail. However, there were some people who came from upper-middle-class backgrounds with servants and were *not* used to "roughing" it or cooking their own food over a campfire. Many were highly educated and used to spending their days studying languages, music, literature, art, and writing. To this point, Sarah Raymond Herndon, who crossed the plains in 1865, wrote in her journal, "While I have been writing Neelie (Cornelia) and Sittie (Henrietta) have been getting supper for a family of twelve, no small undertaking for them, as they have been used to servants and know very little about cooking."[16]

The nineteenth century was the era of letter writing and journal keeping. With no way to capture still images of the journey, people painted pictures with their descriptive written accounts. Similar to the journalists of the Lewis and Clark Expedition, many emigrants left behind detailed accounts of both their lives on the trail and their lives in their new homes in the West. In fact, there are so many primary accounts in the form of letters and journals that it is almost as if people knew the vital importance of recording this moment in history, this mass migration.

The Oregon Trail was filled with young families. Those families often included several small children as well as newly born infants. The historian Susan Butruille explained that the Oregon Trail was known as the family trail, while the California Trail attracted gold seekers and adventurers.[17] There were also single men, sometimes seeking adventure and who may have signed onto a wagon train as a hired hand. Some of the wagon trains were led by former fur trappers and explorers who were familiar with the routes.

Many of the families were enticed by the Homestead Act of 1862 which offered

160 acres of surveyed land for residents who resided on and improved the land for the duration of five years. Along with families seeking the free land, there were widowed or divorced women who could get their own land and independence as promised in the land grant. After the Civil War in 1865, freed slaves and ex-soldiers headed west. Some people without the means of outfitting a wagon simply walked the Oregon Trail on foot or rode on horseback.

Emigrant journals are filled with narratives focused on the hardships and challenges of the trail. For example, water was often mentioned as a subject of complaint. Journal entries reported lack of water, limited water supplies, and toxic water that sometimes led to deadly alkaline poisoning. Abigail Scott Dunway crossed the plains in 1852 and wrote about the scarcity of good water and about passing graves: "We have suffered considerable inconvenience this afternoon in consequence for the great scarcity of good water. The water of the Platte being so muddy and warm that it was impossible to drink it. We however this evening found an excellent spring just in reach of where we wanted to camp and it seems to be it was the best water we had tasted since we left Joe. Passed four graves."[18]

It seems emigrants were constantly battling weather conditions. Mrs. J.E. Goltra wrote, "Had a very heavy wind last night, it might be called a hurricane. Blew down all our tents, had to turn our wagons back to the wind and lock both wheels and run the tongue in the ground to keep the wagon still, came very near blowing our wagon over, scattered our cattle in every direction, next morning we found some kettles and pans that was not lost and some clothing was blown about quarter of a mile."[19]

Mrs. J.T. Gowdy crossed the plains with her mother, her father, seven siblings and three hired men in 1852. Her youngest sister, Frannie, died on the way after drinking bad water from the Platt River. In her personal recollection, Mrs. Gowdy spoke of the heat, the stench of dead livestock, the lack of water, and a limited food supply.

> There was so much sickness and so many deaths. The poor cattle, too, died by the hundreds, starved and overworked, the plains were covered with their carcasses and the air was polluted with their sickening odor. I wonder how any of us lived through it all. Just think of lying with a burning fever in a rough jolty wagon, on a big feather bed put on top of a pile of things all jumbled up with nothing between you and the burning sun but the wagon cover in that smothering dust with sometimes not a drop of fresh water for two days and hardly ever a bit from one camping place to another, and it was often a stagnant pool, with nothing to eat but fat, salt bacon, bread and coffee, cooked on a sage brush or grease wood fire.[20]

Wagon-related accidents and fatalities were often mentioned. Being run over by a wagon seemed to be one of the more frequently mentioned fatal accidents of the Oregon Trail. Mr. Newby wrote about a wagon accident during his overland journey in 1843: "A very bad road. Joel J. Hembree son Joel fel off the waggeon tung & both wheels run over him."[21] Cynthia Cox wrote about an accident on her journey in 1847: "if you ever come to Oregon be shure to have your family waggon made so that yo can get in and out at the hind end on account of the children while we was traveling on big platt their was a boy 8 years old fell out of the waggon when both of the wheles run over his head and killed him instantly."[22]

Some groups of emigrants succumbed to the promises of con men who promised their services in exchange for money or who said they would lead the party to a shortcut. For instance, with 800 miles to go to Oregon City, Tabitha Brown, a 66-year-old retired school teacher and widow who traveled the Oregon Trail in 1846, known as "Grandma

Tabitha Brown," recounted how her party was led astray by a man who promised he would lead them to a cutoff. In Tabitha's words:

> but three of four trains of emigrants were decoyed off by a rascally fellow who came out from the settlement in Oregon, assuring us that he had found a *near cut-off*; that if we would follow him we would be in the settlement long before those who had gone down the Columbia. This was in August. The idea of a shortening a long journey cause us to yield to his advice. Our sufferings from that time no tongue can tell. (He left a pilot with us who proved to be an excellent man; otherwise we never would have seen Oregon.) He said he would clear the road before us; that we should have no trouble rolling our wagons after him; he robbed us of what he could be lying; and left us to the depredations of Indians, wild beasts, and starvation—but God was with us.[23]

Death was a reality on the Oregon Trail. The National Oregon/California Trail Center in Montpelier, Idaho, estimates that there was an average of ten graves per mile on the Oregon and California Trails. A grave stone in Soda Springs, Idaho, marks the burial place of an immigrant family of seven who were killed by Indians and were buried in their own wagon box by trappers and immigrants in 1861.[24] Many of those deaths were the result of diseases and illnesses: dysentery, cholera, measles, mumps, smallpox, tuberculosis, or pneumonia. When a death occurred in a wagon party, the deceased was quickly buried, and the wagons rolled on. Abigail Scott, who was 18 years old when her mother died on the trail, wrote:

> We little thought when last Sabbath's pleasant sun shed upon us his congenial rays that when the next should come it would find us mourning over the sickness and death of our beloved Mother! But it has been even so, our mother was taken about two o'clock this morning with a violent dierrehea attend with cramping, she however aroused no one until daylight when everything was done which we could do to save her life; but her constitution long impaired by disease was unable to withstand the attack and this afternoon between four and five o'clock her wearied spirit took its flight and then we realized that we were bereaved indeed.[25]

More dangers along the Oregon Trail included starvation, dehydration, drowning while making dangerous river crossings, animal attacks, and snakebites. There was accidental discharge of firearms or outright shootings on the trail as tempers flared in the face of daily struggles. Another danger—travelers ran the risk of getting lost on the trail, especially if they attempted shortcuts.

Elizabeth Dixon Smith, her seven children, and her husband, Cornelius, traveled the Oregon Trail in 1847. Her diary chronicles the countless hardships that her family and her traveling companions endured. On July 1, she wrote of an accidental shooting: "today when our hunters came in they brough one dead man he had shot himself last night accidently he left a wife and six mall children the distress of the wife I cannot describe."[26] On September 7, Elizabeth Dixon wrote of two drownings:

> Nooned at Snake river watered our cattle moved on 2 miles and camped, 2 men were left be hind which was always the case with them they had such heavy loads they came up afterwards and while watering some of their cattle swam over the river one of the men swam after them and before he got a cross he sunk to rise no more he left a wife and 3 children the other came runin to camp to let us know some men went back and stayed with them by this time another company had overtaken them next morning my husband took a horse and went back to swim the horse over after the cattle The man that owned the cattle took the horse and swam after the cattle and while coming back by some means got off of the horse and sunk and was seen no more he left a wife and 6 helpless children my husband stood watching him it is supposed that there was a suck in the bottom of the river.[27]

Pioneer Covered Wagon River Crossing, 1870 (iStock.com/bauhaus1000).

On November 19, when her party was near the Columbia River in Oregon Territory, Elizabeth reported that her husband became ill: "my husband is sick and can have but little care rain all day." On November 20, she wrote, "rain all day it is almost an impossibility to cook and quite so to keep warm or dry I froze or chilled my feet so that I cannot wear a shoe so I have to go round in the cold water bearfooted." On November 21 she continued in the journal, "rain all day the whole care of evry thing now falls upon my shoulders I cannot write any more at present."[28]

After traveling all the way from La Porte, Indiana, to Fort Vancouver (in present-day Washington state), Elizabeth and her family were living in a rustic lean-to shack when her husband, Cornelius, died from illness. On February 1, 1848, Elizabeth wrote, "rain all day this day my Dear husband my last remaining friend died." The next day she wrote, "today we buried my earthly companion, now I know what none but widows know that is ow comfortless is that of a widows life espsily when left in a strange land without money or friends and the care of seven children-cloudy."[29] The physical and emotional trials that Elizabeth endured along the Oregon Trail represent the hardships that many emigrants faced as they made their way west. Along with chronicling her hardships, Elizabeth's journal, like many of the other emigrant journals, included entries about music on the trail. On June 19, 1847, she wrote: "made 20 miles evry night we encamped we locate quite a village but take it up the next day we have plenty music with the flute and violin and some dancing."[30]

In 1849, William Birdsall Lorton, a young, adventuresome traveler known for his singing voice, traveled on the Overland Trail as far as Salt Lake City. His detailed journal entries lay bare the many dangers of the trail. For instance, on April 20, 1849, he writes about two men dying from an accidental discharge of firearms. In the same entry, he mentions an after-dinner concert. In his words: "1 man got killed in our rear by his comrades rifle. He was in the brush & the first thing he knew a ball passed through him. I have just rec'd news of another man ahead being killed in the same manner.... After supper we had a concert in our tent in the eve'g, & to help the base, rolling thunder joins the chorus, while clashing through mid-air."[31] In an entry on June 4, Birdsall Lorton notes another danger of the trail—stampeding livestock. "As quick as lightning the spirit of 'stampede' runs along the whole train.... I pulled off my hat and succeeded in turning a team coming full split on our near side."[32]

It was not only the countless dangers, hardships, deaths of family and friends, lack of food and water but also the daily grind, the daily minutia of trail life that wore people down both in body and spirit. Mr. Peter H. Burnett, who traveled on the Oregon Trail in 1843, wrote:

> But there were ten thousand little vexations continually recurring, which could not be forseen before they occurred, nor fully remembered when past, but were keenly felt while passing. At one time an ox would be missing, at another time a mule, and then a struggle for the best encampment, and for a supply of wood and water; and, in these struggles, the worst traits of human nature were displayed, and there was no remedy but patient endurance. At the beginning of the journey there were several fisticuff fights in camp; but the emigrants soon abandoned that practice, and thereafter confined themselves to abuse in words only. The man with a black eye and battered face could not well hunt up his cattle or drive his team.[33]

Many women took to the Oregon Trail because their husbands wanted to go west. At this time in history, women had little or no say in family matters. As a result, many women, against their wishes, were forced to leave behind friends, loved ones, homes, churches, community, and all of the comforts of home. Mrs. E.J. Goltra wrote of her travels across the plains: "Kansas Missouri, April 29th, 1853. Today we started across the dreary plains. Sad are the thoughts that steal over the reflecting mind. I am leaving my home, my early friends and associates, perhaps never to see them again, exchanging the disinterested solicitude of fond friends, for the cold and unsympathizing friendship of strangers."[34]

Some women, such as Mrs. E.J. Goltra, were not happy about uprooting their lives that they had built in the East. They left all of this behind and went off into the unknown. For women, the Oregon Trail experience was particularly grueling because not only did the women have to perform all of their regular duties—among them, cooking, cleaning, and caring for children—but they had to do all of those things on the trail, in dusty conditions, with nothing to cook on but a buffalo chip-fueled campfire.

Through hardships and enflamed tempers, women kept the family unit together, nurtured their children, and tried their best to create moments of civility on the dusty plains. They walked alongside the wagon on travel days, and some even gave birth on the side of the road. Some lost their husbands to accidents or illness along the way. Because these women could not turn back, many were left to drive the wagon, care for the livestock, raise the children and establish a new home in the West on their own.

In some cases, quick weddings took place on the trail, no doubt to help split up the trail and domestic duties. For example, while on the trail in Nebraska, the Rev. Edward Evans Parrish wrote about a wedding on Friday, July 5, 1844: "Sun rose clear. We learn that there was a wedding in camp last night—Mr. John Kindred to Mary King by Rev. Mr. Cave."[35]

Early American Soldiers Pulling a Covered Wagon, 1871 (iStock.com/bauhaus1000).

Thanks to the detailed journal entries left behind, particularly by women, we can read about the experience of life on the trail. Take for example this account given by Luzena Wilson, who traveled west in the 1840s:

Nothing but actual experience will give one an idea of the plodding, unvarying monotony, the vexations, the exhaustive energy, the throbs of hope, the depths of despair, through which we lived. Day after day, week after week, we went through the same weary routine of breaking camp at daybreak, yoking the oxen, cooking our meagre rations over a fire of sage-brush and scrub-oak; packing up again, coffeepot and camp-kettle; washing our scanty ward-robe in the little streams we crossed; striking camp again at sunset, or later if wood and water were scarce. Tired, dusty, tried in temper, worn out in patience, we had to go over the weary experience tomorrow. No excitement, but a broken-down wagon, or the extra preparation made to cross a river, marked our way for many miles. The Platte was the first great water-course we crossed. It is a peculiar, wide, shallow stream, with a quicksand bed. With the wagon-bed on blocks twelve or fourteen inches thick to raise it out of the water, some of the men astride of the oxen, some of them wading waist-deep, and all goading the poor beasts to keep them moving, we started across, The water poured into the wagon in spite of our pre-cautions and floated off some of our few movables; but we landed safely on the other side, and turned to see the team behind us stop in mid-stream. The frantic driver shouted, whipped, belabored the stubborn animals in vain, and the treacherous sand gave way under their feet. They sank slowly, gradually, but surely. They went out of sight inch by inch, and the water rose over the moaning beasts. Without a struggle they disappeared beneath the surface. In a lit-tle while the broad South Platte swept on its way, sunny, sparkling, placid, without a ripple to mark where a lonely man parted with all his fortune.[36]

Children helped to ease the work burden of their mothers and fathers. For those children old enough for chores, their duties included gathering buffalo chips for the cooking fire, packing and unpacking the wagons, and caring for the animals. In addi-tion to these duties, young girls helped their mothers with childcare, cooking, baking, washing dishes, washing clothes, and keeping the wagon clean.

Dangers to children on the trail included wagon accidents and fatalities by either fall-ing out of the wagons or getting run over by a wagon. Some children were accidentally left behind. Some drowned during river crossings, and some were left to fend for them-selves after the death of one or sometimes both parents. Narcissa and Marcus Whitman, mentioned in the previous chapter, whose only child Alice had drowned near their mis-sion home, took in 11 children of deceased immigrants and raised them as their own at the Whitman Mission. Jane Gould Tortillot wrote in her diary on August 3, 1862, about a series of unfortunate events in a neighboring wagon party: "They had just buried the babe of a woman who died days ago, and were just digging a grave for another woman that was run over by the cattle and wagons when they stampeded yesterday. She lived twenty-four hours, she gave birth to a child a short time before she died. The child was buried with her. She leaves a little two year old girl and a husband. They say he is nearly crazy with sorrow."[37]

Those who took to the trail knew they may never return to their loved ones and their homes again. In pursuit of a new life in the West, they left behind family, friends, community, civic organizations, churches, and libraries. They also left behind the opera, the theater, salon gatherings, private music lessons, community bands, sym-phony orchestras and choir societies. Large musical instruments that took center stage in homes on the east coast such as pianos, harps, harpsichords, and large organs were simply too big for the wagon to hold, yet portable instruments such as fiddles, flutes, and guitars made the cut.

The Oregon Trail was a long, arduous route over dusty plains, jagged peaks, across rivers, and miles and miles of rugged travel. Thousands of emigrants died along the way or lost family or friends. At the very least, people endured hardships and challenges that we in our modern world can only imagine. Elizabeth Wood, who traveled the trail in 1851, wrote about the reason for taking the journey: "I have a great desire to see Oregon … the beautiful scenery of plain and mountain, and … the wild animals and the Indi-ans, and natural curiosities in abundance."[38] She also spoke of the fortitude necessary to survive the journey: "people who do come must not be worried or frightened at trifles; they must put up with storm and cloud as well as calm and sunshine."[39]

Lillian Schlissel, a brilliant writer and historian, eloquently summarized the opti-mism, grit and determination of emigrants on the trail: "The qualities of mind and heart that led men and women to choose to make the two-thousand-mile journey are difficult to recapture. An intense hunger for land and for gold and a heady confidence in their own strength combined to catapult the emigrants across the continent. They refused to be discouraged. With boundless, even foolhardy courage, they suppressed the drama of their personal lives for the larger drama that lay before them. And in that moment of exchange, they were buoyant in the faith that the future was expansive and prosperous."[40]

The loss and hardships were endured with humor, faith, courage, camaraderie, the kindness of strangers, the unfettered desire to reach the "promised land," and with the diversion of music. Singing, dancing, playing instruments, and listening to the soothing and familiar sounds of music, which had been a part of everyday nineteenth-century life for so many people in the East, was a powerful way of dealing with the day-to-day loss and struggles on the Oregon Trail. The next chapter explores the musicians, songs, and instruments of the Oregon Trail and the multiple roles that music played in the westward journey.

6

The Music at the Heart
of the Oregon Trail Experience

*When we returned to our tents, & at nine, they all collected & I played on
the guitar, the rest joined in, in loud busts of song seemingly not to think
of the long march they had so short a time, before taken. Here we sat
poring forth out melody til half past nine, when we each retired to our
tents for the remainder of the night wearied out with our long march,
though the day cooler than the one before.*—Ada Vodges, 1869

At the heart of the Westward Expansion lies some 400,000 people who uprooted their lives in pursuit of the dream for a better life in the West. Taking only the bare essentials that would fit into a simple wagon, the emigrants made room for musical instruments right alongside their guns, ammunition, food, and tools. On any given wagon train, travelers might bring along an eclectic collection of portable instruments—from fiddles to flutes and banjos to bugles. The songs of the trail included the sweet melodies of Stephen Foster, romantic ballads, patriotic tunes, and traditional hymns.

As emigrants rolled across the Great Plains, crossed treacherous rivers, and scrambled over the Rockies in the face of countless hardships, music often provided the only spark of light and happiness during what seemed like an endless journey. This chapter brings to light the story of music as a thread that bound people together and highlights the multiple roles music played in the lives of emigrants on the Oregon Trail. Selected emigrant journal entries describe the songs, dances, musicians, and the instruments of the trail and explain how music created community, eased struggles, offered beauty, added comfort, provided solace, and created a link to the world they left behind. The pioneers carried only the clothes on their backs and the bare necessities in their wagons, yet they experienced a rich musical life in the wilderness.

In one role, and perhaps the most important role, music sustained the spirits of the emigrants on the trail by providing solace and an antidote to the countless hardships of the trail.

On August 26, 1865, the *Montana Post* eloquently summed up the role of music in the lives of emigrants:

> A few evenings ago, we were gratified by hearing the most artistically executed music we have listened to for many a day. Four newly arrived Pilgrims sat upon a log, by the wayside, and sang, "Faded Flowers," and "Maggie By My Side," for their own gratification. The time, tune and pathos of the music, arrange as quartettes, was really beautiful. The poor fellows had solace themselves many a time and oft, with the sweet harmony and sentiment of the songs, after a weary day's march over the plains, and, before parting, they united their voices once more in the songs that reminded them of the loved ones in "The Old House at Home."

"The Old House at Home"

Oh! the old house at home where my forefathers dwelt,
Where a child at the feet of my mother I knelt,
Where she taught me the pray'r, where she read me the page,
Which, if infancy lisps, is the solace of age;
My heart, 'mid all changes, wherever I roam,
Ne'er loses its love for the old house at home!

Mrs. Elizabeth Smith traveled on the Oregon Trail with eight children in 1847. She wrote a letter to her friends Mrs. Pauline Foster and Mrs. Cynthia Ames La Porte of Indiana. In the letter she described the ongoing struggles of trail life, the challenges of mothering eight children on the trail, and she also mentioned how the wagon party created a little village every night complete with musical activities involving a flute, a violin, and dancing:

June 17 Made twelve miles. Fell in with eighteen wagons. Broke an axle. Laid by and made a new one. Stood guard all night in the rain.

June 18 Finished the broken axle. Made five miles. Encamped in a circle as is our custom. Put out guards and retired to rest.

June 19 Made twenty miles. Every night when we encamp we make quite a village, but take it up the next day. We have plenty of music with a flute and violin and some dancing.[1]

In 1852, when Mrs. J.T. Gowdy was eight years old, she traveled the Oregon Trail with her mother, her father, and seven siblings. One of her memories included a description of her family singing soothing songs at the end of a long travel day:

My aunt's husband was a good singer and sometimes after supper when everybody, tired with the strenuous day's travel, would be preparing to lay their weary bodies on their hard beds, he would start up some old Methodist hymn; others would take it up and it would seem like an old-fashioned camp meeting was in progress. It must have fallen like a benediction on their over-wrought nerves. My brother was also a fine singer and my sisters, even down to little me could sing. So brother often started up a song, but he did not always sing hymns. Being lively and jolly, his songs were apt to be the same, but they did people good; also sent people to bed in a good humor.[2]

Sarah Herndon made her way across the plains in 1848. Clearly music meant a great deal to Sarah as she made her way west, her journal showcased a multitude of musical events along the trail. In one entry, she wrote about a group of musicians in a neighboring wagon party: "There are several musicians in the McMahan train; Lyde says they serenaded me last night. She says they stood between our two wagons. I think she is trying to tease me."[3] Later in her journal she wrote, "Lyde Walker pleasantly entertained us this evening with songs accompanied with guitar."[4]

Margaret A. Fink traveled the Oregon Trail with her husband in 1850 on their way to the gold fields of California. On June 25, Margaret's party traveled over the South Pass of the Rocky Mountains. She remembers that at the top of the summit there was an American flag flying and also a private post office where emigrants could send letters to friends and family back home. The express charge per letter was $1.00 for a messenger to deliver the letter to the post office in St. Joseph on the Missouri River. Despite a hailstorm, the emigrants celebrated their arrival at the summit with music. Margaret wrote: "Music from a violin with tin-pan accompaniment, contributed to the general merriment of the grand frolic."[5]

Origen Thomson traveled west to Oregon Territory in 1852. He wrote on two occasions how music lifted the spirits of the party and broke up the monotony of the trip.

His first music-related entry mentioned the song, "Uncle Sam's Farm." Thomson wrote, "There were some good singers among us; some had their musical instruments, and these betimes made the solitude ring. The refrain of one favorite song was...."

> *Come along, come along—don't be alarmed;*
> *Uncle Sam is rich enough to give us all a farm.*[6]

In a later entry, Thomson wrote, "We relieved the monotony of our trip by having a singing on our way. Mrs. Lewis rode in our wagon and we 'woke the echoes from their native haunts' by such harmonies as are not often heard in these wilds."[7]

Mary Ringo and her husband, Martin Ringo, traveled the Oregon Trail in 1864 while pregnant with her sixth child. In her journal she mentioned musical activities several times. In one entry she wrote, "June 1st, Wednesday. We laid by today on account of the rain. The gentlemen went fishing and caught a great many fish. We have quite a nice evening, some gentlemen who are camped near us came an played their violins, which is quite entertaining to California travelers."[8]

She mentions the musical friends again a few days later: "June 5, Sunday. While here I washed up all of our dirty clothes, at night our camp friends came and we had some more music. (Stayed here two nights.)"[9] And again, Mary wrote about the local fauna as well as music: "June 11, Saturday. We traveled 5 miles and camped three miles from the Platt river, we have to drive our stock to the river, this place is almost destitute of grass, the soil is sandy we find the cactus and pricky pears grow here and we see numerous little lizards sliding through the grass and one extremely long snake gliding down a hole. Our neighbors again give us some nice music."[10]

On July 30, Mary's husband accidentally shot himself, which left her a single mother of six children with one on the way. Typical of deaths along the trail, the wagon party quickly buried him and moved on. Mary wrote, "And Oh God comes the saddest record of my life for this day my husband accidentally shot himself and was buried by the wayside and oh, my heart it breaking, if I had no children how gladly would I lay me own with my dead—but now Oh God I pray for strength to raise our precious children and oh—may no one ever suffer the anguish that is breaking my heart, my little children are crying all the time and I—oh what am I to do.... After burying my darling husband we hitch up and drive some 5 miles."[11]

Davis Willson traveled west in 1866 with a party of eight men; they were headed to Montana to strike it rich in the gold fields. Davis, 25 at the time, was an avid fiddler and writer. His journal entries reflected the importance of music in his own life and added to the story of music along the Overland Trail.

> We got under way about noon. Came about three miles, when it commenced to rain and went into camp. It broke up about six and I got out my violin. Played awhile, when an old man came along on horseback. He was dried up wrinkled and barefoot. Short, white beard grew on his chin and upper lip resembling bristles. He drove up, looked for a moment, winked, snifted up his nose, and said, "Mighty putty teaune." Hesitating a moment, then winking & snifting again said, "Whear ye from." "New York" we answered Then another wink & sniff, said 'Will y please play a might putty teaun now?'[12]

In another entry, Willson wrote about a musical interaction with an unsavory trail acquaintance whom Willson referred to as "Blow-hard," proving that music appeals to everyone—even the crudest of characters:

Soon Charlie Rich and "Blow-hard" came. Charlie R. and "Blow-hard" Taylor sang and I played accompaniment. "Blow-hard" thought it was "perfectly charming!" "Beautiful" & c &c. "Blow-hard" is a great big, fat, greasy man whom we run on to the other day and is going to Montana with a load of alcohol. He rides a horse and "his man" as he calls him (another fat greasy fellow) drives his ox team. He makes himself rather familiar, is a regular ignoramus but thinks he is a man of more than ordinary capacity and has a fine appreciation of the "fine arts" & the "beautiful"!![13]

Kate Smith and her sister, Jennie, traveled with their family of eight from Independence, Kansas, to Washington Territory in 1879. The sisters kept a journal together and often mentioned comforting violin music as a pleasant diversion on the rugged overland journey. On May 24, near Sand Creek, Kate wrote: "The wind has rose to night it is blowing quite hard. We were favored with music on the violin which was quite a treat. The men have been trying to kill antelope but have failed in every attempt."[14]

Early on her journey, on August 12, the family visited with friends on a ranch near the Blue Mountains. Kate wrote, "We left the Ranch and followed Birch Creek ten miles and stopped for dinner and finding it to be fifteen miles to water remained here all day. It is a very pretty place there is a house right by us the lady of the house played the organ and sang we could hear it quite plain. It sounded quite old fashioned. 10 miles."[15]

On July 27, the sisters both wrote about the challenges of the journey and both mentioned singing as a highlight at the end of the difficult day. Jennie wrote, "This has been another long day I packed all forenoon wrote a letter this afternoon spent the rest of the day with Mrs. Smith some of the boys came around in the evening and we had some music I sang a song with the rest this is a beautiful evening." On the same day, Kate wrote, "Another lonely day Several freight trains passed us the only thing of interest that has happened in the evening there was several songs sang."[16]

In another role, music built a sense of community in the evenings when the emigrants were relaxing after the toils of the day. Henry Brown, an early traveler on the trail, crossed the plains in 1837 with a party of 13 wagons. In his autobiography, he fondly recalls the evening ritual of music within his community of fellow travelers. His description includes singing, fiddle music, dancing, and young boys marching to the beat of a drum:

> The female portion were busy clearing away the remains of the evening meal of preparing for the early morning breakfast. The men, except those who were on guard duty would form circles around the fires, smoking and recounting the incidents of the days travel, singing songs, telling jokes at each others expense; while in another part of the camp, the violin would enliven the air with its notes, to which young and agile feet were keeping time in the merry dance on the soil of the plains, while the boys were marching around playing soldier, led by a youthful drummer, who pounded with might and main on a small specimen of that warlike cymbal. Gradually the stock would lie down and the people retire to dream of home and the dear ones left behind; the camp would become quiet and the fires grow dimmer until its flickering flames expired; no sound would be heard except the low talk of the guards as they made their rounds or the lonesome howl of the prairie wolf as they prowled around the camp.[17]

John G. Abbott, who traveled the Oregon Trail in 1852, fondly remembered the first part of his overland trip: "Everybody enjoyed themselves at first. They would gather around campfires in the evening, sing, tell stories, and talk of the promised land."[18]

James Kirkpatrick, who went west in 1863, was in the first party that attempted to travel the Bozeman cutoff, a rugged and dangerous trail that veered off from the Oregon Trail in present-day Wyoming. He reminisced, "The evenings like the days were fine, campfires enlivened the nighty scene while accordion and violin, varied with song and story, whiled away the pleasant hours."[19]

Sarah Raymond Herndon wrote about the way music, as well as musicians, created a pleasant atmosphere in camp and commented on the healing role of music:

> Mr. and Mrs. Morrison are large-hearted, cheerful people, who seem to be always happy and trying to make others happy. Mrs. Morrison learned that Miss Lyde Walker has her guitar, and sings beautifully, so she invited her to come by their tent and help to entertain a few friends. It was a very pleasant diversion. While Lyde was singing the men and boys from all over the corral came near to listen. When she sang, "The Cottage by the Sea," both inside and outside the tent, there was great applause that terminated in an encore. But no, she would not sing anymore; she murmured something about the rabble, and laid her guitar away.
>
> If I was gifted with a talent, with which I could give pleasure to people, I would certainly do so whenever opportunity was afforded. I would be glad to promote the happiness, and to dispel as much sorrow as possible, in this sorrowful world.[20]

In another role, music added to impromptu church services along the trail. Cecelia Adams and her twin sister Parthenia Blank traveled the Oregon Trail in 1852 and kept a journal together. In one entry, Cecelia wrote about a quick trailside funeral: "Had a very hard wind last night. The sick man is dead this morning. We stop to see him buried.

An illustration of 19th-century instruments from left to right: ten-string guitar, mandolin, and a six-string guitar (iStock.com/MattGrove).

They wrapped him in bed clothes and laid him in the ground without any coffin. We sung a hymn and had a prayer. O! it is so hard to leave friends in this wilderness."[21]

Parthenia wrote about music and a wilderness worship service: "Sunday, Aug. 29. Remain today also. Have a sermon from Captain Hyland who is a Methodist preacher. Feed is not very good, but fear we shall have worse before we have better. Had a good sing today."[22]

Another example of religious music on the trail comes from Benjamin Franklin Owen, who traveled the Oregon Trail in 1853. His original wagon train became known as "The Lost Wagon Train of 1853." This particular wagon train became stranded in the Harney-Malheur Lakes country of Oregon when the party had exhausted their provisions and their ox teams and were unable to move forward. Benjamin was one of the six young men who left the wagon party to look for help and to send back food. He nearly died of starvation in the process. Early on in his Oregon Trail journey he wrote about a religious musical experience:

> July 25th. We traveled about 16 miles crossed Fort Hall Creek, & camped about midway between it, & Portneff River. The McClure Train were in camp about 100 yds from us there was heavy Timber all around us, & when dark came we heard Singing, & the music of an accordion at the other camp, which completely captivated us, we were very naturally drawn to it, & were received kindly, & invited to take part in their devotions. If anyone wants to hear the most beautiful, & thrilling vocal music in the world, let them try it in heavy timber, with some good singers, & a good instrument or two, & my word for it they will have it! One can almost realize heaven is in our midst, to look Back to those days one almost wishes to live them over again.[23]

Another example of the intersection of music and religion on the trail comes from Kate Smith, who wrote about people gathering in her tent to sing Sunday school songs on Sunday, June 8, 1879: "Left camp this morning before breakfast and traveled eight or nine miles before we came to water we then stopped and got breakfast and after discussing the outfit concluded to remain here until morning it is a very pretty place on Crow Creek five miles East of Cheyenne. Have spent the day quite pleasantly. This afternoon quite a number of our neighbors gathered in out tent and sang Sunday School songs It seemed old fashioned."[24]

Ada Vodges traveled the trail with her husband, a cavalryman, bound for Fort Laramie in 1868. Ada was a keen guitarist and brought her instrument along. In her journal she wrote about a specific hymn that lent her comfort during the cross country passage: "I repeated on the road, as I rode along, the hymn 'Guide me on! through Great Jehovah,' which sounded more appropriate to me in this wilderness than ever in my life before, & with more force. What do we know about barren wilderness, in a city church? I had never felt the words, & meaning before as I have done, since I have been on this journey."[25]

"Guide Me on Though Great Jehovah"

Guide me, O thou great Jehovah,
pilgrim through this barren land;
I am weak, but thou art mighty;
hold me with thy pow'rful hand;
Bread of heaven,
Bread of heaven,
feed me 'til I want no more,
feed me 'til I want no more.

In yet another role, music served as accompaniment to dancing on the trail. For example, a group of miners—all men—bound for Idaho to mine for gold, entertained themselves with dancing near Scott's Bluff, Nebraska. The men danced in the males' and females' roles—which is called a stag dance. Julius Merrill wrote: "Good feed at night. Having several fiddlers in our train, we amused ourselves in a 'stag dance' in the eve. That term is applied in the absence of females."[26] At a campsite between South Pass Station and Fort Hall, Julius Merrill wrote, "Having plenty of wood at night, we had a rousing campfire. Gathering around it, we listened to the violin, songs, storytelling, and dancing."[27]

Miners' Ball etching by André Castaigne, 1891, portrays an all-male dance, also known as a "stag dance." The dancers are accompanied by a small accordion (iStock.com/benoitb).

The next day Julius and company had an opportunity to dance with the ladies from a neighboring wagon train. The ladies turned the men down, but undeterred, the Idaho-bound miners danced with each other: "Camped at night within ten miles of Laramie. A Missouri train camped near us and invited us with our music to their corral to dance as they had quite a number of the opposite sex. We gladly accepted the offer. We gave them the first three dances, and upon our being introduced to 'the ladies.' They all refused to dance. We couldn't see the point and formed a 'stag dance,' thinking that as long as we furnished the music, we would dance, ladies or no ladies."[28]

Helen Clark, who traveled the trail in 1860, wrote: "A fiddler comes down from the other camp to see if a dance on the turf cannot be started.... Mr. Upton got down his melodeon and played some—we danced a while and went to bed." Three days later she wrote: "Dora and Mary danced the polka."[29] A melodeon is a type of organ popular in the nineteenth century. The full-size melodion would have been too big to bring along. Helen Clark's journal entry may have referred to either a rocking melodeon or a portable, tabletop melodeon; both are examples of smaller keyboard instruments that would have been suited for overland travel.

Music played an important role in celebrations. Mrs. J.J. Gowdy remembered a Fourth of July celebration on the Oregon Trail in 1852: "A great many folks were camped there, and on the Fourth of July they marched with flags flying, drums beating, and a band composed of several horns, fifes and fiddles."[30]

On July 4, 1866, Theodore Bailey traveled to Montana with a group of four wagons. He wrote about a Fourth of July celebration near the Clark Fork of the Yellowstone. "We fired a National Salute with guns and pistols this evening & had very good music from a band of 2 violins, bass viol & brass horn. the river has been rising all day."[31]

After arriving at South Pass with her wagon party in 1850, Margaret Fink described a musical celebration: "There was a hailstorm at noon, but that did not prevent the assembled company from having an off-hand celebration of our arrival at the summit. Music from a violin with tin-pan accompaniment contributed to the general merriment of a grand frolic."[32]

Regarding the musicians and the ensembles on the trail, people made do with whatever combination of instruments and musicians were available. Soloists, duos, trios, and larger grouping of instruments and singers gathered together to make music, and if there were no instruments, people simply sang a cappella or accompanied themselves with hand clapping.

Guitars, lightweight instruments that didn't take up much space in the wagon, were one of the instruments that was most often mentioned in emigrant journals. Harriet Sherril Ward, who traveled west to California in 1852, was a well-to-do, educated

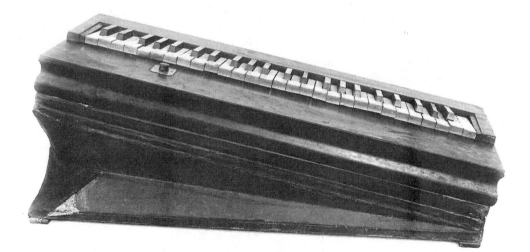

Rocking Melodeon, second quarter of the 19th century, the Crosby Brown Collection of Musical Instruments, 1889. The Rocking Melodeon was a portable keyboard instrument that had to be rocked up and down in order to pump the bellows to sound the reeds (courtesy Metropolitan Museum of Art).

Melodeon, 19th century. Unlike the rocking melodeon, this melodeon did not have to be pumped; a sound was made as soon as a key was depressed (courtesy Jeremy Agnew).

woman who wrote about her daughter Francis, also known as Frankie. "Frankie played the guitar and sang, 'I Have Something Sweet to Tell You.'" Harriet wrote about another young lady, Amelia, who joined her party and got along well with Frankie. "Miss Amelia has her guitar and I hope that all enjoy some pleasant concerts."[33] Perhaps Frankie and Amelia formed a guitar duo who entertained the members of their wagon train.

Violins, like guitars, lightweight and portable, were also frequently mentioned in journals. Sarah Raymond Herndon, who traveled across the plains in 1865, wrote about a musical duo, a married couple who played the violin and the guitar:

> Mr. and Mrs. May—a newly married couple that came into our train at the junction of the roads —are both musicians; several of our young men have fine voices, and with Lyde's guitar, and Mr. May's violin we have an enjoyable musicale away out here in the wilderness. If the Indians had been within listening distance it would be interesting to know what impression the music made upon their minds, as "Music hath charms, etc."* The music this evening has been the happiest feature of the day, for I have to ride in the wagon all day.[34]

On the eve of her westward journey to Fort Laramie, Ada Vodges played the guitar for some of her fellow travelers. "Tomorrow a.m. we move at daylight. This is my first experience in tent life. After dark we all met in Capt. Millers tent, & there we sang until it was time for us to retire for the night. I playing on the guitar."[35]

Along with guitars and violins, the instruments of the trail included bass viols,

---

*The phrase, "Music Hath Charms," a popular expression in emigrant journals, more than likely refers to dialogue from a play by William Congreve (1629–1729), "Music hath charms to soothe the savage beast. To soften rocks, or bend the knotted oak."

harmonicas, accordions, rocking melodeons, banjos, flutes, fifes, tin whistles, drums, bugles, tin pans, and more than likely others that aren't listed here. Elizabeth Dixon Smith wrote about flute and guitar music in camp: "Made 20 miles every night we encamped we locate quite a village but take it up the next day we have plenty music with the flute and violin and some dancing."[36]

James Abby traveled the Oregon Trail in 1850 with a large party of 100 wagons bound for California. In his journal, he wrote about an after-dinner campfire. In the entry he mentioned a variety of instruments including an ophicleide (referred to by Abby as an ophyclide), which is an odd-shaped instrument in the bugle family that slightly resembles a small modern-day euphonium (a small tuba). On April 18, after trying to cook breakfast with wet wood while suffering from a toothache, James Aby wrote the following:

> After eating a hearty supper all hands volunteered and hauled up a big pile of logs for our campfire, around which all seated themselves to hear some music. Billy Reissinger was elected leader of the band. Our music consisted of cornett, ophyclide, trumpet, fiddle, guitar, and a flute. They played "Home Sweet Home," and "Life on the Ocean Wave." How true are the words of the poet, "music hath charms to soothe a savage beast."
>
> Yes, how quick the sweet tones will bring back our warmest recollections of some departed loved ones; what a gush of gentle sorrow will spring up in the bosom when we chance to hear some air that a good old mother used to sing at home years ago! Yes; the son never forgets his home.[37]

Illustration of a fiddle and bow. (iStock.com/channarongsds).

Sarah Raymond Herndon wrote about the bugle signaling the start of Sunday services on the trail: "When the people were gathered, at the call of the bugle, some sat on

Illustration of a 19th-century flute (iStock.com/Nastasic).

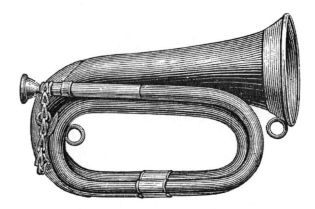

Illustration of a 19th-century bugle (iStock.com/ilbusca).

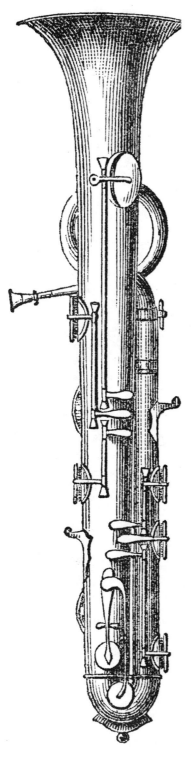

chairs in the shade of wagons, some under umbrellas, some n carriages and light wagons." The same bugle was used to wake up the wagon party in the morning: "We were awakened this morning at the first peep of dawn by the sound of the bugle call."[38] Sarah mentioned the bugle again when her party was near Laramie: "The sounding of the bugle and the echo that reverberated through the mountain gorges this morning was enchantingly sweet and must have driven slumber from every eyelid."[39]

Parthenia Blank, who traveled the Oregon Trail in 1852, wrote about the accordion music played by her twin sister, Cecelia: "Last night we had music and dancing. It makes it seem quite like home to hear the accordion which Cecelia plays most every evening. Not very good roads."[40]

Regarding the style of music popular on the trail, many of the emigrants mentioned exact song titles in their journal entries. Selections included a wide variety of repertoire that mirrors the eclectic tastes of nineteenth-century east coast residents. The songs of the trail included folk songs passed down through the oral tradition; popular songs of the day (e.g., music from Stephen Foster); dance music such as waltzes and polkas; sentimental songs about family and home life; hymns; songs from minstrel shows (the most popular form of entertainment of the time); patriotic songs; opera themes, and spirituals.

Catherine Haun, who traveled across the Plains in 1848, mentioned several songs by name when describing a man in her wagon train named Ralph Cushing: "The latter was the life of the party and a general favorite with the entire train. I see him now

Illustration of an Ophicleide (iStock.com/duncan1890).

in my mind's eye, trudging along; his bright countenance and carefree air, and inspiration. The familiar tunes that he played upon his harmonica seemed to soften the groaning and creaking of the wagons and to shorten the long mils of the mountain road. 'Home, Sweet Home,' 'Old Kentucky Home,' 'Maryland, My Maryland,' 'The Girl I Left Behind Me,' 'One More River to Cross,' seemed particularly appropriate an touched many a pensive heart."[41] Catherine Haun also wrote about music on the Fourth of July: "Patriotic songs were sung, there was music on the violin and Jew's harp, and dancing until midnight."[42]

A little-known topic of Oregon Trail history is the

Illustration of a 19th-century accordion (iStock.com/ ivan-96).

numerous musical interactions between Native Americans and emigrants on the trail. Just as members of the Lewis and Clark Expedition and fur trappers and traders who traveled west in the early 1800s, many of the emigrants on the Oregon Trail mentioned musical observations of Native American music and dance. Some mentioned musical events where emigrants and Native Americans participated in making music and dancing together.

One example comes from Patty Sessions, a Mormon woman who spent the winter of 1847 in the Nebraska Territory before traveling overland to Salt Lake City. While at the Winter Quarters, which was a Mormon community, she wrote about a Native American musical experience. This quote insinuates that Patty and other emigrants listened to Native American music, watched the dances, and also joined in the dance in a type of celebration: "We stay here today many Squaws came today they appear friendly they sing dance and ride around we dance and have music fire two cannons Parley and Taylor feast and smoke with the Chief. Br Grants came in sight to night Mr. Sessions stands on guard."[43]

Claiborne Clayton Walker, who traveled overland from Missouri in 1847, wrote about a musical encounter with Native Americans. On May 18, 1847, his journal entry indicates that Native Americans and emigrants joined together for music making. He wrote: "fine fun here tonight, Indians dancing the War Dance, Fiddes [fiddles] playing Some and Singing Spiritual Songs."[44]

The Peace Treaty Council of 1851, held at Fort Laramie, included U.S. commissioners and over 10,000 Plains Indians. The purpose of the Peace Treaty Council was to ensue peaceful relations between the Plains Indians and emigrants on the trail. Nations that were represented at the council included the Sioux, Cheyenne, Arapaho,

Snake, and Crow, among others. In the eyes of the United States government, the treaty was a success. "Parades of Indian hordes in full array were held, speeches made, presents distributed, the pipe of peace smoked, and by September 17 it had been agreed that peace should reign among the red men and between them and the whites. The white men were to be free to travel the roads and hold their scattered forts, and the Indians were to receive an annuity of $50,000 in goods each year. The council was considered a great success and gave promise of a lasting peace on the plains."[45] However, the treaty did not have lasting success. As the years progressed, Native Americans endured broken treaties, bloody battles, disease, and forced removal from their native lands.

There are some firsthand accounts regarding music and dances that went on during the council. A writer, Mr. Brown, commented about national songs as a group of Indians came into sight at Fort Laramie: "This is much the finest delegation of Indians we have yet seen, and although they are just from a journey of nearly eight hundred miles, they made a most splendid appearance they were all mounted…. They came down the plain in a solid column, singing their national songs."[46] Another report said, "In the afternoon, the Oglala Sioux were hosts to the Snakes, Arapahos and Cheyennes at a great dog feast. The banquet was followed by dancing Feasts and dances were given in most of the other villages and the drumming of the tom toms and the chanting of the revelers continued through the night."[47]

Father De Smet remembered sleeping in his tent near the Shoshone encampment: "the Cheyenne visited the lodges of the Shoshone, who were encamped beside my little tent. Songs and dances were prolonged till daylight and prevented me from sleeping. These amusement among the Indians are perfectly innocent."

Two years after the Peace Council, on June 14, 1853, emigrant Benjamin Franklin Owen wrote about coming to a Sioux village that had 44 lodges. He mentioned three young ladies, a fiddle concert, and friendly relations between the Sioux and the emigrants: "Those three young Indian Women were dressed as finely as the Finest dressed Deerskins, & Beads could make them–They were really beautiful. It was said that they were the Daughters of Chief's. There was one Train there, that had Three men, with Fiddles, all playing in Concert, which, I think, had the effect to Stimulate the zeal of the Indians to their best show of hospitality. They were highly pleased with the music as also the pipe, all the more since The immigrants furnished the Tobacco. Days' drive about 12 M's & camped."[48]

Not all encounters with Native Americans along the trail were peaceful. With the growing number of emigrants taking over land that originally belonged to indigenous people, and exploiting natural resources, some Native Americans retaliated with attacks on wagon parties. For example, on August 20, 1854, a party of 20 emigrants, led by Alexander Ward, camped near the Boise River near present-day Middleton, Idaho. A band of some 200 Shoshone Indians attacked the party and killed everyone except for two young Ward boys. This gruesome event became known as the Ward Party Massacre. Nicholas Lee of Pole County, Oregon, told the story of the tragedy in his ballad, "Snake River Massacre," which was printed in the November 28, 1854, issue of the *Oregon Statesman* newspaper.[49] A contemporary recording of this ballad included a mournful recitation of the words over a simple slow, repetitive accompaniment on a button accordion.[50]

"Snake River Massacre"

A cruel massacre took place
Of late upon the plains.
'Tis hard to describe the place,
It was upon Ward's Train.

While on their way the little band
In harmony progressed,
Nor thought of danger near at hand,
Of quietude possessed.

The savages, they did assail—
Eight men at once were slain;
They had no means to prevail
As eight composed the train.

A wounded lad escaped by chance
The mournful news to tell;
Awakening as if from a trance—
He rose from where he fell.

While eight poor fellows were left dead,
All weltering in gore,
The Indians in haste fled,
The spoil in triumph bore.

Their hatred did not yet abate,
In darker arts indulged—
Most horrible to relate,
The cruelty divulged.

Even to crown the horrible deed
And thus augment their guilt,
The females' cries they did not heed
Until their blood they spilt.

Their cruelty they did portray,
Most shocking, it is true—
Inflicted wounds in every way
That savage art could do.

They did fire and hot irons use,
Hatchets and cudgels, too,
And thus they cut, burned and bruised,
And the poor females slew.

The children met a cruel fate,
As burned to death they were,
And 'tis most shocking to relate
Their mothers present were.

How awful thus for to behold
One's offspring treated so–
Their anguish never can be told,
Their feelings none can know.[51]

Ironically, in the same year, 1854, Dr. J.B. Crane, a California schoolteacher, contributed his own ballad to the canon of tragic songs of the early West. The legend goes, Dr. Crane of California fell in love with his pupil, Susan Newham. He asked Susan for her hand in marriage; she refused, and he killed her. Dr. Crane was tried and condemned to execution in a vigilante court in the mining town of Hangtown, California.

As he awaited his execution, he sang the ballad, and toward the end of the performance, he held out his arms and shouted, "Susan, here I come!"

"Dr. Crane's Song"
(Sung to the tune of "Flow Gently, Sweet Afton")

Come, friends and relations, I bid you adieu,
The grave is now open to welcome me through.
No valleys of shadows I fear on the road,
But angels and waiting to take me to God.

I killed Susan Newham as you have heard tell.
I killed her because that I loved her too well.
Now Susan and I will soon meet at the throne,
And be united forever in the life to come.

Don't weep for me, friends, but dry up your tears,
For I have no sorrows, and I have no fears.
I am eager to go to that far, happy land,
And take my dear Susan again by the hand.[52]

Perry A. Burgess, who was part of a group heading to Montana, wrote about a musical encounter with Native Americans near Laramie Peak on July 6, 1866: "Made one drive, camped for the night among a party of Sioux Indians. There were 400 warriors, beside the old men, women and children. They appeared to be very friendly and peaceable. The chief together with an attendant, took supper with us. We gave them some bread, molasses, and large quantity of new milk. Played some on our violins for their entertainments. Distance to-day 7 mi."[53]

Two days later, near the North Fork of the Cheyenne River, he wrote how Indians had pillaged some of the wagons belonging to his party, and he lost everything except his violin and his rifle. "My chest was in the wagon when that was left. The Indians had torn the cover off from it and taken or destroyed all it contained, my watch, clothing, keepsakes, and small collection of curious petrifications and in fact everything I had with me except my violin and rifle which happened to be in the other wagon."[54]

Easterners were fascinated with stories of emigrants and Native Americans on the Oregon Trail. Several songs were published on the east coast that spoke to this fascination. The cover art for the song, "Ho! for the Kansas Plains," features an emigrant and a Native American.

"Ho! For the Kansas Plains"–Poetry and Music by James G. Clark.

Huzza for the prairies wide and free; Ho! For the Kansas plains;
Where men shall live in liberty; Free from a tyrant's chains.
We spurn at the power and break the rod, Wreaking in guilt and crime;
We bow the knee to none but God, Maker and King of time:
And the brave will round us rally, From the mountain and the valley,
Till the skies with freedom ring, And the world shall hear us sing.

O sweet is the charm of rock and tree; Bright are the flowing rills,
Where we have roam'd in youthful glee, Over the eastern hills:
But we turn from all their beauty, To the call of truth and duty,
And we give our chainless might, To the battle of the right.

Tho' far from the soil of Pilgrim fame, On the Atlantic shore,
Here we will build a noble name, Proud as our fathers wore.
And the faroff Rocky Mountains, With their flashing lakes and fountains,
Shall behold our glory spring, While the world shall hear us sing.[55]

"Ho! For the Kansas Plains," by James. G. Clark. Sheet music cover art depicting a Native American and a pioneer. Published by Oliver Ditson, Boston, 1856 (Kanas State Historical Society).

There were several pieces of music published in the mid-nineteenth century inspired by "Oregon Fever." For example, "My Home's on the Prairie Lee," "Prairie Waltz," "Oregon Quick Step," "Wait for the Wagon," and "Oregon Waltz." "The Girl I Left Behind Me" was a favorite of emigrants on the trail. As is the case for many songs of the trail, there were multiple sets of lyrics that went with the same melody. "The Girl I

Left Behind Me" dates back to an eighteenth-century English folk song, and there were multiple versions of the song floating around on the Oregon Trail. Below are the lyrics to one version found in "Songs and Dances of the Oregon Trail."[56]

"The Girl I Left Behind Me"

I hit the trail in seventy-nine
the herd strung out behind me
As I jogged along my thoughts went back to the girl I left behind me.

(Chorus) Oh that sweet little girl, that pretty little girl, the girl,
The girl you do remind me,
That sweet little girl, that dear little the girl,
the girl I left behind me.

If ever I get off the trail
And the Indians they don't find me
I'll make my way straight back again
To the girl I left behind me.
(Chorus)
The wind did blow and the rain did flow
The hail did fall and blind me;
I thought of that girl, that sweet little girl,
That girl I left behind me.
(Chorus)
She wrote ahead to the place I said
I was always glad to find it;
She says, "I'm true, when you are through
Right back here you will find me."
(Chorus)
When we sold out I took the train
I knew where I would find her.
When I got back we had a big smack
And I ain't no gol-durned liar.

In conclusion, music served multiple roles on the Oregon Trail. People brought heart, fortitude, and passion to the trail as they endured hardships, loss, and countless challenges on the road toward fulfilling their dream for a new life in the West. The music they carried with them provided soulful sustenance on the long road. The many roles of Oregon Trail music included: diversion, entertainment, comfort, solace, a way to remember loved ones, worship, stress relief, a community bond, celebration, and a way to interact with Native Americans. In another role, music marked gruesome historical events as songs were written about unfortunate events that happened along the trail. Many of these ballads were passed down from generation to generation through the oral tradition. In addition, composers and songwriters of the time published songs and melodies inspired by the Oregon Trail experience.

Digging into the music sung and played on the Oregon Trail along with studying musical compositions inspired by the Oregon Trail lends an alternative lens with which to view this epic moment in history. The story of music in the West continued as emigrants arrived at their destinations and continued creating and enjoying rich and varied musical activities on their homesteads and in their early frontier communities—The Place.

We're There!

Music on the Homestead and in Early Frontier Communities

Mr. Waught's benefit on Thursday night drew a very large audience.
The best thing of the evening was Mr. Waught's guitar solo. The snare
drum and the piano imitations were beautiful and the whole piece
aptly chosen and beautifully executed.—Montana Post, 1865

As pioneers settled into their new lives on homesteads and in early frontier communities throughout the mid-to late nineteenth century, musical traditions helped to establish a deep-rooted sense of place. This chapter explores a host of musical activities in the everyday lives of pioneers, including music on the homestead, in bustling frontier towns, in mining camps, in Indian boarding schools, and in the life of an itinerant Methodist preacher.

Life on a homestead was an isolated experience. Moreover, it was a life filled with many trials and hardships as people built their homes, cleared the land, worked their claims, cared for livestock, and planted crops. Homesteads acquired through the Homestead Act of 1862 included 160 acres for a single person and 320 acres for a couple. These large expanses of land meant that frontier homes were spread far apart. If you were a homesteader, your closest neighbor might have been miles and miles away. Get-togethers were a welcome diversion to the isolation and painstaking work of homestead life. Neighbors regularly got together to celebrate the holidays, barn raisings, and weddings or simply to socialize with friends. Homesteaders also got together for the Sabbath. Church took place in open fields, in modest cabins, and in rustic country churches.

All ages readily participated in square dances or breakdowns, which often took place in homes, sometimes on a dirt floor. These dances were often accompanied by a fiddler and a caller who called the dance steps. L.L. Scott, a Kansas pioneer, remembered, "People would come from miles around in lumber wagons, spring wagons, two-wheeled carts, horseback, and afoot. I have known them to come 25 to 30 miles in a hayrack with 15 or 20 passengers.... After dinner there would be speaking of some kind, a ball game, horse racing greased pig catching and other sports for the older people and with a platform dance, both day and night and the men would put up rope swings for the children to play on. Everything was free, just enough money to pay the fiddler was all that was needed."[1] Examples of popular nineteenth-century fiddle tunes that may have been played include: "Turkey in the Straw," "Wagoner," "Arkansas Traveler," "Buy a Broom," and "Fisher's Hornpipe."

Hamlin Garland, a homesteader in Wisconsin, wrote: "Our house was a place of

Anderson sod house, Logan County, Kansas. Three musicians are playing a violin, a violoncello, and an accordion while another man holds a rifle. Isabel, Matilda, and Pete are posed in the front of the house. Created between 1885 and 1890 (Kansas State Historical Society).

Family posed with a fiddler at the Quisenbury Ranch on the Snake River in Nebraska (History Nebraska).

song, notwithstanding the severe toil which was demanded of every hand, for often of an evening, especially in winter time, father took his seat beside the fire, invited us to his knees, and called mother to sing. These moods were very sweet to us and we usually insisted upon his singing for us ... we especially liked 'Down the Ohio.' Only one verse survives in my memory":

> The river is up, the channel is deep,
> The winds blow high and strong.
> The flash of the oars, the stroke we keep
> Down the O-h-i-o

Garland went on about his musical recollections; he wrote of his mother, who "was gifted with a voice of great range and sweetness, and from her we always demanded 'Nellie Wildwood,' 'Lily Dale,' 'Lorena' or some of Roots stirring war songs."[2] (The quote probably refers to George Frederick Roots, an American songwriter who was popular during the Civil War. One of his most popular songs was "The Battle Cry of Freedom.")

When describing the surrounding area and the pioneers of Corvallis, Oregon, George W. Kennedy reminisced, "What places of resort those pioneer stores used to be; and those primitive homes. I cannot describe the open-door hospitality of them, the kindness, the jollity, the oneness of neighborhood life, you might always find in them."[3]

Fremont Nelson homestead, 1900. Elviria with guitar, along with Edgar and Reno Verne (Wyoming State Archives).

George Kennedy fondly remembered religious camp meetings and an enthusiastic preacher who was known for his powerful singing. Kennedy commented, "Sometimes, right in the middle of a song, he would stop short, mount a bench for two or three minutes, his voice, and gesture manner would suggest a thunder bolt let loose…. And then sing:

> While the Angels stand inviting
> The Angels stand inviting,
> To welcome the prodigal home."[4]

George Kennedy also described weekly church services in his homesteading years: "Around the Campfire, in the open yard, before we moved into the cabin, we used to sit and sing old songs of religion. Kennedy wrote that the old standard hymns were sung, and points to a favorite hymn, 'The House of the Lord.'"[5]

> You may sing of the beauty of mountain and dale,
> Of the silvery streamlet and flowers of the vale;
> But the place most delightful this earth can afford,
> Is the place of devotion-the house of the Lord.

Clareta Olmstead Smith recalled stories of pioneer life in the Kittitas Valley of Washington Territory. There were no ministers or preachers around to conduct funerals in what she referred to as her "raw pioneer community." It was up to family, friends, and neighbors to carry out the funeral service, which often included favorite hymns.

At funerals an elderly man of the community would read the Bible verses and say a comforting prayer. A neighbor woman would sing a beautiful old hymn, and the simple service was finished. Favorite hymns were "What a Friend We Have in Jesus" and "Jesus Lover of My Soul." Another lovely old song much used was "The Vacant Chair." This was one of the most popular of the Civil War songs. There were few of the Civil War veteran or members of their families who could not sing at least one of the verses. The melody lingers on after the last note has been caught up and carried away.[6]

Pioneer Adelia Elizabeth Hawkins was a single woman homesteader near Big Sandy, Montana, when she met her husband, Martin Sturm, from Iowa. It was a musical connection. Adelia remembered the story this way: "I was playing piano, a very nice-looking man came to get the mail, he heard me playing and he said, 'Who is that playing?' My mother said, 'It's my daughter,' and he said he hadn't heard any music since he came out about a month ago, so my mother invited him in and he played the violin that he had brought with him. He was from Iowa. My mother invited him over for dinner Sunday night and he brought his violin. This man turned out to be Martin V. Sturm, whom I married within three months."[7]

Adelia and Martin regularly played music together for dances at the granary in town. A collection was taken up for the couple at the end of the night, and they sometimes made $5.00 for the entire evening. Adelia remembered that she was always sad to hear the last musical selection of the evening, which was always the "Home Sweet Home Waltz."[8]

The Reverend Parish stayed for a short time at the Whitman Mission and wrote about the Indians singing during a church meeting: "Moved into the house last evening. More moderate this morning than it has been for some days. We have had the privilege of attending divine service. The Indians' meeting was at eleven o'clock and was interesting to me. The Indians sing well, carrying the parts of music."[9]

As pioneers settled in the West, settlers worked in frontier towns as shopkeepers, bankers, tradesmen, and teachers. A survey of newspapers, biographies, oral histories, personal journals and photographs from these early frontier towns delivers a snapshot of the musical activities of the residents in their early frontier communities. Those activities included dances, concerts, recitals, music lessons, political rallies, celebrations, and church gatherings.

Schools were a popular venue for dances, lectures, literary societies, and political events. In an interview, Mrs. Sarah L. Byrd spoke about a school dance which featured waltzing, square dancing, and the Virginia reel, all of which were danced to the accompaniment of a single Jew's harp:

> When we went to school it wuz in an ol' log house, an' there wuz an empty room, an' there we young uns learned to dance. All the music we had wuz an ol' jewsharp one o' the boys had, an' he could play it perty good … it wuz a grand ball, all decorated an' everythin.' We waltzed some, but mostly it wuz square dances and the Virginia Reel.[10]

Early community newspapers included announcements for local concerts at schools and churches. Alongside the concert announcements, music stores often advertised their offerings such as sheet music, brass band instruments, pianos, organs, accordions, and melodeons. The newspapers also ran advertisements for private music teachers who offered lessons in singing, harp, organ, guitar, violin, piano, organ, and more.

The Handel and Haydn society of Astoria, Oregon Territory, was a typical type of local performance group in a frontier community. On June 3, 1879, the society performed their first concert at the Metropolitan Hall on a drizzly morning. The *Daily Astorian* reported the event was "set with gems from the most popular writers and the execution of it filled the heart of each hearer with joy to know, and to realize, that is was the work of our own friends, the ladies and gentlemen of Astoria." One of the songs performed was "When the Summer Rain is Over" by Donizetti—a fitting selection for the rainy Pacific Northwest.

In Montana territory, Great Falls boasted a thriving musical scene. On Saturday, August 11, 1888, the *Great Falls Weekly Tribune* reported that there was an "agreeable and successful concert" featuring the Heine Family at the Presbyterian Church. The program included the daughter, Miss Evelyn, her mother, Madame Heine, and her father, Professor Heine. "Professor Heine played on the violin 'Cavatina' by Raff and a 'Mazurka,' composed by 'himself.'" Mr. Heine seems to have had a great sense of humor. He also played the tin whistle and performed some imitations of opera singers to the delight of the audience. Madame Heine, a pianist, played "The Brook" by Pape and "Pasquinade" by Gottschalk. Miss Heine sang two popular Scotch songs including "Jamie" and "Coming Through the Rye." Mr. and Mrs. Heine played selections from the opera "William Tell." And the grand finale featured the family trio performing "Home, Sweet Home." As it turns out "Home Sweet Home" was a favorite in the East, on the Oregon Trail and at trails end.

On March 20, 1885, the *Caldwell Tribune* of Caldwell, Idaho Territory, announced an upcoming concert at the public school featuring a variety of 20 musical selections—for orchestra, solo voice, and male quartet. The entire program was listed in the paper along with the price of admission—25 cents. The musical selections included, "Mother's Fool," "Spring Fun," "Kittie's Prayer," "Bachelor Bliss," and "Katydid." The final selection on the program was a short play called "Leap Year in the Village with One Man." Surely the play was a comedy—in the Irish tradition, when it is a leap year, February 29 is the one day when a woman can ask a man to marry her.

An 1870's photograph features the Olympia Band, an ensemble made up of an eclectic combination of instruments including a flute, two banjos, a string bass, a trombone, and a violin. The Olympia Band represents the style of bands that played throughout the West for balls, parties, celebrations, building dedication ceremonies, and community concerts.

Homesteaders and residents of early frontier communities enjoyed musical traditions which, in many ways, were similar to the life they had left behind in the East. On the other hand, mining camps in Idaho, Colorado, Wyoming and Montana were in full swing with a musical life of their own, mainly centered around local saloons. In his book, *The Saloon of the Rocky Mountain Frontier*, author Elliott West explained that the saloon was the social heart-center of a mining camp:

> Even the toughest miners—mostly single men yearned for a touch of music in their rugged mining camps. To satisfy their inhabitants' musical interests, camps often organized amateur orchestras or bands, though the quality was not always the highest. The upbeat selections of the brass band of Ketchum, Idaho, sounded to a local journalist like "a regiment of

Olympia Band, photograph dated 1870–1895. The men in the photograph include W.H. Roberts, C.M. Moore, Charles B. White, Mitchel Harris, Samuel D. Starkwather, Henry Stumer, Theodore Brown, Louis P. Ouellette, and Gus Harris. The musicians hold a baton, a trombone, bass, viol, violin, two flutes, and two banjos (C952.226.41, courtesy Washington State Historical Society, Tacoma, Wash).

tom-cats with their tails tied together and strung on a clothes-line," while its more somber numbers recalled "the last groan of a dying calf. Nonetheless, any amusement was appreciated ... saloon men did their part by giving their facilities over for organizational meetings, hosting balls to raise money for instruments, and featuring professional itinerant musicians when they came through town."[11]

Saloon dances—including hops, flings and masked balls—were especially welcome in the mining towns during the cold, dark winter months and added a touch of elegance to the rustic atmosphere of early mining camps. The miners did not let the lack of women stop them from dancing; the men just filled in for the parts of the women. Elliott West wrote about how the miners learned to dance: "For those untutored in the intricacies of the waltz, schottische, varsovienne, and Virginia reel, dancing academies provided instruction as well as advice in the subtleties of etiquette."[12] The varsovienne, popular form 1850–1870, originated in Poland. It is a slow, elegant dance in three-quarter time.

Miners often composed alternate lyrics to songs that told stories of mining camp life. One such mining song was composed on a stagecoach headed for Leadville, Colorado. The lyrics were to be sung to the melody of "The First Lord's Song" from "H.M.S. Pinafore" a favorite Gilbert and Sullivan comic opera written in 1878. The rewritten lyrics were perfectly at home in a mining town saloon setting:

> When I was a youth and to college went
> I spent all the money that my father sent;
> Fitting up my mind for society
> By filling up my bowels with bad whiskey;
> And I fitted up myself so splendidlee.
> That now I am always on a D.B.D [damn big drunk][13]

James Chisholm, who had worked as a journalist for newspapers in the East, traveled west in 1868 and found himself living in Cheyenne, Wyoming. He described the music scene in Cheyenne: "There is a fiddle scraping and rattling drumming and organ grinding enough to furnish a small Babel."[14] Chisholm, not only a journalist but also a flute player, was asked to play professionally when a passerby heard his flute. James Chisholm wrote: "The other day I took out the flute to give it an airing when the leader of a band happened to see it. On hearing its tones he immediately offered me an engagement to play at a concert hall at seven dollars a night and seemed offended when I declined the offer."[15]

Writer and historian Ruth Anderson wrote about a traveling musician who was a guest performer in a mining town: "One visiting soloist who lived to tell the tale, tells of a conductor conducting with a gun instead of a baton. When asked if the gun was loaded, the conductor replied that it was, so that he could shoot anybody who played a wrong note."[16]

Colonel William Thompson, a pioneer, described a saloon in the mining camp town of Canyon City, Colorado: "The town proper numbered about six saloons to every legitimate business house. Of evenings the gambling hells were a glare of light, and music, both vocal and instrumental, floated out upon the streets to tempt the miners to enter, while away the hour, and incidentally part with their well-earned dust."[17]

Pianos and organs showed up in the West in the 1860s. The instruments were shipped from San Francisco to ports in the Pacific Northwest and hauled overland. They were also carried from the east coast over the Oregon Trail by freight wagon. After

Musicians holding brass instruments and drums pose on the balcony of the Wells Fargo and
Company office and Photograph Gallery in Silver City, Idaho, 1860s (82–2-54, Idaho State
Archives).

the completion of the transcontinental railroad in 1869, they were carried by freight train. One of the first reports regarding pianos came from Davis Willson's journal. He reported seeing a piano in Columbus, Nebraska, en route to Montana by wagon train in 1866:

> Went into camp close outside town [Columbus] about eleven. Saw Indians. Charlie C. [Caldwell] bought a pair of moccasins. Went up town saw Collins—came back to camp with me. Charlie C. had 4 Indian warriors [he was] feeding. Had quite an interesting time with them [Hopkins] Taylor went to one of our neighbors [in Columbus] & tuned their piano, went with him and took violin—had a good time. It is the only piano between Omaha & Denver.[18]

In Kansas, the Hilton family, in particular the mother and the oldest daughter, did not want friends and neighbors back East to see a photograph of their sod house. So they moved their prized possession, the pump organ, outside for the photo session. The organ and the family look perfectly posed in the dirt among the cows, pigs, mules, wagons, corral, and horses.

An enterprising way of selling pianos and organs was the "Piano Car"—a piano showroom housed in a train car that traveled from town to town along the rail line. The "Piano Car" showcased pianos and organs in an inviting artistic parlor-type setting complete with lush carpets, artwork, and comfortable seating. According to *The Western Resources of 1901*, "the train travels through the five states of Washington, Idaho,

David Hilton family of Custer County, Nebraska, posing with the family's organ, 1887. The family did not want to show the old sod house to people back East, but the mother and the daughter wanted to prove that they had an organ (History Nebraska).

Montana, Oregon, and Wyoming. The car invariably makes a sensation when it strikes a town and many a piano is sold that way."

Newspapers were filled with advertisements for music instrument retailers. For example, the *Idaho Semi-Weekly World* ran an advertisement for James A. Phinney and Co., a retailer that sold pianos, organs and sheet music. On the same page there was an advertisement for band instruments, music, and uniforms. The stores also kept the latest sheet music in stock. Pianos were often offered as raffle prizes for charity fundraisers throughout communities in the West, such as Virginia City, Montana Territory. Speaking of Virginia City, according to the *Montana Post* of 1865, the town was looking for a piano tuner: "A gentleman who thoroughly understands his business. Apply at the City Book Store."

Community concerts provided entertainment, a touch of refinement, and a place for friends to meet. For example, on August 19, 1854, *The Pioneer and Democrat* of Olympia, Washington Territory, reported that a group of people were entertained by a vocal program presented by Mr. Clement White at the Washington Hotel. According to the review, his encore included the songs "Cheer Boys, Cheer" and "With Helmet on his Brow." The article also mentioned that Mr. White was staying in town for a few weeks to give vocal and instrumental instruction to "persons desirous of procuring instructions in music."

On February 25, 1865, the *Idaho World* of Idaho City reported on a concert that was held in Pickwick Hall where a full house was treated to music: "Barneys band with their accustomed elegance, filled the balance of the hall with the sweetest of music."

In another example of a community concert, on October 1, 1864, the *Montana Post* of Virginia City reported that a visiting artist, "Mr. Greenwald, formerly musical director of the German opera in San Francisco, will treat the people of Virginia and vicinity to some of the best selected pieces of music, ever produced on any stage. Let everybody turn out and give him a full house, and be assured of his giving entire satisfaction. No pains will be spared to make this entertainment the most select."

On June 20, 1888, the *Bozeman Weekly Chronicle*, of Bozeman Territory, reviewed a concert presented by William H. McKanlass, a well-known African American minstrel show leader, violinist, and cornetist. The paper reported, "McKanlass, the negro musician, held forth with this company at the Palace Theatre and presented his passable specialties. McKanlass's noisy band is a great attraction and has some meritorious performers in it."

A vintage photo of Kansas musicians from the Kansas Historical Society serves as a reminder that music tapestry of the nineteenth-century American West included thousands of African Americans. The photograph does not contain any background information. Perhaps the elegant-looking group may have been a band made up of family and friends. The instruments in the photograph include a violin, guitars, a banjo, and a mandolin. Perhaps the women and some of the young men without instruments were singers with the band. The photograph begs the question: What music were they playing on their instruments? Gospel? Folk songs? Popular songs of the day?

After the Civil War, African Americans moved west in large numbers with the dream of starting their new lives as freed citizens. As many as 6,000 blacks settled in Kansas and Oklahoma in the 1870s, and Nebraska attracted a large number of African Americans in the 1880s. Blacks were not only pioneers but also served in the U.S. Cavalry, and as many as 9,000 African American men rode the range as cowboys in the 1870s.[19]

African American musicians. The four musicians included in this group hold a violin, a banjo, and two guitars. Created by the Lawrence Studio sometime between 1890–1919. The location is unknown; however, the Lawrence Studio was located in Lawrence, Kansas (Kansas State Historical Society).

Nettie Smith was an African American pianist and educator who immigrated with her family to Nicodemus, Kansas, a town established by African Americans after the Civil War. Nettie earned her "Teacher of Music" degree from the Kansas Conservatory of Music in 1883. She served as a church pianist, choir director, and music instructor in Nicodemus, Denver, and eventually in Tacoma, Washington. She is remembered in Tacoma as a pillar of the community. Nettie taught music to many races for more than 50 years and annually presented piano recitals of 45 students or more. Along with her undying dedication to music education, she was known for her beautiful grand piano and her large library.[20]

Singing schools played a part in the musical lives of people in the West. January 27, 1888, the *State Rights Democrat* of Albany, Oregon, reported that six young men were arrested near Crabtree for disturbing a singing-school. On the same page, it was reported that a Professor Mitchell had been teaching a singing-school and had "a good many scholars who are learning very fast."

Theodore Geer wrote about a "singing-school" that took place after the Sunday church service.

As a rule, families brought their luncheon in huge baskets and when the Sunday-school was over everybody repaired to some convenient, shady spot where a meal fit for the gods was served, those not provided with their own luncheon being invited to partake of their neighbors'. Nobody went hungry and no meals were paid for. At three o'clock the singing-school was opened in "Dixie" schoolhouse, where all public meetings were held, and for two hours all the old-time hymns and glee songs were rendered by everybody present in a manner which left nothing to be desired in point of—lung power and enthusiasm. And perhaps those crude efforts were more uplifting than much of the music furnished by the church choirs of to-day, paid for at so much per.[21]

In addition to singing schools, private music teachers flourished, and music teachers made do with whatever space was available for lessons. For example, the *Daily Astorian* announced on September 23, 1877, that Miss Brown was opening a private school at Arrigoni Hotel, where she would also be giving piano lessons for 50 cents per week or $5 per month.

On May 27, 1879, the *Daily Astorian* announced: "We are informed that Prof. E. Cook having severed his connection with the Oregon conservatory of music has opened music parlors on First street, between Main and Salmon, Portland, and was prepared to teach piano, organ, voice building, singing through bass and harmony."

In 1882, the *Wood River Times* of Hailey Idaho advertised that Professor Conrad Zick was offering lessons on the guitar and brass instruments. The *Wood River Times* later ran an advertisement in 1883 for Miss Florence L. Pound, teacher of music, who was accepting students on the piano, organ and harp at "reasonable terms." She listed the Philadelphia Musical Academy as a reference.

Dr. Z.M. Previn was a well-known Oregon pianist, vocalist, and educator who regularly presented concerts in and around Salem, Oregon, where he was also the director of the Conservatory of Music at Willamette University in the late 1800s. The Oregon Historical Society archives holds several compositions by Dr. Previn, including this sentimental ballad expressing the memories of a former comfortable home and a serene family life, "I'll Go Back to Home and Mother." Previn wrote the music to words found in the regional newspaper, the *Oregonian*. On the bottom of the sheet music, there is an advertisement for a dentist, Dr. Maude Tanner, and for the music store, the Wiley B. Allen Company.

> "I'll Go Back to Home and Mother" (Chorus)
> When the songs of the South, 'mid the cotton
> Comes again as of old to my ear
> And my memories, long, long forgotten
> Back to homeland, Mother so dear.

Sometimes students traveled back East to further their music education. For example, on January 26, 1872, the *Albany Register* reported, "Seven young ladies from Oregon have just entered their names as students at the Boston Conservatory of Music." Perhaps these students completed their education in the East and moved back to the West in order to teach, perform, and contribute to the developing cultural scene.

Brass bands were a big part of frontier community life across the West, from military forts to larger cities. According to the *Daily Morning Astorian* on November 21, 1884, "The United States is the greatest country for brass band in the world, but it needs them all. A country that elects a president every four years wants noise." The *Astorian* went on to report, "There were ten brass bands, loud sounding canon, transparencies, torch lights, red fire, rockets, and the greatest enthusiasm." (Transparencies were a popular form of nineteenth-century artwork—illuminated with light and used for celebrations.)

On June 27, 1890, the *Corvallis Gazette* reported, "Don't fail to take super this evening at *the* old college chapel. The brass band will furnish music from 6 to 8 p.m." Likely, some of the most popular Sousa tunes at the end of the 1800s would have been played by brass bands and may have included: "Across the Danube" (1877), "Esprit de Corps" (1878), "Our Flirtation" (1880), "Recognition March" (1880), and "Wolverine March" (1881).

The *Montana Post* of Virginia City ran regular advertisements in the year 1865 for Waugh's Brass and Quadrille Band. The band was available for processions, parties, dances, concerts, and serenades or "in fact for any occasion when a good brass band or orchestra may be employed."

Music was a regular part of community meeting agendas. Take, for example, the meeting agenda for the Farmers Institute, as reported by *The Dalles Weekly Chronicle* of Oregon in 1892:

"The following is the programme of the Farmers' Institute to be held at Wasco the 12th and 13th of May inst., under the auspices of the Wasco and Sherman counties business council."

Thursday, May 12, 9:30 A.M.

- Music.
- Response, the Rev. J.M. Denison.
- Music.
- Response, Prof. H.T. French.
- Music
- Lunch
- Music.
- Industrial education, Wallis Nash.
- Music.
- To What extent the farmers can dispense with the middlemen, P.P. Underwood.
- Music.
- How can the farmers derive the greatest benefit from the experiment station Prof. H.T. French.
- Music.

To the members of the Farmers' Institute, it seems music was as important as informative lectures and business matters. The following day's agenda included music in-between each of the following lectures: business methods of the farmer; horticulture; farm insects; transportation; education of the farmer; cooperation as adapted to the needs of the farmer; green fallowing and green manure; and questions from the question box. The announcement in the newspaper concluded with this comment: "Plenty of music will be on hand and the features of the evening will be among the most interesting parts of the programme."

Music played a starring role in community celebrations. The 1848 Fourth of July celebration in Oregon City, according to the *Oregon Free Press,* announced that the celebration would include a reading of the Declaration of Independence and a "song by a lady and gentleman of this city" and end with benediction music.

The *Montana Post* of Virginia City reported about the opening of a new community venue: "A Grand Opening Ball at the Lyceum with 'delightful music.'" In another example, in celebration of President Lincoln's 1864 election victory, *The Montana Post* of

Music group in Cheyenne, Wyoming. Photograph taken by Joseph Shimitz, undated, from the Meyer's Collection. The musicians are holding guitars, mandolins, and a flute (Wyoming State Archives).

Virginia City reported, "The Union men are having a celebration. Music, bonfires, and speech making are the order of the day, or rather the night."

Music education and the band tradition were also a part of the curriculum at Indian boarding schools, which existed from the 1860s through the turn of the twentieth century. The main goal of these boarding schools was to teach Native American children English and to strip them of their language and culture by learning white "cultural norms" along with skills that were valued by white society. In many of these boarding schools, music was a component of the education. Dancing and making music together had been a large part of indigenous peoples' culture, and the children readily took to playing brass band and stringed instruments. Although the boarding schools and regimented academic programs were not voluntary nor welcome transitions, the children excelled in the music programs which offered a place to make music together, celebrate community, and take pride in their achievements as musicians. Girls were taught to play the piano, guitar, violin, and other parlor-style instruments while boys were typically taught brass instruments and played in wind bands. However, a photograph of the Fort Shaw Band shows girls holding wind instruments including saxophones, flutes, and clarinets.

The Fort Shaw Indian School was located on the Sun River in North Central Montana and had a strong music program and an in-demand performing ensemble. On March 16, 1902, the *Great Falls Tribune* reported on the musical activities at the Fort Shaw School: "The school had a senior band composed of about twenty brass instruments, besides drums, a junior band, a glee club, an orchestra composed of eight pieces;

two violins, a bass viol, two clarinets, a trombone, and two cornets and a mandolin club for girls, which had ten pieces, six mandolins, two guitars, a violin, and one cello."[22]

On June 17, 1900, the *Great Falls Daily Tribune* reported about Robert Bruce from Poplar, Montana, a baritone player who later went on to tour nationally and internationally with the Sousa Band. "The Fort Shaw band has a new member, in the person of Robert Bruce from Poplar. Two years ago he went to Carlisle and it was found, he had no equal in a brass band of sixty young Indians from all over the United States, and today he is the finest Indian baritone player in the world."

In addition to information about the band tradition at Fort Shaw, I encountered several photographs documenting that the Indian brass band tradition thrived in other locations throughout the west. Those images included the Puyallup Reservation Band (Washington), The Tulalip Indian Band (Washington), and the Crow Reservation Band (Montana). The Indian brass band tradition continued into the twentieth century with several accomplished Indian bands such as the North American Indian Concert Band which toured throughout the U.S. and Europe. The informative documentary, *Sousa on the Rez: Marching to the Beat of a Different Drummer*, explores the tradition from the 1800s through contemporary times.

Regarding the children at the Fort Shaw school, in addition to playing their instruments, the students regularly sang hymns with ministers and priests who visited the

Fort Shaw Mandolin Club. The girls hold a variety of string instruments, including mandolins, violins, and guitar. Likely Fort Shaw Indian School. Created circa 1905 (Pac 80-79.M2, Montana Historical Society Research Center Photograph Archives, Helena, Montana).

Father Prando with Crow boys brass band

Father Prando with Crow boys brass band. The boys hold various brass horns (trombone, trumpet, and others), drums, and cymbals. Created between 1845–1906 (035 B05F11.03, of Montana Historical Society Research Center Photograph Archives, Helena, Montana).

school. Reverend Baldwin said, "They would come on Saturday afternoon and have classes for the children with a general assembly on Sunday evenly for the children of both Catholic and Protestant faith."[23]

Mrs. Des Rosier, who worked at the school, remarked, "The children loved to sing in these evening meetings, and when 'Brother Van' came around, their favorite song was, 'Throw Out the Lifeline.'"[24]

"Throw Out the Lifeline"
By Edward S. Ufford

Throw out the life-line across the dark wave!
There is a brother whom someone should save—
Somebody's brother! O who then will dare
To throw out the life-line, his peril to share?

Refrain: Throw out the Life-Line! Throw out the Life-Line!
Someone is drifting away;
Throw out the Life-Line! Throw out the Life-Line!
Someone is sinking today.

Throw out the life-line with hand quick and strong:
Why do you tarry, why linger so long?
See! he is sinking; oh, hasten today
And out with the life boat! away, then away![25]

William Van Orsdel (1848–1919), known as Brother Van, was often referred to as "The Best Loved Man in Montana." Brother Van, an enthusiastic singer, often broke into song during his sermons. He was one of the frequent visitors to the Fort Shaw Indian School and was an early circuit rider—a preacher who rode from town to town conducting church services in barns, schools, and even in the open air. He tirelessly preached the gospel to congregations both large and small—on a steamboat, in saloons, in churches, on rustic homesteads, and in the open air throughout the state of Montana during the latter part of the nineteenth century. When asked by a riverboat captain why he was going to Montana, Brother Van replied, "To sing, to preach and to encourage people to be good."[26]

He stayed true to his word. The beloved and dauntless Brother Van established over 100 churches, six hospitals, a college, and a university during his 47-year Montana ministry (1872–1919). Known affectionately as "Great Heart" by the Blackfeet tribe, he once participated in a buffalo hunt near Choteau, Montana. The event was chronicled by the famous cowboy artist C.M. Russell (1864–1926) in a painting called "Brother Van Shooting Buffalo."

Brother Van claimed he saved a life with his singing. When asked whose life, he replied, "My own." The story goes, Brother Van sauntered into the newly established mining town of Radersburg, between Bozeman and Helena in central Montana. He was dressed for the two-day journey in cowboy clothes and a hat. In the eyes of the Radersburg residents, this stranger walking through the streets, Brother Van, resembled a horse thief on the "wanted-poster" hanging in the post office. Thinking the stranger was the thief, the townsfolk hid behind windows and doors and raised their gun barrels toward the innocent Brother Van. Brother Van raised his arms high above his head, introduced himself, and explained he wasn't the horse thief but a Methodist preacher passing through. Someone in the crowd shouted out, "If you're really Brother Van, you sing 'Diamonds in the Rough,' for us and we'll believe you." To this request, Brother Van belted out "Diamonds in the Rough" as he never had before. And this is how Brother Van saved his own life through music.[27]

"Diamonds in the Rough"

While walking out one evening, not knowing where to go, just to pass the time away, before we held our show,
I heard the gospel mission band singing with all their might; I gave my heart to Jesus and left the show that night.
I used to dance the polka, the schottische, and the waltz;
I loved the theater with all its glittering show and fuss; When Jesus found me, he found me crude and tough,
But praise the Lord, he saved me: I'm a diamond in the rough![28]

Always at the ready with a hymn, Brother Van used song as an expression of joy, love, and faith. When words failed, he would often break into song in the middle of a sermon, delighting parishioners in the process. Brother Van sang songs such as "In the Sweet By and By" and popular hymns of the day from the likes of composers Ira Moody and David Sankey. People loved hearing the old hymns, which reminded them of family, friends, and the communities they had left behind in their old lives before settling in the West. "Diamonds in the Rough" was most often requested by his enthusiastic audiences. Another favorite hymn, written by W.A. Spenser in 1886, came to be known as "Brother Van's Song."

"Brother Van's Song"

Over and Over, yes deeper and deeper
My heart is pierced through with life's sorrowing cry,
But the tears of the sower and the songs of the reaper
Shall mingle together in the joy by and by.[29]

When many of us think of the nineteenth-century American West, our imaginations may turn to the familiar narratives and characters of the Wild West, including roughed-up saloons, grizzled gold diggers, flamboyant madams, tough gamblers, fast-shooting gunfighters, lanky cowboys, grizzled outlaws, brave Indian warriors, and

The Earnest family sitting on the front steps of their home in Fossil, Wyoming, 1899. Mrs. Earnest is holding a guitar, the two girls are holding dolls, and the boy is on a bicycle (Wyoming State Archives).

distinguished-looking U.S. cavalrymen. Indeed, these are all part of the history of the West. However, the West also included an additional western narrative—homesteaders who congregated in a tiny cabin for a fiddling party; miners who took dancing lessons; families and neighbors who gathered in the open air to lay their loved ones to rest with favorite hymns; a young music teacher who taught children to play the piano in the lobby of an Oregon hotel; an African American musician and educator who taught music to hundreds of children in Tacoma, Washington; piano salesmen who rode the rails, selling their wares from town to town onboard luxury train cars full of pianos and organs; brass bands who played for community picnics as well as late-night dance parties; Indian children who excelled at playing a variety of band instruments; and a singing Methodist preacher. As pioneers put down roots and established a sense of place in the West, music served in multiple roles—celebration, distraction, entertainment, socializing, worship, remembering home, education, diplomacy, and as a way to add beauty and joy to daily life.

8

Whoopie Ti Yi Yo

Music and the Real Cowboys in the Old West

When threatening clouds do gather and blinding lightnings flash,
And heavy raindrops splatter and rolling thunders crash;
What keeps the herd from running stampeding far and wide?
The cowboy's long, low whistle and singing by their side.
—From "The Jolly Cowboy," author unknown

Cowboys have long been celebrated in popular fiction, film, songs, and musicals as free-spirited, heroic, strong, and larger-than-life characters. Cowboys have primarily been portrayed as white men; however, the original cowboys represented a melting pot of African Americans, Native Americans, Mexican Americans, and white Americans who all added their own songs and voices to the soundtrack of the Old West. This chapter shines a light on the songs, the singers, the musicians, and the role music played in the era of the trail-riding cowboy.

Nineteenth-century cowboys worked as cowhands on ranches and on a vast network of trails as they drove thousands of longhorn cattle from the south of Texas to grazing lands and markets in points north. In the introduction to his book, *Cowboy Songs and Other Frontier Ballads,* John Lomax set the scene for these songs and the cowboys who sang them:

> In the period from 1870 to 1890 one million mustang ponies and twelve million head of longhorn cattle were driven up the trail from Texas to markets in Kansas, Wyoming, Montana, and other western States. The herds numbered usually from one thousand to three thousand though at times as many as five thousand cattle made up a single train herd. Behind and around and ahead of each bunch of cattle rode a group of men, mostly very young, bold, youthful vikings of the seas of sage grass through which they pushed their way. They came to be known as cowboys-the boys who take care of the cows (from the Spanish *vaquero*). They rode with a song on their lips, voicing youth, the freedom and the wildness of the plains. Hence come cowboy songs.[1]

In 1886, H.F. Fazende wrote a solo piano piece titled, "The Texas Cowboy," which was dedicated to the Stockmen of Texas. While the style of the music—a romantic waltz—had nothing to do with the songs sung by the real cowboys on the trail, the sheet music cover included several images that depicted day-to-day work of cowboys, which included branding, morning roundup, moving up the trail, cutting out, controlling a stampede, and camping at night.[2]

Along the trails, music played a critical role in the workaday lives of the real cowboys. Written accounts and oral histories chronicled the musical lives of the cowboys

"The Texas Cowboy," sheet music published by Thos Goggan & Bro., 1886. The sheet music cover showcases scenes depicting cowboy life, including: "morning round up," "cutting out," "branding," "up the trail," "stampede," and "night in camp" (Library of Congress, Music Division).

and documented the lyrics of many of the songs and tunes of the trail. The song texts vividly told the story of the cowboy life including the dangers, unsavory characters, gambling, drinking, gunfights, dance halls, runaway cattle, sweethearts, religion, life, friendship, and death. One old-time cowboy commented on the cowboy's singing style: "Some of the singers performed in the high-lonesome style of the southern mountain tradition, others used the hard-voiced tenor delivery of the lumberjack, and yet others sang in the mainstream style of the church choir or the music hall."[3]

Who were these cowboys? Most were single, young men attracted to cattle work as a way to make a living. Some were attracted to the nomadic lifestyle, others were looking for adventure, and some were hoping to make a fresh start as ranch hands and cowboys on the trail. One trail driver commented in his record book, "He an' I was the only one in an outfit of twenty-two that had not killed a man."[4]

Cowboys were a culturally diverse bunch and included Civil War veterans, Mexican vaqueros, Native Americans, and freed slaves. (It is estimated that one in four cowboys was African American). Alan Lomax, the son of cowboy music expert John Lomax, wrote about the Black cowboys: "Historians Charles Siringo and Teddy Blue, two noted cowboy historians, said that the best singers and musical cattle handlers were black cowboys from whom they learned their trade in the early days. John Lomax took down many of his finest songs, including, 'Home on the Range' and 'Sam Bass' from Black trail hands."[5]

Mike Searles, known as "Cowboy Mike," is an author and retired history professor who specializes in the history of Black cowboys and buffalo soldiers—African American cavalrymen. In an interview on NPR's "Weekend Edition," Mike Searles commented: "In southeast Texas, you had a large number of blacks who were slaves and had been doing cow work. When freedom comes, it would be just as natural for them to begin to do that work." Searles went on to comment about the integrated crew on the range, "In that environment, you want to have pretty good relations, because that person could elect to help you or not help you in a dangerous situation."[6]

One of the most famous cowboy songs, "Good-by, Old Paint," is credited to Charley Willis, an African American who moved to Texas at the age of 18 and worked as a cowboy on the Bartlett Ranch. In 1871, at the age of 24, he rode the Chisholm Trail from Texas to Wyoming. Charley's great-grandson, Franklin, said, "His voice was real soothing to the cattle, and this is why they wanted him to participate in these big cattle drives, because he would sing to them and just make them relax."[7]

"Good-by, Old Paint"
By Charley Willis

My foot in the stirrup, my pony won't stan',
Good-by, Old Paint, I'm a-leavin' Cheyenne.
I'm a-leavin' Cheyenne, I'm off for Montan';
Good-by, Old Paint, I'm a-leavin' Cheyenne.

I'm a ridin' old Paint, I'm a-leadin' old Fan;
Good-by, old Paint, I'm a-leavin' Cheyenne.
With my feet in the stirrups, my bridle in my hand;
Good-by Old Paint, I'm a-leavin' Cheyenne.

Old Paint's a good pony, he paces when he can;
Good-by, little Annie, I'm off for Cheyenne.
Oh, hitch up your horses and feed 'em some hay,
And seat yourself by me as long as you stay.[8]

Cowboys weren't only "boys" but also women and children who traveled with the cattle drives on horseback or by covered wagons. In one case, a woman, Willie Matthews, curious about life on the trail, worked with a cattle crew for four months disguised as a man. The trail boss commented about this 125-pound cowboy: "I was so pleased with him that I wished many times that I could find two or three more like him."[9] Near Hugo, Colorado, when she had had enough of the experience, Willie, still disguised as a man, asked the trail boss, Samuel Dunn Houston, if he could quit because of homesickness.

A few hours later, at sundown Willie then revealed her true identity to the boss and the rest of the crew. Willie surprised them all by making an appearance in camp as a woman. When she walked into camp wearing a long dress, the cowboys were speechless; they couldn't believe their eyes or their ears as Willie told her story. She explained to the boys that she was the cowboy who had ridden with them for the past four months. Willie said, "Now Mr. Houston, I am glad I found you to make the trip with, for I have enjoyed it. I am going just as straight home as I can go and that old train can't run too fast for me."[10] Mr. Houston and all but one of the boys, who was left behind to look after the cattle, accompanied Willie to her train, which left Hugo at 11:20 in the evening.

Women contributed to the canon of cowboy songs. N. Howard "Jack" Thorp included songs by women and about women in his collection called, "Cowboy Songs," first published as a small pamphlet in 1908. In 1921, he republished the collection and added the stories behind the songs. He included a song by Belle Starr called, "Bucking Bronco," which, according to Thorp, was collected in "Indian Territory." Thorp wrote this explanation above the lyrics: "Written about 1878. Song has been expurgated by me. The author was a member of a notorious gang of out-laws, but a very big-hearted woman. I knew her well."[11] Below are the words to Belle Starr's song, "Bucking Bronco," which is a warning for women to stay away from cowboys. Unfortunately, Thorp did not include the melody to this or any of the other songs in his book, only the words.

"Bucking Bronco"
By Belle Starr

My love is a rider, wild broncos he breaks
Though he's promised to quit it, just for my sake.
He ties up one foot, the saddle puts on,
With a swing and a jump he is mounted and gone.

The first time I met him, 't was early one spring
Riding a bronco, a high-headed thing.
He tipped me a wink as he gaily did go
For he wished me to look at his bucking bronco.

The next time I saw him, 't was late in the fall,
Swinging the girls at Tomlinson's ball:
He laughed and he talked, as we danced to and fro,–
Promised never to ride on another bronco.

He made me some presents, among them a ring;
The return that I made him was a far better thing;
'Twas a young maiden's heart, I'd have you all know
He'd won it by riding his bucking bronco.

Now all you young maidens, wher'er you reside,
Beware of the cowboy who swings the rawhide,
He'll court you and pet you and leave you and go
In the spring up the trail on his bucking bronco.[12]

The notorious Belle Starr was born in Missouri and named Myra Maybelle Shirley. She was a well-educated young woman and an accomplished pianist who graduated from a prestigious school called the Carthage Female Academy in Illinois. After the Civil War threw her family into financial turmoil and forced the sale of the family business, the Shirley family, hoping for a fresh start, emigrated to Texas. In Texas, Myra's life took a turn for the worse as she soon became involved in a series of amorous relationships with one unsavory outlaw after another, including her last husband, Cherokee outlaw Tom Starr. Tom Starr and other outlaws in his gang made their living through unlawful activities including stagecoach robbery, cattle rustling, selling illegal whiskey, and harboring outlaws.

In the end, Belle Starr was ambushed and shot in the back by an unknown killer two days before she turned 41. Though her worst criminal offense was stealing a horse, her reputation as an outlaw grew over the years through dime-store novels and the movie, "The Bandit Queen."[13]

Jack Thorp paid homage to Belle Star and other women outlaws in his poem "Women Outlaws" from his book, *Songs of the Cowboys*:

A studio portrait of Belle Starr, probably taken in Fort Smith, Arkansas. Created in the early 1880s (Wikimedia Commons).

"Women Outlaws"
By Jack Thorp

There's a touch of human pathos,
A glamour of the West,
Round the names of women outlaws
Who have now gone to their rest—

Bronco Sue, Belle Star, and Shudders,
Pike Kate and Altar Doane,
Calamity Jane, Sister Cummings,
And the Rose of Cimmaron.

You've all oft heard the saying,
"I'd go to Hell for you!"
About these women outlaws
That saying was too true.

Each left her home and dear one
For the man she loved the best,
Close by his side on many a wild ride
Through the mountains of the West.

They've played their parts in Western Drama,
On the great unscreened Western stage,
Where the mountains were their platform,
Their stage-setting rocks and sage.

Hunted by many a posse,
Always on the run,
Every man's hand against them,
They fought, and often won.

With a price upon each head,
They'd have to fight and stands,
And die a game as any man
With a gun in either hand.

My hat off to you, women outlaws,
For you did what you thought best,
And the same wild blood that coursed your veins
Has settled up the West.

Whether right or wrong, your spirit
Knew not the word of fear —
And 't is the dauntless courage of your kind
That bred the pioneer![14]

Around 1900, a cowboy named Sam Murray remembered hearing a song at Pecos River at Horsehead Crossing in west central Texas. According to Jack Thorp, the song mentioned by Sam Murray was written circa 1869 by a woman named Kate Childs, known as "Montana Kate." Some of the verses convey the life of the cowboy, while some lament the hardships of women on the California Trail. Cape Horn, mentioned in the text below, was an alternate way to emigrate to the West rather than an overland trail.

California Trail
By Kate Childs "Montana Kate"

List, all you California boys,
And open wide your ears,
For now we start across the plains
With a herd of mules and steers.
Now bear in mind, before you start,
That you'll eat jerked beef, not ham,
And antelope steak, oh, cuss the stuff!
If often proves a sham.

You cannot find a stick of wood
On all this prairie wide;
Whene'er you eat you've got to stand
Or sit on some old bull-hide.

It's fun to cook with buffalo chips
Or mesquite green as corn, —
If I'd once known what I know now
I'd gone around Cape Horn.

The women have the hardest time
Who emigrate by land;

For when they cook out in the wind
They're sure to burn their hand.
Then they scold their husbands round,
Get mad and spill the tea, —
I'd have thanked my stars if they'd not come out
Upon this bleak prairie[15]

The life of the cowboy included countless dangers and hardships such as extreme weather conditions—from hailstorms to blistering heat, stampeding cattle, prairie fires, dangerous river crossings, death by firearm, and long, lonely months on the dusty trail. Cowboys had to be quick thinking, dependable, and knowledgeable about cattle behavior. In 1874, one of the earliest cattlemen, Joseph McCoy, described the typical cowboy: "He lives hard, works hard has but few comforts and fewer necessities. He has but little, if any, taste for reading. He enjoys a coarse practical joke or a smutty story; loves danger but abhors labor of the common kind; never tires of riding, never wants to walk no matter how short the distance he desires to go. He would rather fight with pistols than pray; loves tobacco, liquor and women better than any other trinity."[16]

A record of cowboy songs is largely known through the work of folklorist and cowboy song authority John Lomax, who spent years living among cowboys throughout the West. In 1867, John Lomax, along with his mother, father and six siblings, emigrated to

A group of musicians with their instruments, a pistol, and a rifle from the Turkey Track Ranch near Protection, Kansas. Created between the 1880s and 1890s (kansasmemory.org, Kansas State Historical Society).

central Texas from Mississippi in two wagons. His mother, Susan, recalled: "When we sold our household things, cows, horses, mules, with our land, we had about four thousand dollars in gold. It was given to me to take care of. I made a broad belt, sewed in two rows of twenty-dollar gold pieces. I was to wear it around my waist. I found I could not do it, for it was too heavy. We had a willow basket that held a half-bushel. I tied the belt to one handle, laid it down on the bottom, and tied the other end to the other handle. I never felt so uneasy."[17]

Driven by a desire to capture vanishing cowboy songs, John Lomax tirelessly collected, recorded, and transcribed songs previously known through the oral tradition, songs that would have been lost were it not for his efforts. His collection of songs in his words were "jotted down on a table in the rear of saloons, scrawled on an envelope while squatting around a campfire, caught behind the scenes of a broncho-busing outfit."[18] He also appealed to the general public to help with his research by printing a request in periodicals throughout the West. Through his travels, writings, and lectures, John Lomax became the authority on cowboy songs.

Music played several roles in the lives of the cowboys. Lilting ballads kept the cattle moving along the trail and kept the cowboys awake on the night rounds. Soothing lullabies and traditional hymns kept the cows from stampeding and lulled the herd to sleep at night as the cowboys rode circles around the herd during night rounds. Cowboy Teddy Blue Abbott said: "The singing was supposed to soothe the cattle and it did…. The two men on guard would circle around with their horses on a walk, if it was a clear night and the cattle was bedded down and quiet, and one man would sing a verse of a song, and his partner on the other side of the herd would sing another verse; and you'd go through a whole song that way…. I had a crackerjack of a partner in '79. I'd sing and he'd answer, and we'd keep it up like that for two hours. But he was killed by lightning."[19]

E.H. Elder remembered driving a herd of 3,000 cattle from Clarksville, Texas, to Cheyenne, Wyoming, in 1877. He worked as a cowboy on the trail until 1882 and later recalled singing songs around the campfire at night: "It is good to remember how all the boys gathered round the campfire and told of their experiences. Many is the time I have listened to the chant of the night songs as the boys went around the herd."[20]

Songs such as "Whoopee Ti Yi Yo, Git Along Little Dogies" were used to keep the herd moving during the day, while songs such as "The Cowboy's Dream" were sung at night in order to keep the cows quiet and calm. Joseph McCoy wrote that soothing hymns were the "peculiar forte of a genuine cowboy," that the cowboy, also known as a drover, sang to the cows at night: "Drovers consider that the cattle do themselves great injury by running round in a circle, which is termed in cow-boy parlance, 'milling,' and it can only be stayed by standing at the distance and hallooing or singing to them. The writer has many times sat upon the fence of a shipping yard and sang to an enclosed herd whilst a train would be rushing by. And surprising how quiet the herd will be so long as they an her the human voice … but if they fail to hear it above the din of the train, a rush is made. Singing hymns to Texas steers is the peculiar forte of a genuine cow-boy."[21]

Charles A. Siringo, a cowboy and author who worked cattle on the Chisholm Trail, wrote about a frequent occurrence on the trail—the stampede. He explained, "the herd split up into a dozen different bunches—each bunch going in a different direction. I found myself all alone with about three hundred of the frightened steers. Of course, all I could do was to keep in front or in the lead and try to check them up. I finally about three o'clock got them stopped and after singing a few 'lullaby' songs they all lay down and went to snoring."[22]

John Lomax separated cowboy songs into six main subjects: work, death, love, religion, humor, and heroes. The songs from all of these categories have commonalities in textual meter and musical form. Most of the songs have stanzas (verses) of two, four, five or six lines. The number of stanzas in the songs was continually augmented as cowboys interacted and shared versions of songs along the trail and on ranches. In general, the melodies were simple, spanning an interval of an octave or a tenth, which meant the melodies were in an attainable range for the average voice.

Many cowboy tunes evolved from well-known fiddle tunes, ballads, love songs, and hymns. Some songs were composed on the trail, often combining new words with familiar tunes. For example, the melody of "The Streets of Laredo," or "The Cowboy's Lament," is about a cowboy on his death bed and lives on as one of the most beloved cowboy songs. The melody dates back as far as an Irish ballad from 1790. The following cowboy version of "The Cowboy's Lament" appears in John Lomax's collection of *Cowboy Songs and Other Frontier Ballads*.

"The Cowboy's Lament"

As I walked out in the streets of Laredo
As I walked out in Laredo one day,
I spied a poor cowboy wrapped up in white linen,
Wrapped up in white linen as cold as the clay

Oh, beat the drums slowly, and play the fife lowly,
Play the dead march as you carry me along,
Take me to the green valley, there lay the sod o'er me,
For I'm a young cowboy, and I know I've done wrong.

Let sixteen gamblers come handle my coffin,
Let sixteen cowboys come sing me a song
Take me to the graveyard, and lay the sod o'er me,
For I'm a poor cowboy, and I know I've done wrong.

My friends and relations they live in the Nation,
They know not where their boy has gone.
He first came to Texas and hired to a ranchman,
Oh, I'm a young cowboy and I know I've done wrong.

It was once in the saddle I used to go dashing,
It was once in the saddle I used to go gay,
First to the dram-house, and then to the car house,
Got shot in the breast, and I'm dying today.

Get six jolly cowboys to carry my coffin,
Get six pretty maidens to bear up my pall,
Put bunches of roses all over my coffin,
Put roses to deaden the sods as they fall.

Then swing your rope slowly and rattle your spurs lowly,
And give a wild whoop as you carry me along;
And in the grave throw me and roll the sod o'er me
For I'm a young cowboy and I know I've done wrong.

Oh bury me beside my knife and six-shooter,
My spurs on my heel, my rifle by my side,
And over my coffin put a bottle of brandy,
That's the cowboy's drink, and carry me along.
Go bring me a cup, a cup of cold water,

To cool my parched lips, the cowboy then said;
Before I returned his soul had departed,
And gone to the round-up—the cowboy was dead.

We beat the drums slowly, and played the fife lowly,
And bitterly wept as we bore him along,
For we all loved our comrade so brave, young, and handsome,
We all loved our comrade, although he'd done wrong.[23]

The guitar is often thought of as the instrument of the cowboy. However, according to John Lomax, songs were often sung unaccompanied. If there was an instrument involved, it was often a fiddle or a banjo that had been stored in the chuck wagon. Texas cowboy John Young recalled music-filled evenings in camp:

After supper, the boys not on herd would tell yarns, sing songs, wrestle, and act generally like a bunch of kids, which most we were. Like many of the outfits, ours had a fiddle, and while some artist in spurs, "made it talk," we often put the end gate of the chuck wagon on the ground and then took turns dancing jigs upon it. Or maybe some lad would take the fiddle out to the herd with him and "agitate the catgut" to the tune of "Billy in the Low Ground," "Dinah Had a Wooden Leg," "Hell Among the Yearlin's,'" "Old Rosen the Bow," "Cotton-Eyed Joe," "Saddle Ole Pike," "Sally Gooden," "The Devil's Dream" or some other such favorite. Many a night I have led lake Porter's horse around the herd while he made the longhorns snore to music.[24]

John Young, a cowboy, music enthusiast, and keen observer of cattle behavior, remarked that one "old brindle" wriggled his ears and blew appreciatively when he heard the waltz tune, "One Evening in May." John Young reminisced about the musical night-life on the cattle trail: "Pleasant it was on a warm, clear night to circle slowly around a herd of cattle that were bedded down quiet and breathing deep and out there to catch the strains of a song or fiddle coming from camp, where the fire was like a dim star. But it was pleasanter to be in camp and, while just catching now and then a note from a singer or fiddler on herd, to be dropping off to sleep. As long as a cowboy heard music he knew that all was well."[25]

Lake Porter was a fiddling cowboy on the cattle trail to Kansas in the 1870s and was a friend of John Young. Lake Porter remembered:

Often I have taken my old fiddle on herd at night when on the trail and while some of my companions would lead my horse around the herd I agitated the catguts, reeling off such old-time selections as "Black Jack Grove," "Dinah Had a Wooden Leg," "Shake That Wooden Leg, Dolly Oh," "Give the Fiddler a Dram," "Arkansas Traveler," and "Unfortunate Pup." And say, brothers, those old long-horned Texas steers actually enjoyed the old-time music. I still have the old music box which I use to play in those care-free, happy days.[26]

In one camp, Sam, a beloved African American cook known for his ability to break wild horses, also played the banjo and the fiddle. John Young wrote that at the start of one trail drive, someone stepped on Sam's banjo and broke it. The crew chipped in and bought him a fiddle in a nearby town, which Sam played whenever he got the chance. John Young remembered: "Sam would pick 'Green corn, green corn, bring along the demijohn,' on his fiddle. Among other selections he had a kind of a chant called, 'Dog' that the boys often called on him to give." The first two verses of "Dog":

There was a man who had a dog, a bobtailed ornery cuss,
And this here dog got this here man in many an ugly muss.

The man was on his muscle, and the dog was on his bite;
To touch that bobtail son-of-a gun you were sure to start a fight.[27]

In addition to calming the cows and providing entertainment in camp, music and dancing served as a way for cowboys to let off steam in cow towns along the way. Once the cowboys reached the end of the trail, they shot their pistols up into the air and headed to the local saloon for women, alcohol, music, gambling, and dancing. Joseph McCoy described the cowboy's behavior in the dance hall:

> The cow-boy enters the dance with a peculiar zest, not stopping to divest himself of his sombrero, spurs, or pistols, but just as he dismounts off of his cow-pony, so he goes into the dance. A more odd, not to say comical sight, is often seen than the dancing cow-boy; with the front of his sombrero lifted at an angle of fully forty-five degrees; his huge spurs jingling at every step or motion; his revolvers lapping up and down like a retreating sheep's tail; his eyes lit up with excitement, liquor and lust; he plunges in and "hoes it down" at a terrible rate, in the most approved yet awkward country style; often swinging "his partner" clear off the floor for an entire circle.[28]

McCoy pointed out that many cowboys spent their hard-earned money in the dance hall on women and booze; many of them headed back to Texas after days of frolic and debauchery with only one dollar left of their summer's wages. Alcohol brought out hostilities of some, and many nights ended in gunfire and death. However, McCoy wrote that there were exceptions to the rule: "young men who respect themselves and save their money and are worthy young gentlemen,—but it is idle to deny the fact that the wild reckless conduct of the cow-boys while drunk, in connection with that of the worthless northern renegades, have brought the *personnel* of the Texan cattle trade into great dispute, and filled many graces with victims, bad men and good men."[29]

In the absence of women, cowboys still danced. In one photograph of a room filled with cowboys dancing, the dancers are all men paired up together in what was referred to as a "stag dance." Sometimes the men who were dancing in the women's role tied a white band around their arms.

Cowboy Dance "Stag." Creation date unknown (courtesy *True West* Magazine Archives).

Marvin Hunter offered this explanation about dance calls—the spoken words over the accompaniment of the fiddle or other dance band instruments spoken by a "caller" who gives the dancers direction on which steps to use: "The rhyme dance calls are supplementary to his spoken direction to the dancers, and add almost as much interest and loveliness of the dance as does the music."[30]

> Swing your partners round and round;
> Pocket full of rocks to hold me down;
> Ducks in the river going to ford
> Coffee in a little rag; sugar in the gourd.
>
> Swing 'em early, swing 'em late;
> Swing 'em round Mr. Meadow's gate.
>
> Ladies to the center, how do you do;
> Right hands cross, and how are you!
>
> Two little ladies, do si do,
> Two little gents you orter know.
>
> Swing six when you all get fixed,
> Do si do, ladies like picking up sticks.
>
> Chicken in the bread tray kicking up dough;
> "Granny, will your dog bite?" "No, by Joe."
>
> Swing corners all,
> Now your pardner and promenade the hall.
> You swing me, and I'll swing you;
> All go to' heaven in the same old shoe.
>
> Same old road, same old boy,
> Dance six weeks in Arkansaw.
>
> Walk the huckleberry shuffle and Chinese cling.
> Elbow twist and double L swing[31]

Another kind of dance memory came from cowboy author Nat Love, also known as "Deadwood Dick." Nat Love, born a slave in Tennessee, learned cattle-working skills such as roping, riding, herding, and branding at an early age. At the end of the Civil War, he was 15 years old and a free man. He traveled to Dodge City, Kansas, where he immediately put his cattle skills to work as a cattle driver on the trail between Kansas and Texas. After living the trail life, he found work as a ranch hand along the Gila River in Arizona and eventually became a pullman porter on the railroad. He wrote about his life, including cowboy adventures, in his self-published autobiography, *The Life and Adventures of Nat Love.* In his book, he described a medicine dance of the Pima Indians.

Nat Love told the tale of how he was attacked by the Pima Indians while working as a ranch hand in Arizona. Love claimed he was seriously wounded with gunshots to his leg and breast, but he did not die. Instead, he was taken back to the Pima camp because the Pima Indians respected his strength and thought he had powerful medicine. While Nat Love lived with the tribe and recovered from his wounds, the Pima chief, Yellow Dog, offered Nat Love 100 ponies if he would marry his daughter. Nat Love refused the offer, stole a pony, and rode off into the night. Nat Love described a Pima dancing and medicine ceremony:

As soon as I was well enough I took part in the Indian dances. One kind or another was in progress all the time. The war dance and the medicine dance seemed the most popular. When in the war dance the savages danced around me in a circle, making gestures, chanting, with every now and then a blood curdling yell, always keeping time to a sort of music provided by stretching buffalo skins tightly over a hoop. When I was well enough I joined the dances, and I think I soon made a good dancer. The medicine dance varies from the war dance only that in the medicine dance the Indians danced around a boiling pot, the pot being filled with roots and water and they dance around it while it boils. The medicine dance occurs about daylight.[32]

Alfred Anderson, who worked cattle in the 1870s, told the story of how "Oh Bury Me Not on the Lone Prairie," a well-known tune, was used in a graveside service of an unknown fallen cowboy that one of his crew had found on the trail on the Smoky River in the northwestern part of Kansas. Alfred Anderson told the story: "Myself and several other cowboys were hunting stampeded beeves one day and found the corpse of a cowboy who had come to his death in some manner unknown to us. We decided to bury him there, so we dug a hole and rolled him into it, with but a little burial ceremony. One of the crowd was a good singer and sang the old cowboy song that all of the boys are familiar with, which runs something like this:

> Oh bury me not on the lone prairie,
> Where the coyotes may howl o'er me;
> And dig my grave just six by three—
> But bury me not on the lone prairie.
>
> Yes bury me under an evergreen tree,
> Where the little birds may sing o'er me;
> And dig my grave just six by three—
> But bury me not on the lone prairie."[33]

Alfred Anderson commented further on the burial: "Our hearts were sad when we left that poor unknown boy out there under the sod of that lonely prairie, many miles from habitation. Some mother's boy who went away never to return, some husband or father perhaps who went out into that wild country and lost his life there."[34]

John Lomax collected several work songs of the cowboys, including the work song "Whoopee Ti Yi Yo, Git Along, Little Dogies." John Lomax transcribed this song, sung by Mrs. Trantham, a "wandering gypsy minstrel," at a Texas Cattlemen's Convention in 1910. The term "dogies" referred to in this example are motherless calves that developed swollen bellies from eating grass too soon for their young age. The calves became known as "dough-guts," which probably got shortened to the word "dogie." An alternate theory is that the word "dogie" came from a Spanish word "dogal," meaning halter.[35]

"Whoopee Ti Yi Yo, Git Along, Little Dogies"

As I was a walking one morning for pleasure,
I spied a cow-puncher a riding along;
His hat was throwed back and his spurs were a-jingin,'
As he approached me a singin' this song;

Whoopee ti yi yo, git along, little dogies,
It's your misfortune and none of my own;
Whoopee ti yi yo, git along little dogies,
For you know Wyoming will be your new home.

Early in Springtime we'll round up the dogies,
Slap on their brands, and bob off their tails;
Round up our horses, load up the chuck wagon,
Then throw those dogies upon the trail.

Some of the boys goes up the trail for pleasure
But that's where they git it most awfully wrong;

"In my fighting clothes." Nat Love, also known as "Deadwood Dick." Created 1907 (Library of Congress).

For you haven't any idea the trouble they give us
When we go driving them dogies along.

When the night come on and we hold them on the bed-ground,
These little dogies that roll on so slow;
Roll up the herd and cut out the strays,
And roll the little dogies that never rolled before.

Your mother she was raised way down in Texas,
Where the jimson weed and sand-burrs grow;
Now we'll fill you up on prickly pear and cholla
Till you are ready for the trail to Idaho.

Oh' you'll be soup for Uncle Sam's Injuns,
"It's beef, heap beef," I hear them cry.
Git along, git along, git along, little dogies
You're going to be beef steers by and by.[36]

This song contains typical cowboy language such as "cow-puncher" for cowboy, "git" for the word "get" and "throwed back" for "thrown." The song represents the epic quality found in many cowboy songs with its seven stanzas plus a chorus. The first verse paints a romantic picture of a singing cowboy with silver spurs followed by the chorus, which uses typical cattle call sounds. In the opening lines of the song, the cowboy is introduced. The singing cowboy in the song wears jingling spurs and waves his rope or arms at a wayward cow and coaxes a stray back to the herd with a "yo, yo, yo, yo" and a "yi, yi, yi, yi."

The second verse discusses the order of events before heading up the trail, including branding, bobbing off the tails, rounding up the horses, and loading the chuck wagon—the kitchen on wheels. The third verse implores the herd to move along, "Oh, how I wish you would go on," while the cowboy is telling the cows about their new home—Wyoming. The fourth explains that some boys are in it for the pleasure, but they are mistaken because these "pleasure boys" have no idea what they are in for with the long, slow job of moving cows. The fifth verse tells of bedding down for the night and again comments on the slow herd rolling along. The sixth verse is directed to the dogies, telling them they are leaving the jimson weed and sandburs of Texas for the prickly pear and cholla of Idaho—referring to the different types of vegetation they will be grazing on along the way. In the last verse, the cowboy tells the herd their fate—that they are beef steers, and they will be food for Indians on U.S. reservations.

While "Whoopie Ti Yi Yo" is a song about work, "The Dying Cowboy of Rim Rock Ranch" is a commentary on a cowboy's life, including his horse, friendships, vices, love, death, and the afterlife. In the first verse of "The Dying Cowboy of Rim Rock Ranch," the cowboy says goodbye to his pals, his work, his vices (gambling and drinking), and his home, which has been the prairie. The refrain explains that he is riding away on his "Brown Girl" (his horse) while the sun is sinking—a metaphor for dying. In the second verse he admits to more vices (shooting, gambling, and his wild Irish girl—perhaps someone he met in a saloon). The third verse tells us of the cleaner part of his life—his ranch, the call of the dove—perhaps a metaphor for peace and the girl he loves.

In the final verse, the dying cowboy looks forward to his version of the afterlife referred to here as the final roundup and includes a cabin on a shore. The simple melody matches the tone of the truthful words sung by the cowboy on his death bed.

"The Dying Cowboy of Rim Rock Ranch"

Good-by to my pals of the prairie.
Good-by to the cattle on the trail.
Good-by to the cards and the drinking,
Good-by to the prairies and the vale.

(Refrain)
For I'm riding away on my Brown Girl
Where the sun is singing low;
For I'm riding away on my Brown Girl
Where the sun is sinking low.

Good-by to the cracking of the pistol,
Good-by to the clinking of the spur,
Good-by to the cards and the drinking
Good-by to my wild Irish girl.

Good-by to the yapping of the coyote,
Good-by to the call of the dove,
Good-by to the Rim Rock Ranch,
Good-by to the girl that I love.

Oh, boys when you're far from Rim Rock
You know there's a cabin on that shore,
you can think of the spot where I left you
For the round-up where we all must go.[37]

According to John Lomax, "The Old Chisholm Trail" was the most popular cowboy song. Lomax commented: "This song in all its entirety would give all the possible experiences of a group of cowboys driving a herd of cattle from Texas to Dodge City, Kansas … of all songs, the most universally sung by cowboys."[38] There are more than 50 two-line stanzas and four melodic variations of "The Old Chisholm Trail" printed in *Cowboy Songs and Other Frontier Ballads*. The song has a small range of only five notes, which is why it may have been a favorite—it is an easy song for the average person to sing. Lomax indicates the song should be sung "lustily." Below are the first five stanzas and the refrain:

"The Old Chisholm Trail"

Come along, boys, and listen to my tale,
I'll tell you of my troubles on the old Chisholm trail.

Coma ti yi youpy, youpy yea, youpy yea,
Coma ti yi youpy, youpy yea.

I started up the trail October twenty-third,
I started up the trail with a 2-U herd.

Oh, a ten-dollar hoss and a forty-dollar saddle
And I'm goin' to punchin' Texas cattle.

I woke up one morning on the old Chisholm trail,
Rope in my hand and a cow by the tail.

I'm up in the mornin' afore daylight
And afore I sleep the moon shines bright.[39]

Arguably the roughest cowboy town of the late nineteenth century was Dodge City, Kansas, once called the wickedest city in America. Dodge City was a hub of the cattle market. Cattleman Marvin Hunter told how the city between the years of 1874–1884, with a slew of dance halls and honky-tonks, attracted a variety of disreputable characters including gamblers, buffalo hunters, and unruly cowboys.

Dodge City was also known as the home to the Dodge City Cowboy Band, a brass band organized in 1879 under the direction of Chalk Beeson. The band members, all genuine cowboys, wore flannel shirts, cowboy hats, leather chaps, spurs, and they all carried pistols. The band played in several major American cities including Denver, St. Louis, Chicago, and Kansas City, and Washington, D.C. The novelty of the band made them an audience favorite. Someone asked the conductor why he conducted with a revolver rather than a baton. Chalk Beeson replied, "To kill the first man to strikes a false note."[40] While the band perpetuated the old myth of the wild cowboy in their Wild West cowboy attire, they were reputed to be fine musicians who could readily read sheet music on sight. The band's repertoire included, "Montebello Waltzes," the "Miserere" from "Il Trovatore," and the "Criterion Quickstep."[41] On February 18, 1889, the *Indianapolis Journal* reported, "One of the curiosities of the band is the large steer horns carried by the drum majors. One pair was purchased in 1876 by Manager Beeson for $3. They were taken—from a steer in a Texas trail herd. Since that time Mr. Beeson has refused $150 for the pair, the length from tip to tip measuring five feet seven inches."

In summary, poetic cowboy songs chronicled every aspect of the cowboy's life including work, the dangers of the job, the trail, the cow towns, romances, heartbreaks, prayers, diversions, friendships, and death. The cowboys' daily singing kept the cows moving along the trail, kept the herds from stampeding, put the cows to sleep, and also

A formal view of the manager and members of the Dodge City Cowboy Band of Dodge City, Kansas. Standing: Charles Otero, George Horder, Captain J.S. Welch—Drum Major, unknown, unknown, unknown, unknown; Middle row: unknown, Charlie Makepeace, Jay Drake, Roy Drake—Director, unknown, unknown; Seated: D.M. Frost—editor of the *Globe*, George Meserole, Lou Louber, Charles A. Miller, William G. Visquesney, Chalk M. Beeson—Organizer and Manager, Colonel S.S. Prouty—editor of "The Cowboy"; Boy on ground at left: Harold Jones; Boy at right: Finckey Marsh. Created 1886 (Kansas State Historical Society).

entertained the cowboys both on the trail and in camp. The melodies of the songs were simple, often taken from old folk songs. The song texts, however, continually expanded with added stanzas as the songs were passed from one cowboy to another. At trail's end, cowboys kicked up their heels in dance halls and more formal affairs such as the annual "Cowboy Ball." Through songs and stories of the cowboys, we find representation from lesser-known groups of the American West including women, African Americans, Mexicans, and Native Americans. The life and characters portrayed in cowboy songs went on to capture the imagination of future generations of Americans as the romantic notions of the heroic cowboy and his life became the subject for many artistic mediums including music, television shows, novels, visual arts, musical theater, and film.

9

Music in the Settled West

Three Distinct Frontier
Communities in 1890

*Now don't forget, Lizzie, when you get to the
new world, don't stop in America. You must
go directly to Butte, Montana.*—Mary Hagan

The 1890 census proclaimed that the frontier line of the United States no longer existed and that the West was settled. N. Scott Momaday, essayist, wrote that by the year 1890: "Nearly 17 million people lived between the Mississippi and the Pacific—three times the population of the entire nation when Thomas Jefferson completed the Louisiana Purchase of 1803 and propelled his countrymen toward the western sea."[1] The year 1890 also marked the gruesome Wounded Knee Massacre on the Pine Ridge Reservation in South Dakota, where an estimated 150 Lakota—men, women, and children—died at the hands of the U.S. Cavalry.

In Walla Walla, Washington; Portland, Oregon; and Butte, Montana, circa 1890, residents enjoyed a wide variety of musical experiences. Walla Walla, established in 1856, was a frontier community nestled in the middle of fertile farmland with a musical history steeped in missionary roots. Portland, a gritty port city on the Willamette and Columbia Rivers, established in 1851, enjoyed sumptuous theaters where residents could choose from a variety of weekly operas and concerts. Butte, established in 1874, home of the Copper Kings, was a mining center located in the Rocky Mountains where a group of miners created a nationally recognized and formidable brass band.

Make no mistake, this chapter is by no means a comprehensive look at the musical lives of each of these communities. Rather, this is an attempt to touch on some of the concerts, musical venues, musicians, music, and the role of music in each community around the year 1890, give or take a few years on either side.

Walla Walla, Washington

Walla Walla, according to the Nez Percé who lived in the Walla Walla Valley, means "running waters." Along with the Nez Percé, other indigenous groups that inhabited the Walla Walla Valley of Southeastern Washington included the Cayuse, Walla Walla, and Umatilla. Lewis and Clark encountered the Walla Walla people on their expedition to the Pacific and again on their eastbound return trip.

Following the Lewis and Clark Expedition, fur trappers came west and established

Fort Nez Percé as a major trading post for trappers and local tribes. In 1831 Fort Nez Percé became Fort Walla Walla. Dr. Marcus Whitman and his wife, Narcissa, soon followed the trappers and made their way west in 1836. The Whitmans built a mission on the Walla Walla River which was seven miles west of present-day Walla Walla. Emigrants on the Oregon Trail regularly stopped at the mission for medical care and supplies.

Following the enthusiastic reports about the fertile Walla Walla Valley, thousands of pioneers flocked to the area to establish farms. By 1890, the population of Walla Walla was 4,709, which made it the fifth largest city in Washington state after Seattle, Tacoma, Spokane, and Bellingham.

The center for Walla Walla musical activity was Whitman College, which was first established as Whitman Seminary in 1859, becoming Whitman College in 1889. In 1890, the Whitman music faculty members included Estella Berry, who taught voice along with her colleague Bella Ramsey. The large group of piano instructors included Mrs. Minnie M. Beaven, Georgia William Paul, Ella Maxson, and Blanche Eckler. Harlon J. Cozine was the lead professor of what was referred to as "Voice Culture" and "Theory of Music." Miss Nellie I. Herrick was the head of "Piano and Harmony." Sixty-seven students were enrolled in the music program according to the music department roster.

The demanding voice course included a variety of topics: tone formation, muscular action, the scales and intervals, Bonaldie's "Six Studies of Vocalization," articulation and portamento, etudes, exercises and songs, and Concone's "Vocal Studies." Repertoire included German and Italian singing along with the study of solos and arias from famous operas.

The piano course was equally rigorous and included a year of harmony and theory in addition to technical studies. The student repertoire was chosen from Felix Mendelssohn's "Songs Without Words"; J.S. Bach's "Preludes," "Fugues," and "Inventions"; Frederic Chopin's "Etudes: Op 10 and 25"; and Anton Rubenstein's "Selected Etudes and Preludes."

All of the music students were required to perform in regular solo and ensemble recitals—a requirement that remains the norm in current higher education music programs. The price of music courses ranged from $13 to $16 per term, and private lessons were $24.00 per term. During the term, students could sign up for a piano to practice on for a nominal fee.

Whitman glee clubs, organized as a student social activity for both men and women, were in contrast to Whitman's demanding music programs. A photograph in the Whitman College archives showcases "The First Girls' Glee Club" from 1896.

On June 4, 1890, Whitman College held commencement services at Small's Opera House. According to an archived printed program from the event, the Whitman Chorus sang "Hail to Thee, Liberty!" from *Semiramide*, an opera by Gioachino Rossini. The ladies chorus sang "Heather Rose" by Gustav Hollaender, and Estella Berry sang "When the Sun Is Low" by Carl August Röckel. The commencement service also included "The Class Song" by Grace Ramsay and Harlan J. Cozine and a piano duet, "Invitation au Galop," by Franz Bendel, played by Miss Ramsay and Miss Harford. The class motto was: "*Esse Quam Vidar*"—To be, rather than to seem.

Aside from Whitman's musical groups, one of the most popular Walla Walla performance groups was The Packwood Pierce and Warner String Band. Another group, The Fourth Regiment Band from Fort Walla, located six miles southwest of Walla Walla,

The 4th Cavalry Band at a public gathering at the Union Pacific Railroad Station in Walla Walla, Washington. Creation date unknown (Fort Walla Walla Museum).

often played for public events. A photograph in the Fort Walla Walla Museum archives shows the Fourth Cavalry Band playing for an event at the Walla Walla train depot, circa 1890.

An archived program from 1884 indicates that the citizens of Walla Walla invited soldiers from Fort Walla Walla to a dance. Prior to the dance, there was a promenade concert given by the Second Cavalry Band. The dance portion of the evening included Lancers (a type of square dance), waltzes, quadrilles, schottische, the Virginia reel, the polka, and a rollicking galop at the end of the evening before ending the party with the tune, "Home Sweet Home." As it turns out, "Home Sweet Home" was often mentioned as the last song of the evening throughout the West.

Walla Walla residents regularly attended St. Patrick Church, which had a splendid organ. W.D. Lyman, nineteenth-century southern Washington resident and historian, wrote, "Easter services attracted both worshipers and music lovers—the Catholic church is especially distinguished for its fine organ and superb musical services. Its programs for Christmas and Easter are events which always attract great throngs, both of music lovers and devout worshipers."[2]

Standouts in the Walla Walla music community included Edgar and Alice Fischer. Edgar began his career as the head of the violin department at Whitman Conservatory of Music in 1899. At Whitman, Edgar met Alice Reynolds, an accomplished pianist and singer who was on the piano faculty.[3] The two music educators married and soon after opened their own music school called the Fischer School of Music. The Fischer School was renowned as one of the best music schools in the Northwest. In 1907, Edgar became the first director of the Walla Walla Symphony, which is the oldest continuous symphony west of the Mississippi. Alice took over as conductor of the Walla Walla

Symphony in 1922 when Edgar died at the age of 49.[4] Edgar Fischer was also known for transcribing songs of Northwest Native Americans for the noted photographer Edward Curtis.[5]

Walla Walla resident, Caroline Maxson Wood, was known as "The Jenny Lind of the West." The real Jenny Lind, from Sweden, known as "The Swedish Nightingale," was the most popular singer in Europe and America in the mid–1800s. Wherever she toured, she commanded packed houses. In 1859, Caroline Maxson West, at the age of 16, traveled west on the Oregon Trail with her husband and her parents. The family faced many hardships, including the time Caroline's father was "swept away by the current; men found him half a mile downstream clinging to a branch and nearly unconscious."[6]

Caroline was a vocalist and pianist who performed frequently for the soldiers at Fort Walla Walla as well as for Walla Walla community members and for members of her Seventh-Day Baptist Church. In 1880, she performed for President Rutherford. B. Hayes when he visited Walla Walla.

As an adult, Caroline led the singing at the first Adventist camp meeting in the Northwest in Salem, Oregon. While she and her husband, James, were attending the event, three of their seven children died from the diphtheria epidemic in Walla Walla. Eventually, Caroline taught music at Walla Walla College, a Seventh-Day Adventist college, when it opened in 1892. Her daughter, Grace Reith, also became a music teacher at Walla Walla College.[7]

Walla Walla, like many frontier communities was a melting pot of cultures including Italians, Germans, Russians, Jews, and Chinese. In fact, in 1880, there were over 800 Chinese living in Walla Walla as a result of railroad construction in southern Oregon.[8]

Walla Walla's earliest music venues included Stahl's Opera House and Small's Opera House and Livery Stable. According to the *Walla Walla Union Bulletin* of December 18, 1951, when Small's Opera House first opened in 1884, all of the residents of Walla Walla were about to arrive for a pre–Christmas concert featuring the Sunday school children of the town when the roof collapsed—due to a combination of faulty construction and heavy snow. Mr. William Glasgow, the caretaker, was the only person killed in the accident. Some of the Walla Walla residents declared that the incident was "an act of divine providence." Many more people would have lost their lives had the roof fallen just minutes later. Small's Opera House was rebuilt and served the community for many years as a venue for plays, concerts, recitals, balls, fundraisers, graduations, and community gatherings.[9]

On May 10, 1886, Small's Opera House presented a vocal recital of Miss Marie Stinson. According to an archived printed program, the performance included recitations along with vocal and instrumental solos. The first half of the concert ended with Miss Henrietta Sheets singing "Departed Days" by George Frederick Root. The performance concluded with Miss Marie Stinson singing "Far from Home" by Paul Henrion.[10]

Walla Walla was the birthplace of two important musical women whose careers flourished well into the twentieth century. Emilie Frances Bauer (1865–1926) was a well-known music critic in Portland and later in New York. Her sister, Marion Bauer (1882–1955), was a writer, prolific composer, teacher, and music critic who lived most of her life in New York.

The musical sisters were born to French parents who were both Jewish. Emilie, the eldest child, may have been the first Jewish baby born in Walla Walla. Their father,

This image from the Whitman College Archives in Walla Walla, Washington, is of a Chinese man playing a traditional Chinese instrument called the yue qin, also known as a moon guitar. Created circa 1890 (Whitman College and Northwest Archives).

Jacque, was an amateur musician who played several military band instruments and entertained his family with his beautiful tenor voice and his vast repertoire of operatic arias, frontier ballads, and French songs.[11] He was also a beloved Walla Walla businessman. In his shop, he sold a variety of general merchandise, including sheet music and instruments. Their mother, Julia, a linguist, spoke five languages and taught those languages to eager pupils in Walla Walla.[12]

When Emilie was 14, her parents sent her to San Francisco to study piano. Upon her return to Walla Walla, at the age of 16, she performed in local recitals, taught lessons, and also composed music.[13] She also studied piano for a time at the Paris Conservatory. In all Emilie wrote around a dozen pieces during her lifetime, some under her nom de plume, "Francisco di Nogero," perhaps taken from her middle name—Frances, and Oregon spelled backward.[14] Two of her earliest pieces for piano include "Murmurings from Venice," and "Moonlight on the Willamette." One of her most popular pieces written during her years in New York was a jaunty vocal piece for voice and piano titled, "My Love Is a Muleteer" ("El Arriero"), with English lyrics by Emilie Frances Bauer and Spanish lyrics by Paul Vincent Miller. The piece was first published in 1916 by The Spanish American Music Publishing Company. The sheet music sold out after the first public performance of the song. A.P. Schmidt republished the piece in 1917. The song was a huge success in the United States, Central America, and South America. A recording of this piece, sung in Spanish by José Mardones, is available online at the Library of Congress.[15]

Going back to the early years, the Bauer family moved from Walla Walla, Washington, to Portland, Oregon, in 1890 after the father, Jacque, died from what a Walla Walla statesman referred to as "apoplexy" during a fire in the Walla Walla business district.[16] In Portland, Emilie worked as a music critic for the *Oregonian*, and she also served as the Portland contributor to the *Musical Courier*, a weekly music periodical based in New York. During her Portland years, Emilie wrote, taught piano lessons and organized recitals for her students. Among her pupils was her younger sister, Marion.[17] Emilie Frances moved to New York circa 1896 and became the New York representative for the *Musical Leader* magazine.

Soon after, Marion followed her sister from Portland to New York, then moved to Paris to study composition, and eventually moved back to New York where she became a writer, music critic, composer of more than 150 works, and a music professor at New York University. In 1926, Marion's sister, Emilie Frances, died after she was struck by a car in New York. Marion sunk into a deep state of grief over the loss of her older sister and mentor. It was during this period of mourning that she wrote her most famous piece, *Sun Splendor*, originally written for piano, later arranged for orchestra and performed by the New York Philharmonic in 1947.[18]

On May 8, 1951, New York's Town Hall presented an all-Marion Bauer Concert. A small sample of Marion's compositions include *6 Preludes for Piano, Op. 15, From the New Hampshire Woods, Op. 12, Four Piano Pieces, Op. 21*, and *Sonata for Viola and Piano, Op. 22*. The Bauer sisters represent a story of hardship and loss and a journey from the American West to the East — both moved from Walla Walla to Portland and eventually to New York City, where each thrived as musical pioneers in their individual and diverse musical careers.

Portland, Oregon

Portland, Oregon, founded in 1843, was and remains a major port city just 20 miles from Oregon City, the end of the Oregon Trail. Portland is also ten miles from Fort Vancouver, which was a fur-trading post dating back to 1825. In 1890, the Portland population was 46,385, making Portland the largest city in the nineteenth-century American West. According to the 1890 census record, Portland was 61st in the overall population of the United States. Industries in the Portland area included fishing, lumber mills, wheat farming and cattle ranching. Portland was a hub of transportation because of its proximity to railroads and the Willamette and Columbia Rivers.[19]

On one hand, Portland had a reputation as a gritty and dangerous port city full of unsavory transient characters who arrived by boat at all hours of the day and night. The port was host to an array of illicit activities including opium dens, gambling, prostitution, and gang violence. "The police had their hands full trying to keep order in the Tenderloin and the North End and their street cleaning and sanitation duties were left behind. In 1889, the *Oregonian* declared Portland 'the most filthy city in the Northern states.'"[20]

On the other hand, Portland was a city of earnest, hardworking pioneers who had traveled west on the Oregon Trail. These people were farmers, businesspeople, tradesmen, craftsmen, and educators who valued education, culture, religion, family, and music.

Portland's earliest music school began at St. Mary's Academy, originally known as "The Sisters School." The school was established in 1859 by a group of nuns who were originally from Quebec, Canada. From the earliest days of the school, daily vocal instruction was a part of the curriculum. When the sisters were en route from Quebec, they purchased a piano in New York and arranged for the piano to be shipped from New York around Cape Horn to Portland. To the delight of the nuns and the students, the piano arrived intact in 1860.[21]

Sister Arsenius, one of the pioneering educators, offered these thoughts about the importance of singing to the overall educational plan:

> "The object of vocal music is voice culture. It improves the hearing, and acts on the sensibility by developing and perfecting the power of appreciating the good and the beautiful; it acts also on religious and patriotic feelings. As an art, music is subject to the laws of aesthetics." She wrote that music lessons should have three main purposes: (1) suitable exercise the vocal organs; (2) be simple and harmonious; (3) appeal to the sensibility, elevate the soul, and cultivate good taste.[22]

> Along with a rigorous vocal curriculum, St. Mary's Academy offered instruction on a variety of instruments as well. Private music lessons were offered during the school day at a cost of about $12.00 per term. *The Salem Journal* of February 1900 reviewed an Academy Performance: "The scheme of amusement comprehended a light, three-act drama, the intermission being filled with musical numbers, solos, duets, and orchestra. The musical element of the school is equipped with a splendid orchestra of many young people involving the use of piano, violin, clarinet, ten mandolins, and a bank of guitar, all the major strength of this orchestra was in evidence on this occasion."[23]

One of the earliest colleges in the Portland area, George Fox College, was a Quaker college which offered instruction in vocal and instrumental music. The college opened on September 9, 1891. Inaugural exercises began with choir music and a prayer by Mary Edwards.[24]

St. Mary's Academy class portrait, 1901 (Oregon Historical Society).

Portland High School opened in 1869, and a photo of a coed mandolin and guitar musical group indicates that music was a part of the curriculum.

Portland music venues circa 1890 included the New Park Theatre, formerly "The Casino," where Portland patrons partook in light opera such as the comic opera *d'Olivette* by Edmond Audran. In 1890, the *West Shore* reported: "The Casino has been remodeled and is beautiful both inside and out, the management have adopted the popular scale of prices of 25 and 50 cents, so that everything promises a most successful season of light opera." On January 9, 1890, the *Oregonian* ran an advertisement for the New Park Theatre which featured the J.C. Duff Opera Company in: "Three Grand Spectacular Operas": "Paola," "Queen's Mate," and "Trip to Africa." The opera company included "a female chorus of 24 pretty artists," "a grand male chorus of 20 rich voices, and an orchestra of 15 musicians."

Another prominent venue was the five-story Marquam Grand Opera House which opened in 1890 with Charles Gounod's opera "Faust." The *Oregonian* wrote, "The Grand Marquam Opera House, a temple of drama not surpassed in elegance, comfort, beauty of decoration, and elaborateness of appointments by any playhouse in the east." Later in the year, the Marquam featured Rice and Dixey's Chinese and English Opera, *Pearl of Peking*. According to the *Oregonian* review, "The piece was charmingly staged and richly costumed, and barring the imperfections of some new members in the work of the chorus, the representation was quite a masterpiece."

The 1889 North Pacific Industrial Exposition took place in Portland. The grounds of the exposition included a large musical hall. The grand opening featured the music of Allessandro Liberati, a virtuosic cornet player from New York. "The Stage of the music

Portland High School group with guitars and mandolins. Creation date unavailable (Oregon Historical Society).

hall is set in an elegantly painted grotto and surrounded almost entirely by a semi-circular sounding board which served to intensify the magnificent acoustic properties of the hall ... the entire seating capacity of this hall is between 5,000 and 6,000 persons."[25]

On November 29, 1890, the *Oregonian* listed a week's worth of musical events, as it did every week. This particular week featured two events at the Marquam Opera House which included The Honest Abbot Opera Company singing opera favorites, and Spanish dancers delivering a Spanish-themed musical and dance program. The Cordray's Theatre presented a matinee for women and children of the play "Pique." Corday's Theatre also promoted a minstrel show by the traveling troupe, Gorton's New Orleans Minstrels.

The *Oregonian* reported on another venue that opened in 1890—The Arion Hall, which seated 1,100 people. The opening of the hall kicked off with the overture, "Le Macon," by Daniel Auber and played by the Orchestral Union. The welcome address was delivered in German by Mr. J. Reisacher, president of the Arion Society. The purpose of the society was performing and presenting German songs and upholding the traditions of classical music. The dedication included "The Golden Cross" sung by Mr. P. Wessenger and "The Image of the Rose" and "Osssian," both sung by the Arion male chorus. There was a violin duo, several vocal solos, and a cornet solo called "Remembrance of Prague." The grand finale of the evening was "The Huntsman's Farewell" by Felix Mendelssohn for chorus and orchestra.

Between the years 1880–1890, 4,500 people of Chinese descent lived in Portland, which made Portland the second largest Chinatown in the United States, behind San

Francisco. The Chinese contributed their own culture, songs and instruments to the Portland music scene. In 1887, W.H. Scott described the Portland Chinese Quarter, including traditional music, and instruments:

> To strangers there is nothing more attractive than the Chinese quarter. This comprises about three blocks on Second street, Alder being their cross street. The buildings which they occupy are mainly of solid brick, put up in the first place largely by Americans, but on long leases to the Chinese merchants and have been fixed over according to their convenience and ideas of beauty. They are intensely oriental in their general air, with piazzas of curved roofs, highly ornamented with yellow, white, and vermillion paint, paper globes, and gewgaws. Red paper inscribed with characters in black serve as signs, and are pasted numerously over doors and windows. On gala days the entire area is lit up by lanterns or gaily ornamented with paper, and thin, peevish tones of their flutes, fiddles, and falsetto twang of their gongs.[26]

Portland churches, along with weekly services, regularly presented public concerts and recitals. For example, on October 27, 1890, the Unitarian Church presented the Mendelssohn Quintet Club. The grand finale was "Gypsy Rondo" by Franz Haydn. On June 10, 1890, the *Oregonian* reported, "The Centenary M.E. Church was filled to overflowing last evening with a cultivated audience to hear the concert of Flora Batson, the noted colored singer, assisted by local talent." According to the review, "Huntsman's Horn," by Charles Allen White, was one of the audience's favorite pieces. Miss Batson's voice "resounded like a silver bugle cheering the hounds in pursuit of game." The concert was described as "one of the best ever given in East Portland."

Hoyt and Company sold high-quality musical instruments such as pianos, organs, sheet music and music books. On January 1, 1890, the company ran an advertisement in

Professor C.V. Theill playing guitar. Professor Theill was a guitar teacher in the Portland area. Creation date unavailable (Oregon Historical Society).

the *Oregonian* which spoke of Portland's collective love of music: "Never before have the people of Portland been so thoroughly appreciative of music, pure and simple, and of music and arts as during the past year."

Butte, Montana

In 1890, the population of Butte, Montana, was 10,723 people. Butte was originally established as a mining camp in the year 1864, and the town was once known as "The Richest Hill on Earth." Copper was the cash cow of the Butte mining industry from around 1882 and into the twentieth century. Butte was home to the famous Copper Kings—Augustus Heinze, Marcus Daily, and William A. Clark, industrial businessmen who became astoundingly wealthy on the backs of the miners who worked around the clock in the treacherous Butte mines.

In the year 1890, Butte was a city of wide ethnic diversity. The "No Smoking" signs in the Butte's mines were written in 14 languages. First and foremost, Butte was as an Irish town. In addition to the Irish, the ethnically diverse population included Chinese, Scots, Swiss-Italians, Cornish, Germans, Croatians, Serbians, African American, Slovenians, Swedes, Italians, Lebanese, Greeks, Mexicans, Danes, and Jews. The Congregation B'nai Israel Temple, built in 1903, is the oldest synagogue in Montana still used for worship. Ethnic groups were divided by neighborhoods surrounding the center of Butte. "The Cabbage Patch," located on the east side, was Butte's shanty town, "home to bootleggers, prostitutes, widows, alcoholics, drug users, new immigrants, downtrodden minorities, and anyone else who didn't quite manage to fit into 'civilized Butte.'"[27] Each of these neighborhoods, undoubtedly, had musical traditions steeped in their countries of origin. Imagine the citizens of Butte playing music and dancing in their individual neighborhood. The musical mixture may have included Irish ballads, Lebanese lullabies, Greek folk songs, Swedish dance tunes, the strum of Mexican guitars, Chinese string music, and Jewish Klezmer songs.

In 1890, there were nearly 400 Chinese living in Butte's Chinatown. The thriving Chinese community included tailors, physicians, laundries, grocery stores, shops, and restaurants—including noodle bars. The transcontinental railroads were built with Chinese labor, which is one of the reasons why such a large population of Chinese was living in the West in the late 1800s. Undervalued and scorned by the U.S. government, the Chinese laborers' contribution to the American West was forgotten with the passing of the 1882 Chinese Exclusion Act. The act was passed to keep Chinese workers out of the U.S. and to make it impossible for those already living in the country to become eligible for naturalization.

Today, the Mai Wai Museum provides visitors access to the Wah Chong Tai (Beautiful Old China) building, built in 1899, and the Mai Wah (luxurious, beautiful) building, built in 1909. In these buildings, the Wah Chong Tai Noodle Parlor and the Mai Wah Noodle Parlor delivered bowls of steaming noodles to the Chinese community and to the citizens of Butte. The Mai Wah Museum showcases several Chinese artifacts from the nineteenth and early twentieth centuries, including a collection of Chinese musical instruments. Among the collection of drums and bells is the *suona*. The museum description explains, that the *suona*, also called a *laba* or *haidi*, is identified by its conical wooden body, tubular copper mouthpiece and small double reed. The *suona* has a distinctively loud and high-pitched sound and is used frequently in Chinese traditional music ensembles, particularly those that perform outdoors.

Outside of the Butte-Silver Bow Public Archives, a selection of quotes about Butte are carved into the cement walls surrounding the building, including this quote by

Richard K. O'Malley: "The town grew out on the side of the Hill, and it was Butte all at once, out of the copper womb."

A booklet distributed by the Northern Pacific Railway in 1888 described Butte as follows:

The city is a bee-hive of industry; $500,000 per month is paid out to the workmen in its mines and smelters. Work goes on continually day and night the year around, and one hundred and fifteen smoke-stacks can be counted from one point belonging to its smelters. New mines are, being continually discovered and opened up, so there is almost no limit to the continued development of its mineral treasures. The city is well built and contains many imposing business houses and elegant residences belonging to its mining millionaires.

Theodore Roosevelt visited Butte in 1903 and remarked, "Butte was mercurial.... The wicked, wealthy, hospitable, full blooded little city welcomed with wild enthusiasm of the most disorderly kind." And what better segue into the musical life of Butte than this quote by an anonymous Butte woman? "Butte people measure their wealth in the richness of their culture, their value as workers, and their strength in family."

Indeed, Butte was known as a cultural hub of the West. Talented artists, performers and musicians readily flocked to the rough and tumble mining town with

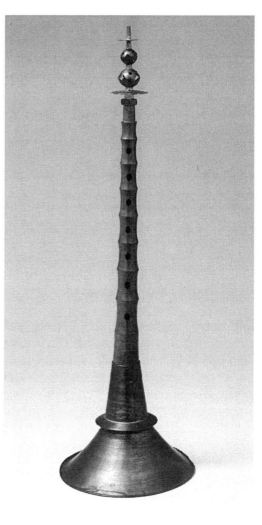

Suona, 19th century. The suona has a penetrating sound and is used for processions, military functions, and popular music (Metropolitan Museum of Art).

a reputable arts scene. Butte bands and musicians could easily find work on any night of the week in the town that never slept. Butte miners and citizens loved to dance. Dance halls were a popular and affordable form of entertainment for the hard-working Butte crowd.

Along with music in the public and private schools of Butte, music lessons were readily available. A booklet of business listings distributed by Western Resources states: *Butte, Montana at the Dawn of the Twentieth Century* listed at least 20 musician/educators in the collection of Butte professional profiles.[28] Take, for example, this profile of Professor Russell H. Ballard, cello soloist: "a clean cut, suave, courteous gentleman, and he has friends here." Another Butte gentleman, Professor J.C. Coombs, was a "Dancing Master" at Renshaw Hall, "The leader in his line." Professor Joseph R. Hebaus, musician of brass and stringed instruments: "is originally from Hungary and obtained his musical education abroad. He has played in the best orchestras in the country and Europe."

Professor Leo C. Bryant was a music teacher who specialized in violin and piano on 1 Tuttle Block. "He puts heart and soul into all he does and he is conscientious, painstaking and of marked ability in his profession."

Several women music professionals were featured alongside the men in the *Butte at the Dawn of the Twentieth Century* booklet. Mrs. F.C. Bowen was a pianist and music teacher who also professionally preserved flowers. Mrs. Bowen, originally from Montreal, was described as, "keenly intelligent and she never spares herself, her pupils make rapid progress." She also played for dancing schools and parties and had a knack for preserving flowers for use in weddings and other functions. Miss Mayme Vivian, a harpist, originally from Chicago, was described as having "complete command of this beautiful instrument and she has attained a reputation which extends far beyond the state." Mrs. Edna M. Hill, teacher of piano and organ, taught a studio of 40 pupils and served as the organist at St. John's church. "She puts heart and soul into her work, and she is a type of the finished, up to date, successful musician."

The diverse group of professional musicians and music teachers was revered and celebrated. The thriving musical scene at the turn of the twentieth century indicates that Butte was anything but a cultural wasteland. On the contrary, Butte was filled with hardworking artistic professionals cheered on by a community of music, dance, and arts lovers who appreciated and sought out their musical talents.

More than likely, it was the Montana Music Company on 119 Main that provided many of the instruments for Buttes' music professionals and hobbyists. The Montana Music Company claimed to carry the largest stock of musical goods in Montana. An advertisement for the store, circa 1900, indicated that the store carried pianos, organs, sheet music, instruction books, guitars, mandolins, zithers, banjos, and music boxes.

The most outstanding musical group of the late 1800s was the Butte Mines Band, which was started in 1887 by the visionary bandleader, Sam Treloar, who served as director of the band for 41 years. The original name of the band was the Boston and Montana Mine Company Band, and was made up of workers from The Boston and Montana Copper and Silver Mining Company. In the beginning, Sam Treloar worked out a deal with the powers that be so that members of the band could work the coveted day-time mining positions which freed up their evenings to rehearse and give concerts. In return, the band performed free concerts to the mine owners and employees.

At first, the band had only six members and did not give public performances for a year and a half. During that time, they diligently practiced and built up to 18 members. When they finally performed, they were a terrific success and were soon in demand across the state of Montana. The band was a source of pride for Butte residents, and the miner musicians regularly played for celebrations, parades, and for visiting dignitaries.

In 1890, the band was installed as the regimental band for the Montana National Guard. In 1896, they were invited to perform at the National Democratic Convention in Chicago and were invited again to perform for the 1900 Convention held in Kansas City. Regarding the Kansas City National Convention, a Butte resident said, "When the proper moment arrived and the flags were drawn aside amid tremendous excitement, it was the Boston and Montana Band that came down the center of the aisle playing 'Dixie' as a fitting climax to the impressive scene."[37]

The band was a celebrated success at the conventions. Audiences were surprised that such an accomplished band came from the wilds of Montana. A Kansas City newspaper wrote, "The men are all practical miners, engaged in different duties about the mines, and are a fine body of men."[29] Nineteenth-century Butte resident Harry Freeman wrote, "The band brought a sense of community pride and unity to Butte. The band has had no little part in eliminating baneful class distinctions throughout the city, its entire personnel having long ago demonstrated that as high culture can work below ground as above it."[30]

The Alice Band, started in 1880 under G.W. Pierce, was another Butte band with a national reputation. Friday, September 1890, the *Daily Intermountain* reported that The Alice Band, The Boston Montana Band, and a third band—The Black Eagle Band, under the baton of M. Bornhardt from Great Falls, Montana, all played for the 1890 Montana State Republican Convention.

One of the first arts venues of Butte was the Renshaw Music Hall built in 1881—a three-story building with a grocery store on the bottom and a theater on the top. The venue, managed by actor John Maguire, was used for theater productions. John Maguire arrived in Butte in 1875 and

Miss Mayme Vivian, a harpist and music instructor featured in the *Western Resources Magazine*, Butte, Montana, 1901 (courtesy Butte-Silver Bow Public Library).

first entered the Butte performance scene with his one-man shows, which he presented to workers in the mining camps. Another music venue in Butte was the Curtis Music Hall which was built in 1892. In the 1920s, the hall became a housing facility for transient miners.

Maguire's Grand Opera House, which later became known as the Murray Grand Opera House, was built in 1882. The opera house was the brainchild of two Irish immigrants. One was John Maguire, who had earlier opened the Renshaw Hall. The other was James Murray, one of the wealthiest men in Butte and in the state of Montana, who generously supported Butte theater and music. Another wealthy Butte businessman, William Clark, financed the building of the opera house along with James Murray. The opera house presented entertainers from all over the country. Arts pioneers Murray and Maguire inspired other producers to move to Butte and start up their own theaters and production companies.

In addition to a variety of public venues, many of the private Butte mansions had ballrooms and music rooms for concerts and dance parties. One such building was the Clark Chateau, built in 1898. The Chateau was geared toward music. For example, some of the rooms were decorated with hand-painted wallpaper featuring musical instruments. The Chateau had a trap door for lifting the piano to the top floor. The legendary

Butte Mines Band with Director Sam Treloar in the center of the front row. Photographer Smithers C. Owen. Creation date, 1937–1939 (03010.02, Butte-Silver Bow Public Archives).

ballroom was the sight of performances, parties, and all-night dances. In 1917, the Chateau became the home for the Butte College of Music where students studied guitar, piano, voice, clarinet, flute, elocution, and more. Music instructors not only taught at the Chateau, but they also lived in rooms on the third floor.

On January 15, 1895, 10:00 p.m., the community of Butte suffered an unthinkable tragedy when 57 people, including seven firemen, perished in what came to be known as the "The Great Explosion." The tragedy started out as a fire in the Butte warehouse district. The fire department and several volunteers answered the call of the fire alarm, and while attending to the fire, the scene erupted into a series of explosions that blew an iron roof off of one of the warehouses. The explosion launched metal, shrapnel, chicken wire, and construction debris into the air, which mowed down anyone in the area as it all came crashing down to the ground. The human carnage included fireman, volunteers, and Butte citizens who happened to be in the wrong place at the wrong time.

The community of Butte was heartbroken by the tragedy, and the funeral was attended by fireman from around the state. In the Butte-Silver Bow Archives, there is a piece of sheet music titled, "Butte's Fatal Explosion," which was written by two sisters: Miss Ella T. Henneberry when she was 23 and Miss Margaret M. Henneberry when she was 21. The piece is dedicated to the memory of the lost, and the lyrics tell the entire story of the Butte Explosion. The sheet music was never published, and there is no record of the song ever being performed.

"Butte's Fatal Explosion"

(first verse) 'Twas fifty-five minutes past nine in the evening,
On the fifteenth of January ninety-five,
That firemen of Butte in Montana, State

Were call'd to extinguish a fire;
And the great and gallant firemen,
Like heroes true and brave,
Made ev'ry effort that they could
All property to save.

What means this large gath'ring of people?
But Hark! What deaf'ning sound is that which fills the air?
'Tis an explosion caused by powder,
Between South Butte and Butte City proper.
Fiercer still the fatal blast throws out its heated breath,
And holds many of Buttes citizens
Within the arms of death.

(chorus) Honor the names of the fireman brave,
Who lost their lives, the city to save,
The husband and the father;
The brother and the son,
Have left behind a record of duty nobly done,
The names of the lost heroes;
will live on in our hearts with pride,
And we shall ne'er forget Butte's firemen,
Who for duty bravely died.

(second verse) The people rushed from their homes in wonder,
To a scene they can never, never forget,
And witnessed the explosion of powder,
Which to them will be a lifelong regret;
That night 'mid black'ning ruins,
Oh! God, what a sight to be seen,
The dead all unshapely were lying
where once joy hath reigned supreme.
Loud are the lamentations heard throughout the land,
For the widow's and the orphans,
Of that true and loyal band,
Of that true and loyal band,
May God in this hour of sorrow come to the widow's aid,
Caring to for the orphans
Which this fatal explosion hath made.
(repeat Chorus)[31]

Music was central to the heart of the communities and played an important role in establishing a sense of place in Walla Walla, Portland, and Butte. In churches, organ and choral music enhanced weekly services and religious holidays. Music was taught as part of the school curriculum in both private and public institutions. Music stores provided instruments and sheet music for hobbyists and professional musicians. Private music teachers offered instruction on a variety of instruments including piano, voice, harp, violin, and guitar. Newly established musical venues, which in some cases rivaled elaborate performance halls in the East, presented visiting artists as well as local talent. The people of Walla Walla, Portland, and Butte incorporated music as an important aspect of everyday life, cultivated new music traditions, and added a sense of beauty to their frontier communities through music. The music-related stories, people, and songs found in these communities contributed to the overall diverse musical history of the American West.

10

Western Inspiration

Scholars, Composers, and Musicians

Who doesn't know what I'm talking about
Who's never left home, who's never struck out
To find a dream and a life of their own
A place in the clouds, a foundation of stone

Many precede and many will follow
A young girl's dreams no longer hollow
It takes the shape of a place out west
But what it holds for her, she hasn't yet guessed.

She needs wide open spaces
Room to make a big mistake
She needs new faces
She knows the high stakes

—"Wide Open Spaces" by Susan Gibson.
(Permission courtesy of BMG)

The West evokes images of wide-open landscapes, independence, freedom, and new beginnings. In 1993, songwriter Susan Gibson captured a contemporary vision of the West with her song, "Wide Open Spaces." The Chicks recorded the song in 1998, and it became the CMA (Country Music Association) Single of the Year. The lyrics touch on dreams, unknown challenges, family, personal growth, and the desire for wide-open spaces that can be found in the West.

Susan Gibson, an exemplary contemporary musical artist, found creative inspiration in the West. She grew up in Texas but spent every summer of her youth in Montana where her family had a cabin on Flathead Lake. She attended the University of Montana for a couple of years as a forestry student before returning to Texas and embarking on her music career. During her time at the University of Montana, Susan returned to Texas during Christmas break, and it was then that she wrote, "Wide Open Spaces." In an email exchange, she shared her background story with me: "On my first Christmas back home in Texas, I furiously scribbled these lyrics on my mom's kitchen table and then went back for my second semester of school. A couple weeks later, my mom sent me a care package that had the notebook in it. I found the lyrics and put some music to them and that became the song."[1]

One of the lines in the song "Wide Open Spaces"—*She traveled this road as a child*—Susan explained, speaks of the road that took her up to Montana from Texas every summer of her youth. The "she" in another line of the song refers to Susan's mother—*it didn't seem like that long ago*, when *she stood there and watched her own folks go*. Like Susan, her mother also attended the University of Montana. Susan's mother took the train from northeastern Nebraska to Montana and watched her folks get smaller and smaller in the distance as her train pulled away from the platform.

I asked Susan if the West continues to inspire her song writing. She explained, "I think so—I don't know if someone looking in would think that, but going west is always going home for me. And I write about my family, those bonds and memories that I have had longer than any others. Being in the West—Flathead and Glacier Park and even that drive through Wyoming to get there—that sense of space, that natural world with where the natural laws are upheld and the metaphors that are in nature—that all came from my time heading west. It's the path of the sun, so probably, you know, a powerful draw."[2]

Just as Susan Gibson found musical inspiration in her experiences in the West, ethnomusicologists, composers, musicians, educators, and music scholars—throughout the past century to today—have dipped into that same inspirational well. This chapter shines a light on some of these musically minded people who turned their inspiration into books, recordings, compositions, and performances that both honor and build on the diverse traditions laid down by Native Americans, fur trappers, missionaries, pioneers, cowboys, and early musicians from the era of the Westward Expansion.

The first group of people who looked to the West at the end of the nineteenth century were musical ethnologists, also known as ethnomusicologists, including Alice Fletcher, Natalie Curtis, Frances Densmore, and Thurlow Lieurance, to name a few. After the forced relocation of Native Americans to reservations, musical scholars rushed to create a permanent record of traditional Native songs, stories, and legends that for centuries had been passed down through the oral tradition. Ethnomusicologists of the time believed that the musical and cultural traditions of native people were in danger of being lost forever due to the fracturing of traditional Native American communities. With the goal of musical preservations, ethnomusicologists traveled throughout the West, often living with native people as they dove deep into the exploration of Native music, ceremonies, and culture. The ethnomusicologists often sought out the best singers from each tribe in order to transcribe and record the songs to the highest degree of accuracy possible. Ethnomusicologists, who for the most part were non–native people, often transcribed the song that they heard into standard musical notation, and they also recorded using cumbersome wax cylinder phonograph devices.

Writer, historian, and authority on American music Richard Crawford pointed out in *An Introduction to America's Music* that this system of collecting songs, though a valuable form of preservation, was fraught with three major issues. First, the data in the form of documented songs, dances, and beliefs was not complete. Secondly, the format of preservation by ethnomusicologists was accomplished with recording devices or by written notation. This is in contrast to the oral tradition—the traditional way that Native American songs and dances were passed down from generation to generation. The third issue was that the music and traditional stories of Native Americans were filtered through the beliefs and observations of non–Indian people. Despite these issues, the work of these early ethnomusicologists remains a valuable record of early Native American music making and traditions.[3]

In July of 1898, at the Congress of Musicians held in Omaha, Nebraska, for the first time a group of Omaha Indians sang some of their Native songs to an audience of mostly trained musicians. This event was important because it illustrated the importance of

Native American song as an integral part of music history, and according to ethno-musicologist Alice Cunningham Fletcher, "This unique presentation not only demonstrated the scientific value of aboriginal songs in the study of the development of music, but suggested their availability as themes, novel and characteristic for the American composer."[4]

Alice C. Fletcher was one of the pioneering ethnomusicologists who collected songs from native people in the American West. Fletcher also worked as an agent for the Bureau of Indian Affairs; in this position, she managed land allotments for the Omaha and the Nez Percé. In 1900, she published *Indian Story and Song,* a book which included a variety of songs from several tribes and the backstory of each song. The songs were written out in standard musical notation and included the original words in Native languages. Fletcher said, "I have transcribed several hundreds of Omaha songs, and have also taken down songs of the Dakotas, Otoes and Poncas, tribes belonging to the same linguistic family as the Omahas…. Indian songs I have discovered travel far, and those of one tribe are soon home in another."[5] The songs in her book were harmonized by Edwin C. Tracy and J.C. Fillmore, and they were published as piano music with text.

Like ethnomusicologists who followed her, Alice Fletcher attempted to record the songs exactly as she heard them, without embellishments. In the introduction to *Indian Story and Song* she wrote: "Many of the stories and songs in this little book are now for the first time published. All have haven gathered directly from the people, in their homes, or as I have listened to the earnest voice of the native priest explaining the ancient ceremonials of his fathers. The stories are close translations, losing only a certain picturesqueness and vigour in their foreign guise; but the melodies are exactly as sung by the Indians."[6]

Another early musicologist, Theodore Baker, transcribed songs of the Iroquois, Cheyenne, Comanche, Dakota, Iowa, Kiowa and Ponca tribes. Baker wrote a doctoral dissertation based on his studies. American composer, Edward MacDowell, used some of the themes transcribed by Baker in one of his most popular orchestral works, titled, "(Indian) Suite No. 2, Op. 48," which was published in 1897 and included five movements: "Legend," "Love Song," "War Times," "Dirge," and "Village."[7] Shortly after the orchestral suite was released, the work was also arranged for four-hand and solo piano by Otto Taubman.

Dr. Frances Densmore, born in 1867, a musician, photographer, ethnomusicologist, and authority on Native American music, devoted her life's work to preserving vanishing songs of indigenous North American peoples. Her research featured songs from the indigenous people of the western United States including the Sioux, Navaho, Chippewa, Northern Ute, Makah, Mandan and Hidatsa. Densmore wrote 20 books, including *The American Indians and Their Music*, published in 1926. In this book she wrote, "Music is closely intertwined with the life of every race. We understand the people better if we know their music and we appreciate the music better if we understand the people themselves."[8]

Francis Densmore collected over 2,000 wax cylinder recordings of Native American songs. She remained dedicated to putting her informants and singers "entirely at ease in discussing a subject, and never allow the form of a question to suggest a possible answer. Care was taken also to avoid an impression of seeking anything sensational or of tracing a similarity to the beliefs or traditions of the white race."[9] With her body of work, she established the Smithsonian Densmore Collection, which is currently held at the Library of Congress. Many of her field recordings have been digitized and are available at the LOC website. (See recommended listening, Appendix B, for more information.)

Natalie Curtis, born in 1875, was a classically trained pianist, ethnomusicologist, and writer who became fascinated with Native American music in 1903 after a trip to the American Southwest. In her work as an ethnomusicologist, she traveled from village

Ethnologist Francis Densmore playing a recording for Piegan Indian Mountain Chief, 1916 (Library of Congress).

to village in the American West and studied indigenous music and cultural traditions. Rather than use a wax cylinder recorder, she transcribed traditional songs, note by note, with pen and paper into standard music notation. In 1902, she published *The Indians' Book, Authentic Native American Legends, Lore, and Music.* Theodore Roosevelt, impressed with the work of Natalie Curtis, wrote the forward to her collection: "These songs call a wholly new light on the depth and dignity of Indian though, he simple beauty and strange charm — the charm of a vanished elder world — of Indian poetry."[10] Several of the melodies found in her book inspired her former teacher Ferruccio Busoni in his 1914 composition—"Indian Fantasy, op. 44" for solo piano and orchestra.

In 1921, Natalie Curtis, age 46, traveled to Paris and gave a lecture-concert of Native American songs at the Sorbonne to an audience of musicians and scholars from around the world who were fascinated with her transcriptions as well as her performance of the songs. During her lecture, she sang in several of the original Native American languages. During her stay in Paris, her life was cut short when she was hit by a taxicab while crossing the street.

Musicologist Thurlow Lieurance, born in 1878, was an ethnomusicologist, composer, and devotee of Plains Indian flute music. He collected Native American flutes and had a direct connection to the Northern Cheyenne courtship flute, which was discussed in the first chapter of this book. In the early twentieth century, John Turkey Legs, the Northern Cheyenne flute master of his era, shared his music and the legend of the flute with Lieurance, who made a wax cylinder recording of Turkey Legs playing his flute on the reservation near Lame Deer, Montana, in 1912. The Library of Congress holds the original recording, catalogued as "Flute Song." The quality of the recording is poor, but the slow-moving flute song can be faintly heard over the sound of a howling wind. The song stays within a span of an octave and contains long, sustained notes. Based on the Turkey Legs recording, Lieurance composed a piece for solo piano called "Indian Flute Call and Love Song."

Thurlow Lieurance taught music at Wichita State University and traveled throughout the United States presenting lectures, musical performances of his compositions, and demonstrations of Native American flutes and songs. His large collection of flutes is currently housed at Wichita State University. When Gene Spangler attended Wichita State, he worked with Lieurance as a lighting operator for his flute performances and lectures. Spangler commented on the concerts: "We never did the same thing twice in exactly the same way. They were theatrical type concerts." Spangler continued, Lieurance "stood by the piano and played the flutes ... and occasionally one or two Indians played."[11]

According to Gene Spangler, Thurlow Lieurance's most ambitious undertaking was a performance for the Episcopal National Convention in Kansas City, Missouri. Spangler remembered: "He took all the Indians, chorus, and orchestra. This tour was made on the train. He had to buy upper berths for the bass fiddles. When we got to Kansas City, he put the Indians in cabs and told the drivers not to stop until they were at the hotel."[12]

The aforementioned ethnomusicologists, and more specifically their research, transcriptions and recordings contributed to a musical compositional trend, circa 1880–1920, called the "Indianist" movement. Just as McDowell composed his "Indian Suite," inspired by Native American melodies, other non-native composers working in this genre incorporated Native American melodies into classical-style music compositions for orchestras, string ensembles, vocal solos, choral works, and solo piano pieces. This trend was largely inspired by the Czech composer Antonín Dvořák, who suggested that American composers incorporate homegrown folk music—in particular, music of Native Americans and African Americans—into their compositions. Composers of the Indianist movement included Charles Wakefield Cadman, Arthur Farwell, Arthur Nevin, Carlos Troyor, Thurlow Lieurance, and many others.

While ethnomusicologists, to the best of their abilities, carefully recorded and transcribed authentic Native American songs precisely as they were sung or played, Indianist-style composers liberally mined the collections of songs for compositional ideas. These composers modified and manipulated original Native American melodies to fit into recognizable classical-style modalities, rhythms, and time signatures. Traditional Native American songs were played on indigenous flutes, sung a cappella, or sung with the simple accompaniment of drums or rattles. Indianist composers added harmonies, accompaniments, and in many cases, English words to traditional songs and arranged them for piano, small string ensemble, choral ensembles, and orchestras. While some of the compositions may have retained a small portion of the Native American melodies, most were idealized, embellished, and stretched beyond recognition. The resulting compositions were playable by classically trained musicians, and the repertoire appealed to established concert audiences who were used to hearing European-style art music.

In the years 1901–1911, Arthur Farwell, the leading Indianist composer, established and managed a publishing company called the Wa-Wan Press. In Farwell's words, the Wa-Wan Press was "an enterprise organized and directly conducted by composers, in the interests of the best American composition. It aims to promote by publication and public hearings, the most progressive characteristic, and serious works of American composers, known or unknown, and to present compositions based on the melodies of American folk-songs."[13]

For the name of his press, Farwell took inspiration from an Omaha ceremony which honors peace and fellowship. Wa-Wan in the Omaha language means "to sing to someone." In 1906, with the Wa-Wan Press, Farwell published his composition inspired by the same ceremony, *Impression of the Wa-Wan Ceremony of the Omahas* for solo piano which contains: "Nearing the Village," "Song of Approach," "Laying Down the Pipes," "Raising the Pipes," "Invocation," and "Song of Peace."

Carlos Troyor wrote *Traditional Songs of the Zuñis*, which was published by the Wa-Wan Press. In the introduction to Troyor's book, Arthur Farwell wrote about the objective of the Wa-Wan Press: "The hunger of art growth in a new country is never appeased until every available source of new art life and especially folk expression, has been seized upon and assimilated. Read art history. The Wa-Wan is seizing upon the wealth of primitive song in America, upon the new or the serious or daring expression of American composers, is tracking down songs of the soil still unrecorded. Materialistically America is sufficiently conquered. We have wrested a living from the soil from the East to West, and now we must rest from its treasure of poetry."[14]

In 1901 Farwell published the book, *American Indian Melodies*. Farwell's publication included several songs previously published by Alice Fletcher in her 1900 publication, *Indian Story and Song from North America*. Farwell credited Fletcher in the introduction of his book, *American Indian Melodies*: "The writer wishes to make grateful acknowledgement to Miss Fletcher, without whose previous labors, and whose present assistance and suggestion, this work could not have been undertaken. Gratitude is due as well to Mr. Francis La Flesche, whose name must permanently be connected with the history of Indian music and whose unfailing aid and influence among the members of his race made possible the accomplishments of Miss Fletcher's task."[15]

A comparison of the two publications illustrates two different approaches to presenting Native American music in written form. Alice Fletcher presented the cultural background and stories behind the songs and included used Native languages in the song texts. Farewell treated the songs in a different manner. He used the Native American melodies that had been carefully collected and researched by Alice Fletcher and turned those melodies into elaborately harmonized, modified, expressive character pieces that would appeal to a curious American audience interested in hearing and playing "exotic" Native American music. In the introduction to his book, Farwell said the composer "should consult, not merely this melodic structure, but the poetic nature of the particular legend occurrences, which they qualify or interpret, or upon religious ceremonies of which they form a part."[16]

Arthur Farwell's Indianist output included songs for piano and voice, solo piano, choral pieces, and orchestral works. His most famous piece was "The Old Man's Love Song," first arranged for solo piano and later arranged for SATB (soprano, alto, tenor, bass) as well as for symphony orchestra. Regarding the compositional treatment of "The Old Man's Love Song," Farwell explained: "'The Old Man's Love Song' gives expression to a mellowed love of life, born of years of benign and ennobling existence, voices at dawn in the presence of peaceful nature. It is a tribute, in song, to the spirit of love and beauty in the world. The dreamy and idyllic prelude is but a floating breath. This song, with its phrases like the notes of birds, and its pastoral musings, is singularly self-explanatory."[17]

Charles Wakefield Cadman, a contemporary of Arthur Farwell, composed dozens of pieces inspired by Native American melodies. Incidentally, none of his works were published by the Wa-Wan Press but by other American music publishers. One of his most popular works was *Four American Indian Songs* for piano and voice, published in 1909 with text written by Nelle Richmond Eberhart. Eberhart wrote most of the texts for Cadman's works. The first song in the suite, and also one of Cadman's most popular songs, "From the Land of Sky-Blue Water," was based on Omaha tribal melodies collected by Alice C. Fletcher. The second piece in the suite, "Dawn is Stealing," based on an Iroquois melody, was collected by Dr. Theo Baker. The third piece is "Far off I Hear a Lover's Flute," based on an Omaha flageolet "Love Call," collected by Alice Fletcher. The final piece in the suite, "The Moon Drops Low," based on an Omaha melody, was also collected by Alice C. Fletcher.

The terms flageolet, whistle, and flute were often used interchangeably by ethnologists. Alice Fletcher wrote about the musician and the flageolet featured in "Far off I Hear a Lover's Flute": "The native flageolet has proved a trusty friend to many a youth to whom nature has denied the power of expressing in vocal melody his fealty to the maiden of his choice. With its woody tones he rivalled the birds as he sounded his love-call from the hills and made glad the heart of the girl, who, catching the signal, awaited his coming at the spring.

There are many bits of music composed for this little instrument, which, in spite of its inaccuracies of pitch, arising from imperfect construction, are not without hints of beauty."[18]

Another popular Cadman composition, *Thunderbird Suite*, originally written for piano and later scored for orchestra, was intended as incidental music for the play,

Thunderbird. The *Thunderbird Suite* includes "From the Village," based on an Omaha melody collected by Alice C. Fletcher, and "Nuwana's Love Song," based on a Blackfeet tune that was collected by photographer and ethnologist Walter McClintock.

Along with his compositional output, Charles Wakefield Cadman also collected field recordings of the Omaha with the help of Alice Fletcher and Francis La Flesche. La Flesche, of Omaha, French, and Ponca descent, was the first Native American ethnologist. Many of the recordings collected by Cadman, Fletcher, and La Flesche are available online at the Library of Congress. In 1893, Fletcher and La Fleshe published *A Study of Omaha Music*. La Flesche, Cadman, and Nelle Richmond Eberhart collaborated on an opera based on the life of the Omaha people titled, *Daoma,* but the opera was never produced.

Tsianina Redfeather Blackstone, also known as Princess Redfeather, was a star soloist soprano of Creek and Cherokee descent who toured, performed, and collaborated on musical projects with Charles Wakefield Cadman. As a young student, she was recognized as an aspiring musician while attending a tribal school in Oklahoma. She was sent to Denver to study piano with her teacher, John Wilcox, who introduced her to Cadman. At the age of 16, she began touring with Cadman and performed his compositions in traditional dress, braided hair, and her signature hand-beaded headband.

Tsianina Redfeather and Cadman toured throughout the United States, Canada, and Europe. During World War I she entertained American troops who were on the front line of battle. A surviving black-and-white silent film from 1918 features Tsianina confidently singing and playing a lap slide guitar while mesmerized American soldiers listen to the performance.[19] She was best known for her performances of Cadman's compositions "Land of Sky-Blue Water" and "Indian Love Call."[20]

In addition to her performances, Tsianina Redfeather also collaborated with Cadman and librettist Nelle Eberhart on the opera *The Robin Woman* (*Shanewis*), which premiered in the years 1918 and 1919 with the Metropolitan Opera Company of New York. The opera became a popular production among American audiences in the 1920s, and Tsianina Redfeather performed the lead role in Denver and Los Angeles. She lived to be 102 years of age.

Another standout Native American musician was Zitkála-Šá (Red Bird), a Dakota Yankton Sioux woman born in 1876 who collaborated with composer William F. Hanson on another Native American-themed opera called *The Sundance Opera*. Throughout her life, Zitkála-Šá served in many roles, including classically trained musician, teacher, writer, speaker, community organizer, and influential political activist. According to writer Terry Lee Marzell, Red Bird's efforts helped in granting U.S. citizenship status to indigenous people in 1924. According to Marzell, she also worked toward increased educational opportunities, improved treaty rights, and substantive lands claims for Native Americans. In addition, she crusaded against the use of the hallucinogenic drug, peyote, which was widely used in Native American religious ceremonies. Zitkála-Šá believed the drug interfered with "sensible attention to education and religion."[21]

When Zitkála-Šá was eight years old, she and seven other children were taken from the Yankton Sioux Indian Reservation in South Dakota by Quaker missionaries to attend the White's Indian Labor School in Wabash, Indiana, an Indian boarding school. The purpose of the boarding school was to assimilate Native American children into the lifestyle of white people. In general, Indian boarding schools traumatized Native American children, who were forced to leave their homes and give up all aspects of their native

Tsianina Redfeather Blackstone, a singer and performer of Creek and Cherokee ancestry. Created between 1910–1915, Bain News Service photograph collection (Library of Congress).

culture including language, music, dancing, clothing, and their given Native American names. They were also forced to cut their hair. At this school, Zitkála-Šá was given the name Gertrude Simmons. She continued her studies at Earlham College in Indiana where she stood out as an award-winning orator and was also known for her beautiful singing voice and her excellent musicianship on the violin and the piano.

At the age of 20, Zitkála-Šá was hired to teach music and to serve as a band leader and lead violin soloist at the Carlisle Indian Industrial School in Pennsylvania, a large Indian school that enrolled up to 1,000 students annually. In 1900, Gertrude and the Carlisle Band traveled to Paris for the International Exposition. In Paris, Zitkála-Šá, as featured Carlisle violin soloist, dazzled audiences with her musical performances.

From Carlisle, Gertrude moved to Boston to further her music education at the New England Conservatory of Music. In 1902, she moved back to South Dakota and worked as a clerk at the Standing Rock Reservation, where she met Raymond Bonnin, also a Yankton Sioux. The pair married, had a son and moved to the Uintah-Ouray Reservation in Utah where she worked as a music teacher. While in Utah, she met William F. Hanson, whom she collaborated with on *The Sun Dance Opera,* a romantic opera based on the Indian Sun Dance. Zitkála-Šá contributed the libretto and the songs for the opera. In order to capture the Native American songs precisely, Zitkála-Šá played traditional Sioux songs from South Dakota including love songs, medicine chants, and game songs on her violin. Hanson transcribed the melodies into standard music notation and then turned the original transcriptions into orchestral arrangements. The songs for the opera also included flute melodies that Hanson had transcribed from songs that Zitkála-Šá played on her native flute. The flute was a wedding gift from her husband.

The Sun Dance Opera debuted in 1913 at the Orpheus Hall in Vernal, Utah, with a cast of non-native classically trained singers along with native Ute singers and dancers from the nearby Uintah-Ouray reservation. At the time, traditional Native American dances, including the sun dance, scalp dance, and war dance, were punishable offenses according to the United States "Code of Indian Offenses" established in 1883.[22] It wasn't until 1978 that the American Indian Religious Freedoms Act was established to protect and preserve Native American religious expressions and traditions.[23]

Around 1920, Zitkála-Šá and her husband moved to Washington, D.C., to work in the Office of Indian Affairs where she was known for her writing and political activism. In 1938, just a few months after her death, *The Sun Dance Opera* was presented by the New York Opera Guild at the Broadway Theatre.[24]

Zitkála-Šá, "Red Bird," also known as Gertrude Bonnin—at age 22 during a period when she taught at the Carlisle Indian School in Pennsylvania. Artist: Joseph Turner Kelly, 1898 (National Portrait Gallery).

The performance was attended by 150 members of the New York Society of American Indians dressed in full Native American regalia. Today, the Brigham Young University Library holds the complete score of the opera.[25]

Following the twentieth-century work of musicologists and composers inspired by Native American songs and traditions, there are current Native American composers and musicians who blend traditional American Indian music with European-style classical music into Amerindian music. For example, composer George Quincy is a Juilliard-trained composer and conductor of Choctaw heritage. Quincy's many works include *Choctaw Nights*, for chamber ensemble which was recorded by The New York 5 and released by Albany Records in 2002. He wrote another composition titled, *The Choctaw Diaries,* a concerto for Native flute and orchestra which was released by Albany Records in 2008, with Timothy Archambault playing the Native flute. In a 2008 interview with the *Juilliard Journal,* George Quincy commented that he draws inspiration from nature and incorporates traditional Native American instruments such as the water drum and the rain stick into his compositions.[26]

Jared Tate is an award-winning American Indian classical composer and pianist of the Chickasaw Nation whose orchestral works have been performed by several major U.S. orchestras. On September 23, 2005, the *Washington Post* wrote about a concert at the Kennedy Center featuring his composition, "Iholba": "You could hear the quiet prayer, sense the heartbeat and feel the wind in Tate's 'Iholba' (The Vision). Tate's connection to nature and the human experience was quite apparent in this piece, which is based on traditional Chickasaw song, with original poetry sung in Chickasaw."[27]

American Indian musical artist R. Carlos Nakai, of Navajo-Ute heritage, an 11-time Grammy-nominated Native American flutist, scholar, and author, has released over 50 recordings. Nakai plays traditional Native American flute music as a solo artist and collaborates with a variety of jazz, classical, and world music artists mixing traditional music with a variety of genres including new age, world-beat jazz, and classical. His 2014 solo recording, *Canyon Trilogy,* went platinum (over 1,000,000 copies sold).[28]

Nakai commented on his life in music in his online biography, "Our primary importance as musicians is trying to tell people that history can't be changed, but the future can be. Personally, I feel I should try to contribute something that would encourage people to change, to become more positive about our situation, to reorganize and reorient ourselves together instead of continuing to build walls."[29]

Nakai has brought the Native American flute into the concert hall with over 30 performances with symphonies and chamber orchestras. On September 18, 2004, he was the featured soloist with the Omaha Symphony for the premier of a Philip Glass composition that was inspired by the Lewis and Clark Expedition—*Piano Concerto No. 2.* The concerto consists of three movements. The first movement, "The Vision," according to Philip Glass, is a "musical steamroller" signifying the energy and resolve that Lewis and Clark brought to the expedition.[30]

Ashley Hassebroek of the *Omaha World-Herald Bureau* reviewed the premier of the concerto and described the second movement: "The slower second movement, 'Sacagawea,' based on the Shoshone Indian who became Lewis and Clark's companion, has arguably the most mesmerizing musical themes of the piece. The slow, brooding duet between the American Indian flute and the piano features a traditional Shoshone musical theme as well as a middle section that is quicker and delightfully disjointed."[31]

The final movement, "The Land," expresses the vast area of land explored by Lewis and Clark. Philip Glass commented on the final movement, "I wanted this final movement to reflect also the expanse of time—what the land was before the expedition, and what it became after."[32]

Many twentieth-century composers found inspiration in the vast landscape and the dreaminess of the American West, including Antonín Dvořák, the famous Czech composer who resided in the United States in the years 1892–1895 and wrote *The New World Symphony.* In 1894 he composed *American Suite, Op. 98,* for solo piano, which was later arranged for solo piano with orchestra. The five-movement composition portrays the expansive Iowa prairie, Native American dancing, and African American banjo playing.[33]

Leo Sowerby composed *Prairie* in 1929 for orchestra. The work was based on the Carl Sandburg poem "Prairie" and is meant to evoke the vastness of America's Midwest. The score includes these words from the original Sandburg poem:

> Have you seen a red sunset drip over one of my cornfields, the shore
> of night stars, the wave lines of dawn up a wheat valley?
> Have you heard my threshing crews yelling in the chaff of a strawpile and the
> running wheat of the wagonboards, my cornhuskers, my harvest hands hauling
> crops, singing dreams of women, worlds, horizons?[34]

In 1944, twentieth-century German-born American composer Lukas Foss composed *The Prairie,* a 50-minute, seven-movement composition for solo and duet voices with chorus based on the same Sandburg poem. The Boston Modern Orchestra Project (BMOP) recorded the epic piece in 2008 and described it as "an iconic work of American classical music that embodies the hardships and optimism that defined a generation of men and women braving industrialization in America."[35]

Dave Brubeck (1920–2012), the great American jazz pianist and composer, grew up on a cattle ranch in Northern California. He worked after school and summers as a cowhand on the ranch, and beginning at the age of 14, he played jazz in rural towns such as Angels Camp, Murphys, and Sutter Creek. Brubeck wrote about his earliest musical influences, "In the evenings, my father often played the harmonica (cowboy style) and my mother played the piano (classical style). These two diverse traditions produced in me a jazz style that was individual, and compositional style that in an amalgam of a variety of early influences."[36]

In 1946, Brubeck composed *Reminiscences of Cattle of the Country* for solo piano, inspired by those early years of growing up on the cattle ranch and listening to the music of his mother and father. The set includes: "Sunup," "Breaking a Wild Horse," "The Fairgrounds," "Look at My Pony," "The Chickens and the Ducklings," and "Dad Plays the Harmonica."

Aaron Copland, beloved American composer, wrote several compositions with pioneer and cowboy themes. Though an urban New York composer, he had a familial connection to the West—his mother had roots in rural Illinois, where she grew up among cowboys, ranchers, and Native Americans.[37] Copland's Western-themed compositional output includes the ballets *Rodeo* and *Billy the Kid.* He also composed an orchestral suite titled *Prairie Journal* in 1937. He composed the score for the movie *Red Pony,* based on a John Steinbeck novel about California ranch life, and two shorter Western-themed works, including "My Head Is in the West" for voice and piano and "The Young Pioneers" for solo piano. The folk melodies used in his two sets of *American Songs* for voice and piano may have been some of the same folk songs that were sung on the Oregon Trail and in early frontier communities, such as "Simple Gifts," "Long Time Ago," and "The Little Horses."

Along with Aaron Copland, other twentieth-century composers, including Roy Harris, Samuel Barber, and Virgil Thomson, all composed works based on frontier folk melodies and cowboy songs. For example, all four composers mentioned here and perhaps others have woven the well-known melody "Streets of Laredo," also known as the "Cowboy's Lament," into their musical compositions. Copland wove the melody into his ballet, *Billy the Kid*. Roy Harris included the melody in his *American Ballads* for solo piano. Samuel Barber repurposed the same melody in the third movement of his solo piano suite, *Excursions,* and Virgil Thomson used the melody in his suite for solo piano, *The Plough That Broke the Plains*.

Still today, the West continues to inspire contemporary musicians and composers. For instance, in 1993, collaborators Eric Houghton and the late Robert Marquis of Princeton New Jersey wrote a musical called *Pioneer Songs*, which documents the optimism, hardships, uncertainty, hope, and triumphs of pioneers on the Oregon Trail. Eric Houghton wrote the music, while Bob Marquis wrote the lyrics and narration. At the time, Marquis was studying piano with Houghton at the Westminster Conservatory. The songs in the musical tell the story of the first crossing of the 2,000-mile Oregon Trail/California Trail.

The work is based on the 1841 group of pioneers known as the Bidwell Party, who traveled on the Overland Trail from Sapling Grove, near Westport, Missouri, to Northern California. In particular, the story follows Ben and Nancy Kelsey, a young married couple who were members of the original Bidwell Party. *Pioneer Songs* conveys important events that occurred during the Bidwell Party crossing in 14 songs: "Gathering," "Beckoning," "Proposal," "Preparation," "Marriage Vows," "Farewell," "Departure," "Doin's of the Day," "The Prairie," "The Oxen," "The Desert," "The Mountains," "Petition," and "Celebration."

Pioneer Songs premiered in Princeton New Jersey in August of 1993, just before Bob Marquis passed away five months later. There were a handful of other performances in St. Louis, Chicago and New Jersey. Then in 2016, Eric Houghton amended the work and added a chorus to several of the movements and presented *Pioneer Songs* again, this time at the Princeton Meadow Church and Event Center in Princeton. In 2018 the production was presented at the War Memorial in Trenton, New Jersey, where audiences raved about the performance.[38] Future performances of *Pioneer Songs* are in the works, and musical scores with narration are available from the publisher, Art of Sound Music.

Another contemporary artist who draws from the musical history of the Old West is Dom Flemons, Grammy award-winning vocalist, multi-instrumentalist, and historian known as "The American Songster." In 2018, he released *Dom Flemons Presents Black Cowboys* on Smithsonian Folkways Recordings, a collection of songs inspired by nineteenth-century African American cowboys and pioneers. The 60-minute recording, accompanied by a 40-page booklet of liner notes, is available at Smithsonian Folkways.[39] The booklet includes photographs and an extensive narrative about Black Americans of the Old West and highlights several prominent African American historical figures, including Addison Jones, a respected trail boss out of New Mexico; cowboy Nat Love, known as "Deadwood Dick"; and Bill Picket, who invented the rodeo sport of bulldogging. Flemons also spotlights songwriter Charley Willis, who contributed "Good-by, Old Paint" to the cannon of well-known cowboy songs.

In the CD liner notes, Flemons points out: "Many people see the West as the birth-place of America. If they only see it as the birthplace of white America, it means basically that all other people are interlopers—they're not part of what makes an American. But if they understand that African Americans were cowboys, even Native Americans were cowboys, Mexicans were cowboys, it really opens the door for us to think about America as a multiethnic, multiracial place. Not just in the last decade or century, but from the very beginning."[40]

Some of the songs on the recording include "Going Down the Road Feeling Bad," "Good-by, Old Paint," "Lonesome Old River Blues," "Old Chisholm Trail," and "Black Woman," a field-holler (an African American work song) that Flemons included in honor of the thousands of Black women who built schools, churches, and shaped communities in the early days of the Western frontier. He highlights women such as Mary Fields, known as "Stagecoach Mary," or "Black Mary," a gun-toting, whiskey-drinking, cigar-smoking, rough-talking entrepreneur who, as an independent contractor on a star route (a rural mail delivery route), delivered U.S. mail via stagecoach in Montana through blizzards and blistering heat. She was the first African American star route carrier in the United States.[41] Flemons composed "He's a Lone Ranger" based on the first African American U.S. Marshall, who may have been the inspiration for the legend of the Lone Ranger.[42]

Dom Flemons is one of the many contemporary artists and composers whose work shines a light on the music and people who played a part in the era of the Westward Expansion. Through the decades, the landscape, characters, and vision of the West have inspired musical artists whose work echoes the diversity of people and the place that is the American West. The musical thread is long, beginning with the first indigenous people, followed by members of the Lewis and Clark Expedition, missionaries, fur traders, explorers, emigrants, settlers, teachers, preachers, cowboys, composers, as well as contemporary musical artists who continue adding their own creative contributions into the unfolding musical story of the great American West.

Epilogue

From the first sound of indigenous bone flutes thousands of years ago, *Music in the Westward Expansion* touched on Native American music, fiddling and dancing of the Lewis and Clark Expedition, music of the fur trappers, French songs of the voyageurs, traditional hymns of the missionaries, tunes of the emigrants on the Oregon Trail, musicians in early frontier communities, songs of the cowboys, and finally, the musical lives of three communities: Walla Walla, Washington; Portland, Oregon; and Butte, Montana.

My goal for writing this book was twofold. First, I wanted to tell the rich and far-reaching story of the Westward Expansion through the lens of music. The history of the Westward Expansion is part of our collective American history and a story worth retelling—the good and the bad. The story of music in the Westward Expansion is a fascinating, yet little-known narrative that is an important American story. Secondly, I wanted to inspire readers to add more musical experiences into their own twenty-first-century lives. The stories found throughout the book prove that musical experiences create energy, spark conversations, bring people together, and touch people's hearts. What was true at the time of the Westward Expansion remains true today.

Each group that traveled west brought heart to the experience as they wove their unique thread into the musical tapestry that was as diverse as the people and experiences of the nineteenth-century American West. The following "Heart List" highlights the many roles that music played as people established a new sense of place.

Heart List

Music provided:

- Celebration
- Comfort for people (and restless cattle)
- Community connection
- Creative outlet
- Diplomacy
- Diversion
- Entertainment
- Expression of cultural identity
- Expression of friendship
- Expression of joy
- Expression of love
- Expression of sorrow
- Historical records of events
- Memories of home
- Sense of place
- Solace
- Worship

The multiple roles of music from the era of the Westward Expansion, as outlined in the "Heart List," have direct bearing on our modern lives. As I write this epilogue, we are dealing with a global pandemic. In this time of death, pain, isolation, and uncertainty, people have turned to music as one of the ways to express a variety of emotions—anger, sorrow, tenderness, hope, loneliness, solidarity, fear, gratitude, frustration, and love. Music has provided a way to connect with one another in this unimaginable crisis, even if that connection, for the most part, is through the computer screen.

In Italy, one of the first countries hit hard by the Coronavirus, Italians stood on their balconies at designated hours to honor medical workers by singing traditional Italian songs and playing instruments—violins, accordions, guitars, trumpets, harps, flutes, oboes, drums, tubas, cooking pots, and wooden spoons. Opera singers sang arias such as "Nessum Dorma" from the opera, *Turandot*. Other countries, including Portugal, Spain, and the U.S., followed Italy's example of singing and playing musical instruments in order to show solidarity and to honor workers on the front line. Video footage from New York shows residents gathered at their windows singing Beatles favorites, including "Hey Jude" and "Yellow Submarine." They also sang the Smokey Robinson song, "My Girl," and the old spiritual "We Shall Overcome." Classical, jazz, and popular musicians have performed online concerts which have provided beauty and comfort in these troubled days. Arts organizations from across the U.S. have offered online concerts, theater productions, and educational programs. A group of Berklee music students, each working in isolation for their part of the recording, created a video of "What the World Needs Now Is Love." In this unprecedented time, we need music more than ever. Musicians and arts organizations are answering the call with creativity, collaboration, and generosity.

During the pandemic, weekly music lessons and seasonal recitals continue in an online format for many students and teachers, including me. Students and their parents are delighted to keep this connection going as a form of joy, diversion, and because the weekly lessons add a sense of familiarity to this trying time. Today, as I was teaching an online piano lesson in my studio, my daughter was in another room of the house having an online lesson with her violin teacher. Throughout this crisis, we are witnessing the power of music to bring joy, provide comfort, offer hope, and help people feel connected. Clearly, music matters!

Just as music enriched the lives of Lewis and Clark, fur trappers, emigrants on the Oregon Trail, pioneers on homesteads, and citizens of early frontier communities, music enrichment remains relevant in our modern world. Most recently, during the global COVID-19 pandemic, the multiple roles and benefits of music have taken center stage as people from around the world are connecting online through music. The lyrics of the Stephen Foster Song "Hard Times Come Again No More" ring true today.

"Hard Times Come Again No More"

Let us pause in life's pleasures and count its many tears
While we all sup sorrow with the poor.
There's a song that will linger forever in our ears,
Oh, hard times, come again no more.

'Tis the song, the sigh of the weary.
Hard times, hard times, come again no more.
Many days you have lingered around my cabin door.
Oh, hard times, come again no more.

While we seek mirth and beauty and music light and gay.
There are frail forms fainting at the door.
Though their voices are silent, their pleading looks will say.
Oh, hard times, come again no more.

There's pale drooping maiden who toils her life away
With a worn heart, whose better days are o'er.
Though her voice would be merry, 'tis sighing all the day,
Oh, hard times, come again no more.

'Tis a sigh that is wafted across the troubled wave
'Tis a wail that is heard upon the shore
'Tis a dirge that is murmured around the lowly grave
Oh, hard times, come again no more.

Beyond the "Heart List," numerous scientific tests and studies show the positive effects of music on the brain. Music positively impacts brain functions including cognitive and motor skills and spatial reasoning. Playing and listening to music literally lights up the brain and has been found as a way to help people who suffer with neurodegenerative diseases, including Alzheimer's and Parkinson's. The Alzheimer's Society has a "Singing for the Brain" program which helps people to sing songs they know and love in a supportive environment.

Playing an instrument and listening to music can help with depression, reduce anxiety, ease pain, improve sleep quality, boost productivity, and possibly slow down the aging process. The list of benefits goes on and on. An internet search of "music and the brain" yields nearly 1,000,000 results.

Singing releases endorphins associated with feelings of pleasure, improves mood, exercises the lungs, improves circulation, and may even help with snoring. Singing in a group reduces stress, builds social connections, and may even increase life expectancy. The voice is the one instrument we carry with us at all times. With the multiple benefits of singing, it's a wonder we're all not walking around singing 24 hours a day.

Time and time again, at dinner parties, in coffee shops, in yoga class, and on the bus, I've met people who ask me what I do for a living. I say, "I'm a professional musician, and I teach music." An animated conversation ensues. The subject of music stirs up something in many people I have come across. Most people have some opinion about music, and it's usually that they don't have enough in their lives, they are sad they gave up on playing an instrument, they want to take up an instrument, they want their child to start lessons, or they want to tell me about a concert they just attended. Here are some of the comments I have heard along with some of the responses that I have given:

COMMENT: "I wish I wouldn't have stopped taking music lessons when I was young."
RESPONSE: "It is never too late to jump back into music lessons, the most important thing is to start."
COMMENT: "I miss having music in my life. I'm too busy."
RESPONSE: "Make time for music in your life every day. Sing a song, play an instrument, go out and listen to live music, listen to a beautiful piece of music in your home, beat on a drum. These all qualify as musical experiences that will enrich your life."
COMMENT: "I'm not musically talented."
RESPONSE: "We are all born with the ability to make music. What matters is a desire to participate in some type of musical activity. Music is available to EVERYONE! Musical experiences are out there for all of us to enjoy, not just the chosen few."
COMMENT: "I had a terrible experience in school with a teacher who told me I wasn't talented."
RESPONSE: "That was an unfortunate experience, but that doesn't have to be your reality. This experience is in the past; move past it, and don't let that one comment keep you away from all of the benefits of music."

COMMENT: "When I retire, I'd like to have more music in my life."

RESPONSE: "Why wait until you retire. If you start now, you will have years of musical study under your belt before retirement, which will enrich your retirement years."

The time to add meaningful musical experiences into your life is now. It doesn't have to be expensive, and it doesn't have to take a lot of extra time. The rewards will be great. I implore you to attend music events, host a house concert, learn an instrument, sing in a choir, go out dancing, or advocate for music in schools and in your community. For a jumping off point on how to enrich your life with music or on how to expand your musical activities, start with the appendices in the back of my book, which include a song list from each chapter, suggested recordings for listening, a small collection of songs that were mentioned in the book in sheet music form, and ideas for adding musical experiences into your life.

Americans are no longer rolling along a 2,000-mile dirt road in covered wagons, battling cholera, or setting up homesteads on rocky outposts. Yet, today, we live in difficult times that challenge the human spirit. Through singing, playing instruments, attending musical events, and advocating for the arts, we can create beauty, experience joy, express sorrow, celebrate humanity, respect one another, and find common ground in what connects us.

> *The life of the arts, far from being an interruption, a distraction, in the life of the nation, is close to the center of a nation's purpose—and is a test to the quality of a nation's civilization.*—John F. Kennedy

Appendix A

Selected Songs and Musical Works

Works indicated with (*) are available in sheet music form at the Library of Congress website (loc.gov/notated-music).

Preface

Moonlight Sonata (Ludwig van Beethoven)
"Old Dan Tucker" (Traditional)*
"Twilight and Mist" (James Horner)

Chapter 1: Northern Cheyenne Love Songs

"Amazing Grace" (Traditional)
"Hohiotsitsi No-otz" (Morning Song) (Cheyenne)
"Meshivotzi-No-otz" (Baby-Song) (Cheyenne)
"Wunk-Hi Na-Wan" (Love-Song) (Winnebago)

Chapter 2: The Genesis: The Lewis and Clark Expedition (1804–1806)

"Au Clair de la lune" (Traditional)*
"La Belle Catherine" (Traditional)
"Barbara Allen" (Traditional)
"Boil the Cabbage" (Traditional)
"Chester" (William Billings)
"Come Thou Fount of Every Blessing" (Robert Robinson)*
"Come Ye Sinners Poor and Needy" (Joseph Hart)*
"The Cuckoo" (Traditional)*
"Devil's Dream" (Traditional)*
"Fisher's Hornpipe" (Traditional)*
"Go Down Moses" (Traditional)
"Jolie Blonde" (Traditional)
"Kedron" (Charles Wesley)
"My Days Have Been So Wondrous Free" (Parnell/ Hopkinson)*
"Oh Dear What Can the Matter Be" (Traditional)*
"Old French Hornpipe" (Traditional)
"Pretty Saro" (Traditional)
"The Rose Tree" (Traditional)
"Whiskey Before Breakfast" (Traditional)
"Yankee Doodle" (Traditional)*

Chapter 3: Trailblazers: Explorers, Mountain Men, and Missionaries

"Awake and Sing the Song" (William Hammond)
"Crazy Jane" (Traditional)*
"Dans mon chemin" (Traditional)
"Derriere chêz nous, y a un etang" (Traditional)
"Fandango Variado" (Dionisio Aguado)
"Jarabé Tapatío" (Jesus González Rubio)
"The Lass with the Delicate Air" (Traditional)
"Leather Britches" (Traditional)
"Red River Jig" (Traditional)
"Supper Waltz" (Traditional)
"Watchman, Tell Us of the Night" (John Bowling)*
"The Wayworn Traveler" (Traditional)
"Ye Banks and Braes O'Bonnie Doon" (Traditional)*
"Yes, My Native Land" (Samuel Francis Smith)

Chapter 4: Setting the Stage for the Oregon Trail: American Musical Life and Oregon Fever (circa 1830–1850)

"L'Ahambra Waltz" (Madame de Goñi)
"Beautiful Dreamer" (Stephen Foster)*
"The Blue Juniata" (Marion Dix Sullivan)*
"Come All Ye Fair and Tender Girls" (Traditional)
"The Esmerelda Polka" (Jos. Labitzky)*
"Home, Sweet Home" (John Howard Payne and John Duff Brown)*
"I Will Go West" (J.A. Butler, J. A./J.P. Barrett)*
"Indian's Prayer" (I.B. Woodbury)*
"Jeanie with the Light Brown Hair" (Stephen Foster)*
"Jesus, Lover of My Soul" (J.M. Chadwick)*
"Nobody Knows the Trouble I've Seen" (Traditional)*
"Oh Fly to the Prairie" (James Mitchell)*
"The Old Granite State" (The Hutchinson Family)*
"La Prima Donna Waltz" (Justin Holland)*
"Rock of Ages" (Augustus Toplady)*
"Rock O' My Soul" (Traditional)*
"Simple Gifts" (Joseph Brackett)
"Sometimes I Feel Like a Motherless Child" (Traditional)
"Wondrous Love" (Traditional)*
"Woodman, Spare That Tree" (H. Russell)*

Chapter 5: Life on the Oregon Trail

No songs are mentioned in this chapter.

Chapter 6: The Music at the Heart of the Oregon Trail Experience

"The Cottage by the Sea" (J.R. Thomas)*
"Faded Flowers" (James Power)*
"The Girl I Left Behind Me" (Traditional)
"Guide Me on Though Great Jehovah" (Traditional)
"Ho! For the Kansas Plains" (James Clark)*

"I Have Something Sweet to Tell You" (Heinrich/Osgood)*
"A Life on the Ocean Wave" (Charles Grobe)*
"Maggie by My Side" (Stephen Foster)*
"Maryland My Maryland" (C. Munzinger)*
"My Old Kentucky Home" (Stephen Foster)*
"The Old House at Home" (Thomas Bayly)*
"One More River to Cross"(Traditional)
"Oregon Quick Step" (A. Metz)*
"The Oregon Waltz" (William Bradbury)*
"Prairie Waltz" (C.H, Weber)*
"Uncle Sam's Farm" (Hutchinson/Barker)*
"Wait for the Wagon" (Traditional)*

Chapter 7: We're There! Music on the Homestead and in Early Frontier Communities

"Across the Danube" (John Philip Sousa)
"Arkansas Traveler" (Colonel Sanford C. "Sandy" Faulkner)
"The Brook" (Willie Pape)*
"Buy a Broom" (Walter Hewitt)*
"Cavatina" (J. Raff)*
"Cheer Boys Cheer" (Henry Russell)*
"Diamonds in the Rough" (Traditional)
"Down the River, Down the Ohio" (E.P Christy)*
"The First Lord's Song" (Gilbert and Sullivan)
"Home, Sweet Home Waltz" (Francis Rziha)*
"The House of the Lord" (E.A. Barnes)
"I'll Go Back to Home and Mother" (Leo Friedman/Mary Beales)*
"Jesus, Lover of My Soul" (Henry Tucker)*
"Katydid" (Traditional)*
"Lily Dale" (H.S. Thompson)
"Prayer of the Dying Californian" (E. W. Denison)*
"Turkey in the Straw" (Traditional)*
"The Vacant Chair" (Henry Washburn)*
"Wagoner" (Traditional)
"What a Friend We Have in Jesus" (Joseph Scriven)

Chapter 8: Whoopie Ti Yi Yo: Music and the Real Cowboys in the Old West

"Billy in the Low Ground" (Traditional)
"Bucking Bronco" (Belle Star)
"California Trail" (Kate Childs "Montana Kate")
"Cotton-Eyed Joe" (Traditional)
"The Devil's Dream"(Traditional)
"Dinah Had a Wooden Leg" (Traditional)
"Dog" (Traditional)
"The Dying Cowboy of Rim Rock Ranch" (Traditional)
"Good-by, Old Paint" (Charlie Willis)
"Hell Among the Yearlin's" (Traditional)*
"Montebello Waltzes" (Vaas)*
"Oh Bury Me Not on the Lone Prairie" (Traditional)
"The Old Chisholm Trail" (Traditional)

"Old Rosin the Bow" (Traditional)
"Saddle Ole Pike" (Traditional)
"Sally Gooden" (Traditional)
"The Streets of Laredo" (Traditional)
"Texas Cowboy Mazurka" (H.F. Fazende)*
"Whoopee Ti Yi Yo, Git Along Little Dogies" (Traditional)
"Women Outlaws" (Jack Thorp)

Chapter 9: Music in the Settled West: Three Distinct Frontier Communities in 1890

"Butte's Fatal Explosion" (E.T. Henneberry/M.M. Henneberry)
"The Class Song" (Grace Ramsey/Harlan Cozine)
"Departed Days" (George Frederick Root)*
"Far from Home" (Paul Henrion)*
"The Golden Cross" (Traditional)*
"Gypsy Rondo" (Franz Joseph Haydn)
"Hail to Thee Liberty" (Gioacchino Rossini)
"Heather Rose" (Gustav Hollaender)*
"The Huntsman's Farewell" (Felix Mendelssohn)
"The Image of the Rose" (G. Reichardt)
"Invitation au Galop" (Franz Bendel)
"Le Macon" (Daniel Auber)
"Moonlight on the Willamette" (Emilie Frances Bauer)*
Sun Splendor (Marion Bauer)
"When the Sun Is Low" (Carl August Röckel)

Chapter 10: Western Inspiration: Scholars, Composers, and Musicians

American Ballads (Roy Harris)
American Indian Melodies (Author Farwell)*
Billy the Kid (Aaron Copland)
"Black Woman" (Dom Flemons)
The Choctaw Diaries (George Quincy)
"He's a Lone Ranger" (Dom Flemons)
Iholba (The Vision) (Jared Tate)
Indian Fantasy, op. 44 (Ferruccio Busoni)
"Indian Flute Call and Love Song" (Thurlow Lieurance)
"Indian Love Call" (Charles Wakefield Cadman)
Indian Suite (Edward McDowell)
"Land of Sky-Blue Water" (Charles Wakefield Cadman)
"The Old Man's Love Song" (Arthur Farwell)
Piano Concerto No. 2 (Philip Glass)
The Plough That Broke the Plains (Virgil Thomson)
Reminiscences of Cattle of the Country (Dave Brubeck)
Thunderbird Suite (Charles Wakefield Cadman)
"Wide Open Spaces"(Susan Gibson)

Epilogue

"Hard Times Come Again No More" (Stephen Foster)*
"Hey Jude" (The Beatles)

"My Girl" (Smokey Robinson)
"Nessum Dorma" (Giacomo Puccini)
"We Shall Overcome" (Traditional)
"What the World Needs Now Is Love" (Burt Bacharach)
"Yellow Submarine" (The Beatles)

Appendix B
Suggested Recordings

This list includes recorded music representative of each chapter along with information on where to purchase the recordings. Many of the recordings are also available on streaming platforms, as indicated below. Please note, this is not an exhaustive list; this is a point of entry for your own musical exploration. Some of the recordings may be available from other retailers and on other streaming platforms that are not mentioned here.

Chapter 1: Northern Cheyenne Love Songs

Ashland Singers, *Northern Cheyenne War Dance,* Indian House IH 4201, 1974, LP (Indian House).

Fire Crow, Joseph, *Cheyenne Nation,* Makoché, 2000, audio CD (Amazon, Spotify, Apple Music).

Locke, Kevin, *The First Flute,* Makoché, 1999, audio CD (Amazon, Spotify, Apple Music).

Chapter 2: The Genesis: The Lewis and Clark Expedition (1804–1806)

Discovery String Band, *Most Perfect Harmony, Lewis and Clark, A Musical Journey Discovery,* Big Canoe Records, 2003, audio CD (Amazon, Bartonpara.com).

The New Columbia Fiddlers, *Fiddle Tunes of the Lewis and Clark Era,* Voyager Records, 2002, audio CD (Amazon, Apple Music, Spotify, Voyager Records).

Slosberg, Daniel, *Pierre Cruzatte, a Musical Journey Along the Lewis and Clark Trail with Daniel Slosberg,* Native Ground Music, 2003, audio CD (Amazon, Native Ground Music).

Various Artists, *Lewis and Clark: The Journey of the Corps of Discovery* by Ken Burns, Original Soundtrack Recording, RCA, 1997, audio CD (Amazon, Apple Music, Spotify).

Chapter 3: Trailblazers: Explorers, Mountain Men, and Missionaries

Blegen, Theodore Christian, *Songs of the Voyagers,* Minnesota Historical Society Press, 1998, audio CD (Amazon, MNHS Press).

O'Dette, Paul, Andrew Lawrence-King, Pedro Estevan and Pat O'Brien, *Jácaras!—18th Century Spanish Baroque Guitar Music of Santiago de Murcia,* Harmonia Mundi, 1998, audio CD (Amazon, Spotify, Apple Music).

The Red River Ramblers, *Métis Fiddle Music,* The Red River Ramblers, 2020, MP3 (Amazon, Apple Music, Spotify).

Rose, Victor, *Vic's Picks: Old-Time Métis Fiddle Tunes,* The Gabriel Dumont Institute of Native Studies and Applied Research, 2010, audio CD (Gabriel Dumont Institute of Native Studies and Applied Research).

Various Artists. *Beautiful Beyond: Christian Songs in Native Languages Presented by the National Museum of the American Indian,* Smithsonian Folk Ways Records, 2004, audio CD (Smithsonian Folkways Recordings, Amazon, Spotify, and Apple Music).

Chapter 4: Setting the Stage for the Oregon Trail: American Musical Life and Oregon Fever (circa 1830–1850)

DeGaetani, Jan /Gilbert Kalish, *Songs by Stephen Foster,* Nonesuch, 2008, audio CD (Amazon, Spotify, Apple Music).

Jabbour, Alan, compiler, *American Fiddle Tunes, Various Artists,* Library of Congress, 2012, digital audio available at: https://www.loc.gov/item/2016655239/ (Amazon).

Kruisbrink, Annette, *Guitar Music by Women Composers,* Les Productions, sheet music book and audio CD (Sheet Music Plus, JW Pepper).

Mesney, Dorothy and Myron McPherson, *The Parlour Piano: Popular Songs of the 1800's,* Folkways Records, 1978, LP (Amazon, Apple Music, Smithsonian Folkways Records, Spotify).

Various Artists, *Anthology of American Folk Music,* Edited by Harry Smith, Smithsonian Folk Ways Recordings, 1997, digital audio available at https://folkways.si.edu/anthology-of-american-folk-music/african-american-music-blues-old-time/music/album/smithsonian (six CDs and book available at Smithsonian Folk Ways).

Chapters 5 and 6: Life on the Oregon Trail and The Music at the Heart of the Oregon Trail Experience

American Hymns Singers, Come Home, Rediscovering Old American Hymns Volume 1, MSR Classics, 2006, audio CD (Amazon, Apple Music, Spotify).

Jones, Clark, *Early American Folk Music and Song,* Folkways Records, 1982, audio CD (Amazon, Apple Music, Smithsonian Folkways Recordings, Spotify).

Taylor, Darryl, Brent McMunn, *How Sweet the Sound,* Albany Records, 2010, audio CD (Amazon, Spotify, Apple Records).

Various Artists, *Ken Burns Presents The West Soundtrack,* Sony Classical, 2007, audio CD (Amazon, Spotify, Apple Records).

Various Artists, *Pa's Fiddle, Charles Ingalls, American Fiddler,* arranged by Joe Weed, Highland Records, 2012, audio CD (Amazon, Apple Music, Spotify).

Williams, Phil and Vivian, Dance Music of the Oregon Trail, Voyager Recordings, 2000, audio CD (Amazon, Apple Music, Spotify, Voyager Records).

Chapter 7: We're There! Music on the Homestead and in Early Frontier Communities

Holcomb, Roscoe, *An Untamed Sense of Control,* Folkways Records, recorded 1961–1973, released 2003, audio CD (Amazon, Apple Music, Smithsonian Folkways Recordings, Spotify).

Mao, Ellie, *An Anthology of Chinese Folk Songs,* Folkways Records, 1963, LP (Amazon, Apple Music, Smithsonian Folkways Recordings, Spotify).

Montgomery, Little Brother, *Church Songs: Sung and Played on the Piano by Little Brother Montgomery,* Folkways Records, 1975, LP (Amazon, Apple Music, Smithsonian Folkways Recordings, Spotify).

Sousa, John Philip, *The March King,* Legacy International, 2007, audio CD (Amazon, Apple Music, Spotify).

Summers, Andrew Rowan, *Hymns and Carols,* Folkways Records, 1951, LP (Amazon, Apple Music, Smithsonian Folkways Recordings, Spotify).

Chapter 8: Whoopie Ti Yi Yo: Music and the Real Cowboys in the Old West

Flemons, Dom, *Black Cowboys*, Smithsonian Folkways Recordings, 2018, audio CD, Vinyl 2xLP (Amazon, Apple Music, Smithsonian Folkways Recordings, Spotify).

Fredrickson, Dave, *Songs of the West*, Folkways Records, 1961, LP (Amazon, Apple Music, Smithsonian Folkways Recordings, Spotify).

Houston, Cisco, *Cowboy Ballads*, Folkways Records, 1952, LP (Amazon, Apple Music, Smithsonian Folkways Recordings, Spotify).

Moffat, Katy, *Cowboy Girl*, Western Jubilee, 2001, audio CD (Amazon, Apple Music, Smithsonian Folkways Recordings, Spotify).

Reed, Ray, *Ray Reed Sings Traditional Frontier and Cowboy Songs*, Folkways Recordings, 1977, LP (Amazon, Apple Music, Smithsonian Folkways, Spotify).

Chapter 9: Music in the Settled West: Three Distinct Frontier Communities in 1890

Boldin, Deborah, Irina Muresanu, Virginia Eskin, *Marion Bauer*, Albany Records, 2001, audio CD (Albany Records, Amazon).

Chestnut Brass Company and Friends, *Tippecanoe and Tyler Too. A Collection of American Political Marches, Songs, and Dirges*, Newport Classic, 1992, audio CD (Amazon, Discogs).

Drake, Susan, *Arabesque 19th Century Romantic Harp Music*, Hyperion Records Limited, 1986, audio CD (Amazon, Apple Music, Spotify).

Robertson, Walt, *American Northwest Ballads*, Folkways Records, 1955, LP (Amazon, Apple Music, Smithsonian Folkways Recordings, Spotify).

Various Artists, *As I Roved Out (Field Trip-Ireland)*, Folkways Records, 1960, LP (Amazon, Apple Music, Smithsonian Folkways, Spotify).

Chapter 10: Western Inspiration: Scholars, Composers, and Musicians

Archambault, Timothy, and George Quincy: Pocahontas at the Court of King James the I and Choctaw Diaries, Lyrichord Discs Inc., 2008 audio CD (Amazon, Apple Music, Spotify).

Bernstein, Leonard, with the New York Philharmonic, *Copland: Billy the Kid*, RODEO, CBS Great Performances, 1988, audio CD (Amazon, Apple Music, Spotify).

Bohuslav Martinu Philharmonic, *Orchestral Music of Edward MacDowell*, Albany Records, 2006, audio CD (Amazon, Apple Music, Spotify).

The Chicks, *Wide Open Spaces*, Monument, 1998, audio CD (Amazon, Apple Music, Spotify).

Freeman, Paul, with the Czech National Symphony Orchestra, *Prairie: Tone Poems by Leo Sowerby*, Cedille Records, 1997, audio CD (Apple Music, Discogs, Spotify).

Gibson, Susan, *Remember Who You Are*, CD Baby, 2017, audio CD (Amazon, Apple Music, Spotify).

Nakai, R. Carlos, *Canyon Trilogy*, Canyon Records, 2014, audio CD (Amazon, Apple Music, Spotify).

The New York 5, *Choctaw Nights: Chamber Music of George Quincy*, Albany Records, 2003, audio CD (Amazon, Apple Music, Spotify).

Parker, William, *Old Song Resung: William Parker Sings Ives, Griffes, Farwell, and Cadman*, New World Records, 1995, audio CD (Amazon, Apple, Spotify).

Thomas, Lisa Cheryl, *Arthur Farwell Piano Music*, Volume 1, Toccata Classics, 2012, audio CD (Toccata Classics, Spotify).

Various Artists, *Healing Songs of the American Indians*, recorded on location by Frances Densmore, Folkways Records, 1965, LP (Amazon, Apple Music, Smithsonian Folkways, Spotify).

Appendix C

Musical Scores

Baby-Song (Lullaby)

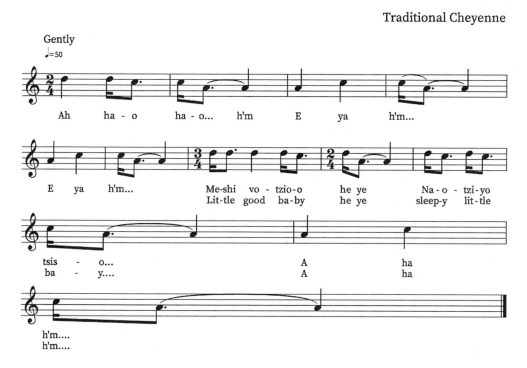

Meshivotzi No-otz Baby Song. As sung by Winunahe (Chief Woman) and transcribed by Natalie Curtis in *The Indians' Book*, Harper and Brothers, 1907.

La Belle Catherine

Arrangement inspired by a version of "La Belle Catherine," on The Sessions (website), 2021 (https://thesession.org/tunes/4625).

Red River Jig

Traditional Métis Fiddle Tune

Red River Jig. As played by Léon Robert Goulet / Victor 216568 / 1928, Traditional Tune Archive (website) https://tunearch.org/wiki/TTA.

The Blue Juniata

Marion Dix Sullivan, 1846

Verse 2
Gay was the mountain song of bright Alfarata,
Where sweep the waters of the blue Juniata.
Strong and true my arrows are, in my painted quiver.
Swift goes my light canoe, a-down the rapid river.

Verse 3
Bold is my warrior good, the love of Alfarata,
Proud waves his snowy plume, along the Juniata.
Soft and low he speaks to me, and then his war cry sounding,
Rings his voice in thunder loud, from height to height resounding.

Verse 4
So sang the Indian girl, bright Alfarata,
Where sweep the waters of the the blue Juniata.
Fleeting years have borne away, the voice of Alfarata,
Still sweeps the river on, blue Juniata.

The Blue Juniata. Arrangement based on the original sheet music at the Library of Congress. Mary Dix Sullivan, "The Blue Juniata," Oliver Ditson, 1846. Notated Music, https://www.loc. gov/item/sm1846.410250/.

I Will Go West!

Lyrics: Ezekiel Jones and William Geer

Music: J.P. Barrett

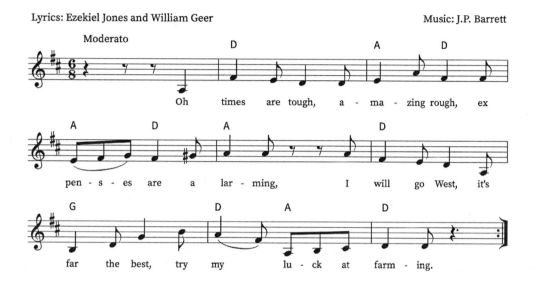

I Will Go West! Arrangement based on the original sheet music at the Library of Congress. J.P Barrett, words by Ezekiel Jones and William Geer, "I Will Go West," J.A. Butler, 1875, https://www.loc.gov/item/sm1875.10352/.

I Have Something Sweet to Tell You

"I AM TALKNG IN MY SLEEP"

Words by Mrs. Frances S. Osgood   Music by James E. Magruder

Verse 2
O shut your eyes so earnest,
Or mine will wildly weep;
I love you! I adore you!
But I'm talking in my sleep.

Chorus:
For I know I am but dreaming
When I think your love it mine
And I know they are but seeming,
All the hopes that round me shine.

I Have Something Sweet to Tell You. Arrangement based on the original sheet music for guitar and voice, "I Have Something Sweet to Tell You," Mrs. Frances S. Osgood and James E Magruder, F. D. Benteen, 1851, https://www.loc.gov/item/sm1851.500810/.

Bucking Bronco

Words by Belle Starr, circa 1878

Music by Laura Dean, 2021

The first time I met him, 'twas early one spring
Riding a bronco, a high-headed thing.
He tipped me a wink as he gaily did go,
For he wished me to look at his bucking bronco.

The next time I saw him, 'twas late in the fall,
Swinging the girls at Tomlinson's ball:
He laughed and he talked, as we danced to and fro,–
Promised never to ride on another bronco.

He made me some presents, among them a ring;
The return that I made him was a far better thing;
'Twas a young maiden's heart, I'd have you all know,
He'd won it by riding his bucking bronco.

Now all you young maidens, wher'er you reside,
Beware of the cowboy who swings the rawhide,
He'll court you and pet you and leave you and go,
In the spring up the trail on his bucking bronco.

Bucking Bronco. Words by Belle Starr found in *Songs of the Cowboys*, N. Howard "Jack" Thorp, Houghton Mifflin Company, 1921. Music by Laura Dean, 2021.

Good-Bye, Old Paint

Charley Willis

My foot in the stir - rup, my pon - y won't sta, - n' good - bye old Paint I'm a lea - vin' Chey - enne. I'm a - leav - in' Chey - enne, I'm off for ta - n', good - bye old Paint, I'm a leav - in' Chey - enne.

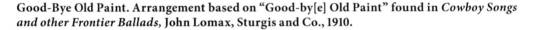

Good-Bye Old Paint. Arrangement based on "Good-by[e] Old Paint" found in *Cowboy Songs and other Frontier Ballads,* **John Lomax, Sturgis and Co., 1910.**

Home Sweet Home

Poem by John Howard Payne

Music by Sir Henry Bishop

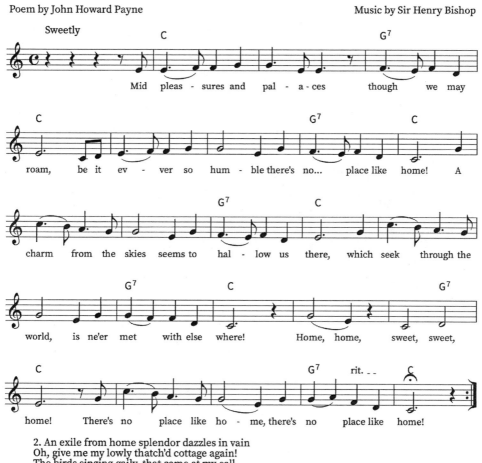

2. An exile from home splendor dazzles in vain
Oh, give me my lowly thatch'd cottage again!
The birds singing gaily, that came at my call,
Give me them, with peace of mind, dearer than all!

Home, home, sweet, sweet home!
There's no place like home, there's no place like home!

Home Sweet Home. Arrangement based on the original sheet music, "Home, Sweet Home,"
by Bishop and Payne, Brainard's Sons, S. Cleveland, 1883 (https://www.loc.gov/resource/
sm1883.17251.0/?sp=).

Hard Times Come Again No More

Stephen Foster

Hard Times. Arrangement based on "Hard Times Come Again No More," Stephen Foster, *Stephen Foster Song Book,* selected and edited by Richard Jackson, Dover, 1974.

Appendix D

Meaningful Musical Experiences: Ideas to Get You Started on Your Own Musical Journey

Whether you are a professional musician, a hobbyist, or a music enthusiast, the following ideas are jumping off points for enriching your life with musical activities!

Hands-on Music Making Experiences in the Home and Community:

- Attend sing-alongs or hire a musician (a guitarist or a pianist) for a casual sing-along with friends, neighbors, and family. Pass out song sheets to attendees.
- Dance! Dance in the home, take lessons, attend community dances. Dancing is usually accompanied by either live or recorded music.
- Give the gift of music: tickets to musical events, music lessons, sheet music, a gift card to your favorite music store, or a musical instrument. (A harmonica, ukulele, recorder, or small percussion instruments are inexpensive choices.)
- Hire a musician or an ensemble to provide background music for family gatherings, outdoor events, or special celebrations. If cost is an issue, consider hiring local high school or college students who are in the early stages of their performance careers.
- Host a house concert—invite a local musician or ensemble into your home to give a concert for family and friends. The audience usually pitches in to cover the musician's fee. For more information, check out the following organizations that organize house concerts such as: Concerts in Your Home (https://concertsinyourhome.org), Undiscovered Music (https://undiscoveredmusic.net/venues/house_concerts), Listening Room Network (https://listeningroomnetwork.com).
- Join a choir. Many community and church choirs don't require an audition.
- Join a community band, orchestra, ukulele ensemble, guitar group, or other instrumental groups.
- Keep a collection of percussion instruments handy for impromptu drumming sessions with family and friends. Percussion instruments and kits are readily available at your local music store or online. You can also make your own with buckets, empty containers filled with rice, or other repurposed items.
- Learn to play an instrument. It's never too late! If you want to learn an instrument, take private or group music lessons. Teachers are out there; to find one, inquire at a local music store or music school. You may also contact your local branch of MTNA (Music Teachers National Association). Many community colleges and community centers offer private and group instruction.

189

If you are a "do-it-yourself" kind of learner, utilize "teach yourself" books, YouTube videos, and pre-recorded (often free) online lessons.

- Listen to music on LP records, CDs, or online platforms such as YouTube, Apple Music or Spotify.
- Listen to NPR music broadcasts, which feature a variety of musical styles such as: *Tiny Desk Concerts, American Routes, Alt.Latino, Mountain Stage, All Songs Considered, World Cafe, Thistle and Shamrock,* and *Jazz Night in America.* Check your local NPR station for programming details.

Attend Musical Events in Your Community. Once you start looking, you will find that is correct live music opportunities are abundant in your community, many of them with free access.

- art fairs
- breweries
- churches
- coffee shops
- colleges and universities
- community centers
- farmers markets
- high schools
- house concerts
- libraries
- local choirs, bands, orchestra concerts
- museums
- music and cultural festivals
- musicals
- open mic nights
- operas
- recitals
- street fairs
- summer outdoor musical events
- symphonies
- wineries

Chapter Notes

Preface

1. Ambrose, *Undaunted Courage*, 359.

Introduction

1. PBS, *The West*.

Chapter 1

1. Webb, "Northern Cheyenne Flute Maker."
2. *Billings Gazette*, "How the Cheyenne Men Wooed Their Soulmates."
3. Mader, *The Road to Lame Deer*, 28.
4. *Ibid.*, 33–34.
5. Jay Old Mouse, online interview, June 25, 2020.
6. Jackson, "Oral Histories of Cheyenne Descendants," Volume II, 73.
7. *Ibid.*, 74.
8. Old Mouse, personal interview, August 13, 2017.
9. Old Mouse, online interview, June 25, 2020.
10. *Ibid.*
11. Stands in Timber, *Cheyenne Memories*, 215.
12. Jay Old Mouse, personal interview, August 13, 2017.
13. Stevens Funeral Home, "Jay Old Mouse Obituary," 2020.
14. Stands in Timber, 63.
15. *Ibid.*, 63.
16. Monaghan, "Cheyenne and Lakota Women," 16.
17. Stands in Timber, 64.
18. *Ibid.*
19. *Ibid.*
20. *Ibid.*, 69–70.
21. *Ibid.*, 115.
22. Fitzgerald, ed., *The Cheyenne Indians: Their History and Lifeways*, 115.
23. *Ibid.*
24. *Ibid.*
25. *Ibid.*
26. Curtis, *The Indians' Book*, 153.
27. *Ibid.*, 261.
28. Crawford, *Flute Magic*, 5.
29. Wapp, "Smithsonian Folklife Festival."
30. Ortiz, *American Indian Myths and Legends*, 275–278.
31. Arcapello, *Native American Nations Map*, 2017.
32. Page, *In the Hands of the Great Spirit*, 42.
33. Ralph, "World's Oldest Known Musical Instruments."
34. Goss, "Anasazi Flutes."
35. Little Chief, "Musical Instruments."
36. Curtis, *The Indians' Book*, xv.

Chapter 2

1. Mussulman, "Music on the Trail."
2. Meriwether Lewis, William Clark, et al., October 19, 1805, entry in *The Journals of the Lewis and Clark Expedition*. https://lewisandclarkjournals.unl.edu/item/lc.jrn.1805-10-19.
3. Meriwether Lewis, William Clark, et al., June 25, 1805, entry. https://lewisandclarkjournals.unl.edu/item/lc.jrn.1805-06-25#lc.jrn.1805-06-25.01.
4. Meriwether Lewis, William Clark, et al., March 30, 1805, entry. https://lewisandclarkjournals.unl.edu/item/lc.jrn.1805-03-30#lc.jrn.1805-03-30.02.
5. Meriwether Lewis, William Clark, et al., August 18, 1804, entry. https://lewisandclarkjournals.unl.edu/item/lc.jrn.1804-08-18#lc.jrn.1804-08-18.02.
6. Meriwether Lewis, William Clark, et al., June 18, 1806, entry. https://lewisandclarkjournals.unl.edu/item/lc.jrn.1806-06-08#lc.jrn.1806-06-08.03.
7. Meriwether Lewis, William Clark, et al., September 26, 1804, entry. https://lewisandclarkjournals.unl.edu/item/lc.jrn.1804-09-26#lc.jrn.1804-09-26.03.
8. Olds, "Music of the Lewis and Clark Expedition," 9.
9. Apel, *Harvard Dictionary of Music*, 447.
10. Meriwether Lewis, William Clark, et al., January 1, 1805, entry. https://lewisandclarkjournals.unl.edu/item/lc.jrn.1805-01-01#lc.jrn.1805-01-01.02.
11. Meriwether Lewis, William Clark, et al., August 30, 1804, entry. https://lewisandclarkjournals.unl.edu/item/lc.jrn.1804-08-30#lc.jrn.1804-08-30.05.

12. Mussulman, "The Greatest Harmony," 4.

13. *Ibid.*, 6.

14. Kuntz, "The Traditional Tune Archive."

15. Zierke, "Pretty Saro."

16. Song of America, "My Days Have Been."

17. Hunt, "Merry to the Fiddle," 16.

18. Meriwether Lewis, William Clark, et al., May 18, 1804, entry. https://lewisand clarkjournals.unl.edu/item/lc.jrn.1804-05-18#lc.jrn.1804-05-18.06.

19. Meriwether Lewis, William Clark, et al., June 11, 1804, entry. https://lewisandclarkjournals.unl.edu/item/lc.jrn.1804-06-11#lc.jrn.1804-06-11.01.

20. Meriwether Lewis, William Clark, et al., August 16, 1804, entry. https://lewisand clarkjournals.unl.edu/item/lc.jrn.1804-08-16#lc.jrn.1804-08-16.03

21. Meriwether Lewis, William Clark, et al., August 20, 1804, entry. https://lewisand clarkjournals.unl.edu/item/lc.jrn.1804-08-20#lc.jrn.1804-08-20.05

22. Hymnary.org, "Come the Fount."

23. Meriwether Lewis, William Clark, et al., August 30, 1805, entry. https://lewisand clarkjournals.unl.edu/item/lc.jrn.1804-08-30#lc.jrn.1804-08-30.04.

24. Meriwether Lewis, William Clark, et al., September 26, 1804, entry. https://lewisand clarkjournals.unl.edu/item/lc.jrn.1804-09-26#lc.jrn.1804-09-26.01.

25. Meriwether Lewis, William Clark, et al., September 26, 1804, entry. https://lewisand clarkjournals.unl.edu/item/lc.jrn.1804-09-26#lc.jrn.1804-09-26.03.

26. Ambrose, 182.

27. Meriwether Lewis, William Clark, et al., December 25, 1804, entry. https://lewisand clarkjournals.unl.edu/item/lc.jrn.1804-12-25#lc.jrn.1804-12-25.04.

28. Crum, "Newe Hupia: Shoshoni Poetry," 5.

29. *Ibid.*, 34.

30. Meriwether Lewis, William Clark, et al., April 26, 1805, entry. https://lewisand clarkjournals.unl.edu/item/lc.jrn.1805-04-26#lc.jrn.1805-04-26.01.

31. Meriwether Lewis, William Clark, et al., July 4, 1805, entry. https://lewisandclarkjournals.unl.edu/item/lc.jrn.1805-07-04#lc.jrn.1805-07-04.01.

32. Meriwether Lewis, William Clark, et al., April 26, 1805, entry. https://lewisand clarkjournals.unl.edu/item/lc.jrn.1805-08-26#lc.jrn.1805-08-26.01.

33. Ambrose, 300.

34. *Ibid.*

35. Meriwether Lewis, William Clark, et al., October 16, 1805, entry. https://lewisand clarkjournals.unl.edu/item/lc.jrn.1805-10-16#lc.jrn.1805-10-16.02.

36. Meriwether Lewis, William Clark, et al., October 26, 1805, entry. https://lewisand clarkjournals.unl.edu/item/lc.jrn.1805-10-26#lc.jrn.1805-10-26.02.

37. Meriwether Lewis, William Clark, et al., November 16, 1805, entry. https://lewisand clarkjournals.unl.edu/item/lc.jrn.1805-11-16#lc.jrn.1805-11-16.02.

38. Meriwether Lewis, William Clark, et al., December 25, 1805, entry. https://lewisand clarkjournals.unl.edu/item/lc.jrn.1805-12-25#lc.jrn.1805-12-25.02.

39. Meriwether Lewis, William Clark, et al., April 16, 1806, entry. https://lewisand clarkjournals.unl.edu/item/lc.jrn.1806-04-16#lc.jrn.1806-04-16.02.

40. Meriwether Lewis, William Clark, et al., April 23, 1806, entry. https://lewisandclarkjour nals.unl.edu/item/lc.jrn.1806-04-23#lc.jrn.18 06-04-23.02.

41. Meriwether Lewis, William Clark, et al., April 28, 1806, entry. https://lewisand clarkjournals.unl.edu/item/lc.jrn.1806-04-28#lc.jrn.1806-04-28.03.

42. Mussulman, "Medicine Songs."

43. Meriwether Lewis, William Clark, et al., June 8, 1806, entry. https://lewisandclarkjour nals.unl.edu/item/lc.jrn.1806-06-08#lc.jrn.1806-06-08.02.

44. Meriwether Lewis, William Clark, et al., August 17, 1806, entry. https://lewisand clarkjournals.unl.edu/item/lc.jrn.1806-08-17#lc.jrn.1806-08-17.01.

45. Meriwether Lewis, William Clark, et al., Sept 14, 1806, entry. https://lewisand clarkjournals.unl.edu/item/lc.jrn.1806-09-14#lc.jrn.1806-09-14.01.

46. Lavender, "The Way to the Western Sea."

Chapter 3

1. Pike, *Exploratory Travels in North America*, 45.

2. *Ibid.*, 50.

3. *Ibid.*, 112.

4. Lewis, "Crazy Jane."

5. Pike, 336.

6. *Ibid.*, 337.

7. *Ibid.*

8. *Ibid.*, 253.

9. Peters, *The Life and Adventures of Kit Carson*, 241–242.

10. Gregg, *Scenes and Incidents*, 242.

11. *Ibid.*, 243.

12. Apel, *Harvard Dictionary of Music*, 307.

13. Pelissier, *Pelissier's Columbian Melodies*, XXI.

14. Olsen and Sheehy, eds., *The Garland Handbook*, 185.

15. Don Quijote, "Jarbe Tapatio."

16. Irving, *The Works of Washington Irving*, 178.

17. *Ibid.*, 180.

18. Bradbury, *Travels in the Interior*, 12.

19. *Ibid.*, 96.

20. James, "Account of an Expedition," 127.
21. Grinnell, *Bent's Old Fort and Its Builders*, 29.
22. Dary, *Seeking Pleasure in the Old West*, 22.
23. Hamilton, *My Sixty Years on the Plains*, 117.
24. *Ibid.*, 183.
25. Beckwourth, *The Life and Adventures*, 107.
26. *Ibid.*, 322.
27. *Ibid.*,451.
28. *Ibid.*, 188.
29. Loukinen, *Medicine Fiddle*.
30. Wiseman, phone interview, March 13, 2020.
31. Inbody, "The Keeper of the Métis Heritage."
32. Morin, cassette tape performance.
33. Wiseman, phone interview, March 13, 2020.
34. Caves, "Founder of Elks Here."
35. *Ibid.*
36. Whitman, PBS, "The Letters and Journals."
37. *Ibid.*
38. *Ibid.*
39. Herndon, *Days on the Road*, 13.
40. Dunton, "Music at St. Mary's Academy," viii.
41. Whitman, PBS, "The Letters and Journals."
42. *Ibid.*
43. Penrose, *At Waiilatpu: Impressions and Recollections*, 9.
44. Farnham, *Part I of Farnham's Travels*, 44.
45. Penrose, 19.
46. Whitman, "Marcus and Narcissa Whitman Collection," 1838.
47. Tate, "The Narcissa Prentiss House."

Chapter 4

1. Newman, "Martin," 2–3.
2. Mattfeld, *Variety Music Cavalcade*, 66.
3. Wyeth, *The Public School Singing Book*, 150–151.
4. *Merrian Webster Dictionary.*
5. Peters, "William Henry/Master Juba Lane."
6. Dobney, "The Legacy of Guitar Virtuoso."
7. *Ibid.*
8. Crumm, "Complicted Life of 'Simple Gifts' Anniversary."
9. Crawford, *America's Musical Life*, 255.
10. Philharmonic Society, "Archives New York Philharmonic Society."
11. Miller, *Women of the Frontier*, 5.
12. Barrett and Geer, "I Will Go West," 1875.

Chapter 5

1. Dary, *The Oregon Trail*, xiii.
2. Parkman, *The Oregon Trail Sketches*, 9.
3. Butruille, *Women's Voices*, 13.
4. Brown, "Traveling on the Oregon Trail," 11.
5. Flora, "The Emmigration: Fort Laramie," Newby, July 28.
6. Abby, *American Frontier: A Trip*, 18.
7. Parrish, *The Oregon Trail Diary*, 48.
8. Abby,19.

9. Johnson, "The Journal of," 52.
10. Schlissel, *Women's Diaries*, 203.
11. Geer, "The Ragens."
12. Blevins, "Alexander Blevins' Reminiscence."
13. Smedley, *Across the Plains*, 52.
14. Thornton, *Oregon and Caliornia in 1848*, 260.
15. Butruille, 24.
16. Herndon, *Days on the Road*, 14.
17. Butruille, 24.
18. Holmes, *Covered Wagon Women* (Volume 5), 59.
19. Goltra, "Journal kept by Mrs. E.J. Goltra," 4.
20. Gowdy, "Crossing the Plains Personal Recollections," 5.
21. Newby, "Fort Laramie," July 18.
22. Cox, "Oregon Trail Letter."
23. Holmes, *Covered Wagon Women*, Volume 1, 51–52.
24. Oregon California Trails Association.
25. Tompkins, "In Their Own Words."
26. Holmes, Volume 1, 122.
27. *Ibid.*, 132–133.
28. *Ibid.*, 143.
29. *Ibid.*, 146.
30. *Ibid.*, 120.
31. Johnson, "Journal of a Young," 52.
32. *Ibid.*, 55.
33. Burnett, "The Great Migration," May 22.
34. Goltra, 3.
35. Parrish, 28.
36. Wilson, "Luzena Stanley Wilson, '49er."
37. Schlissel, 233.
38. *Ibid.*, 99.
39. *Ibid.*
40. *Ibid.*, 72.

Chapter 6

1. Geer, *Fifty Years in Oregon,*135.
2. Gowdy, *Crossing the Plains: Personal Recollections*, 6.
3. Herndon, *Days on the Road*, 112.
4. *Ibid.*, 125.
5. Holmes, *Best of Covered Wagon*, 78–79.
6. Thomson, *Scenes, Incedents and Adventures*, 8.
7. *Ibid.*, 41.
8. *Ibid.*, 270.
9. *Ibid.*, 271.
10. *Ibid.*
11. *Ibid.*, 280–281.
12. Doyle, *Journeys to the Land*, 581.
13. *Ibid.*, 582.
14. Smith, *Kate and Jennie Smith*, May 24.
15. *Ibid.*, August 15.
16. *Ibid.*, July 27.
17. Brown, J. *Henry Brown*, 5–6.
18. Abbott, "Crossing the Plains," 3rd paragraph.
19. Doyle, 125.

20. Herndon, *Days on the Road*, 78.
21. Webber, *The Oregon Trail Diary*, 30.
22. *Ibid.*, 55.
23. Owen, "Benjamin Franklin Owen."
24. Smith, Kate, July 8.
25. Vogdes, *The Journal of Ada*, 70.
26. Merrill, *Bound for Idaho*, 82.
27. *Ibid.*, 56–57.
28. *Ibid.*, 57.
29. Schlissel, *Women's Diaries*,128.
30. Gowdy, 5.
31. Doyle, 478.
32. Anderson, "Music on the Move," 28–29.
33. Schlissel, 105.
34. Herndon, 83.
35. Vogdes, 52.
36. Holmes, 120.
37. Abby, April 18.
38. Herndon, 159.
39. *Ibid.*, 102.
40. Webber, 25.
41. Schlissel, 179–18.
42. *Ibid.*, 181.
43. Holmes, Volume 1, 173.
44. Purvine, Purvine, and Miller, "Purvine-Walker Papers," 6.
45. National Park Service, "The Fort Laramie Treaty Council."
46. Hafen and Young, *Fort Laramie and the Pageant*, 189.
47. *Ibid.*, 185.
48. Owen, July 14.
49. Slim Chance Music, "The Ward Party Massacre."
50. *Ibid.*
51. Burt, *The Minstrelsy of Murder*, 264–265.
52. *Ibid.*, 271–272.
53. Doyle, 561.
54. *Ibid.*, 563–564.
55. Clark, "Ho! For the Kansas Plains."
56. Williams, *Songs and Dances of the Oregon Trail*, 12–13.

Chapter 7

1. Dary, *Seeking Pleasure in the Old West*, 152–153.
2. Hamlin, *A Son of the Middle Border*, 46–47.
3. Kennedy, *The Pioneer Campfire in Four Parts*, 56–57.
4. *Ibid.*, 180.
5. *Ibid.*, 156.
6. Smith, *The Trail Leads West*, 159–160.
7. Carter, *Montana Women Homesteaders*, 70.
8. *Ibid.*, 75.
9. Parrish, *Oregon Trail Diary*, 72.
10. Wrenn, "Pioneer Life (Wrenn 1936-39)," 5.
11. West, *The Saloon*, 8.
12. *Ibid.*, 87.
13. *Ibid.*, 3.
14. Chisholm and Homsher, *South Pass*, 34.
15. *Ibid.*

16. Anderson, "Music on the Move," 33.
17. Thompson, 59.
18. Doyle, *Journeys to the Land of Gold*, 584.
19. Wishart, "Encyclopedia of the Great Plains," 2011.
20. Broussard, "History Commentary: Nettie Craig Asberry," 2005.
21. Geer, *Fifty Years in Oregon*, 250.
22. Greer, 50.
23. *Ibid.*, 52.
24. *Ibid.*, 58.
25. Hymnary, "Throw Out the Lifeline."
26. Lind, *Brother Van Montana Pioneer*, 37.
27. *Ibid.*, 72.
28. *Ibid.*, 68–69.
29. *Ibid.*, 188–189.

Chapter 8

1. Lomax, *Cowboy Songs and Other Frontier Ballads,* 1986 edition, xxiii.
2. Fazende, "Texas Cowboy Polka Mazurka."
3. Lomax, *Cowboy Songs and Other Frontier Ballads*, xviii.
4. *Ibid.*, 1.
5. *Ibid.*, xviii–xix.
6. Searles, radio interview, December 4, 2010.
7. *Ibid.*
8. *Ibid.*, 12–13.
9. Hunter, *The Trail Drivers of Texas*, 64.
10. *Ibid.*, 66.
11. Thorp, *Songs of the Cowboys*, 14.
12. *Ibid.*, 14–15.
13. Trimble, "Bandit Queen Belle Starr."
14. Thorp, 170–171.
15. *Ibid.*, 18–20.
16. McCoy, *Historic Sketches of the Cattle Trade*, 10.
17. Lomax, 1986 edition, xii.
18. Lomax, 1910 edition, xxiv.
19. PBS, *The West, Program 5, Cowboys*.
20. Hunter, 467.
21. McCoy, 101.
22. Siringo, *A Texas Cowboy*, 53.
23. Lomax, 1986 edition, 417–419.
24. Dobie and Young, *A Vaquero of the Brush Country*, 91.
25. *Ibid.*, 91–92.
26. Dary, 120.
27. Dobie and Young, 138–139.
28. McCoy, 139.
29. *Ibid.*, 141.
30. Hunter, 301.
31. *Ibid.*
32. Love, 101.
33. Hunter, 415.
34. *Ibid.*
35. Lomax, 1986, 4–5.
36. *Ibid.*
37. *Ibid.*, 98–99.
38. *Ibid.*, 28.
39. *Ibid.*, 28–29.

40. Westermeier, "The Dodge City Cowboy Band."
41. *Ibid.*

Chapter 9

1. Momady, *The West: An Ilustrated History*, 394.
2. Lyman, *An Illustrated History of Walla Walla*, 199.
3. Reed, *Legendary Locals of Walla Walla*, 67–68.
4. Walla Walla Symphony, "Our History."
5. Reed, 67.
6. Johnson, "Caroline Maxson Wood."
7. *Ibid.*
8. Chin, "A Shadow of the Past."
9. Drazan, "Images of the City."
10. *Ibid.*
11. Pickett, *Marion and Emilie Frances Bauer*, 5.
12. *Ibid.*, 3.
13. *Ibid.*, 5–7.
14. *Ibid.*, 91.
15. Mardones, "El arriero, My love is a muleteer," audio recording, 1918.
16. Pickett, 8.
17. *Ibid.*, 11.
18. Pickett, "Portland Youth Philharmonic Preview."
19. PDX History, "Early Portland."
20. Portland Police Museum and Historical Society, "Samuel B. Parrish."
21. Dunton, "Music at Saint Mary's Academy," 15.
22. *Ibid.*
23. *Ibid.*, 37.
24. Beebe, *A Heritage to Honor*, 5.
25. Scott, *History of Portland, Oregon*, 436.
26. *Ibid.*, 437.
27. Gibson, "Ethnic Butte," map, 2008.
28. Western Resources, "Butte, Montana."
29. Freeman, *A Brief History of Butte*, 37.
30. *Ibid.*
31. Henneberry, "Butte's Fatal Explosion," 1895.

Chapter 10

1. Gibson, "Writing 'Wide Open Spaces,'" email from Gibson to author, December 18, 2020.
2. *Ibid.*
3. Crawford, *An Introduction to America's Music*, 237.
4. Fletcher, *Indian Story and Song*, vii.

5. Fletcher, *A Study of Omaha Music*, 9.
6. Fletcher, *Indian Story and Song*, viii.
7. Chase, "The 'Indianist' Movement in American Music," 2.
8. Densmore, *The American Indian*, 7.
9. Densmore, "Teton Sioux Music Bulletin," 7.
10. Curtis, *The Indians' Book*, xix.
11. Hensley, "Thurlow Lieurance Indian Flutes," 4.
12. *Ibid.*
13. Farwell, "Impression of the Wa-wan Ceremony," 20.
14. Troyer, *Traditional Songs of the Zunis*, 4.
15. Farewell, *American Indian Melodies*, 8.
16. *Ibid.*, 2.
17. *Ibid.*, 3.
18. Fletcher, 68.
19. Critical Past, "Tsianina Redfeather, World War 1," video clip, 1918.
20. Heard Museum Guild, "Princess Tsianina Redfeather."
21. Marzell, *Chalkboard Heroes Twelve Courageous*, 61–62.
22. Zotigh, "Native Perspectives."
23. Hafen, "A Cultural Duet Zitkala Ša," 103.
24. *Ibid.*
25. Hanson Papers, "William Hanson Papers, part 1."
26. Currie, "George Quincy: Finding a Native Voice."
27. Wein, "'Iholba': Haunting Wind Music."
28. Nakai, "R. Carlos Nakais Biography."
29. *Ibid.*
30. Barnes, "Philip Glass Compositions. Piano Concerto No. 2."
31. Hassebroek, "Wise Music Classical: Reviews."
32. Barnes.
33. Horowitz, "Dvorak in America."
34. Crociata, "Symphonic Poems by Leo Sowerby," album booklet,1996.
35. Boston Modern Orchestra Project, "Lukas Foss: The Prairie."
36. Brubeck, *Reminiscences of the Cattle Country*, sheet music, 1980.
37. Minnesota Public Radio, "Aaron Copland: Writing the Soundtrack."
38. Houghton, "Pioneer Songs."
39. Smithsonian Folk Ways Recordings, "Dom Flemons."
40. Flemons, *Black Cowboys* liner notes, 6.
41. *Ibid.*, 16.
42. *Ibid.*, 25.

Bibliography

Abbey, James. *A Trip Across the Plains, in the Spring of 1850, being a daily record of incidents of the trip ... and containing valuable information to emigrants.* [Tarrytown, N.Y. Reprinted W. Abbattt 1933.] Pdf. Retrieved from the Library of Congress, February 28, 2021. https://www.loc.gov/item/33009652/.

Ambrose, Stephen. *Undaunted Courage: Meriwether Lewis, Thomas Jefferson, and the Opening of the American West.* New York: Touchstone, 1996.

Apel, Willi. *Harvard Dictionary of Music Second Edition, Revised and Enlarged.* Cambridge, Massachusetts: Belknap Press of Harvard University Press, 1972.

Axtell, Juliet L. *Gospel Hymns in the Nez Perce Language.* Washington State University Libraries Manuscripts, Archives and Special Collections, 1896. Retrieved from the Plateau Peoples' Web Portal Accessed February 27, 2021. https://plateauportal.libraries.wsu.edu/digital-heritage/gospel-hymns-nez-perce-language-page-40%20().

Barnes, Paul. *Philip Glass Compositions: Piano Concerto No. 2 "After Lewis and Clark,"* 2019. Accessed February 27, 2021. https://philipglass.com/compositions/piano_concerto_2/

Barrett, J.P., William Geer, and Ezekiel Jones. "I Will Go West!" Boston: J.A. Butler, 1875. Retrieved from Library of Congress. https://www.loc.gov/item/sm1875.10352/.

Berrett, Joshua, and Alan Lomax. "Introduction ." *Cowboy Songs and Other Frontier Ballads.* J.A. Lomax. New York: Macmillan, 1986.

Billings Gazette (video). "How the Cheyenne Men Wooed Their Soulmates with the Courtship Flute." Accessed February 27, 2021. https://www.youtube.com/watch?v=iTSQisrPqs8.

Boston Modern Orchestra Project. "Lukas Foss: *The Prairie.*" Accessed February 21, 2021. https://bmop.org/audio-recordings/lukas-foss-prairie.

Brubeck, Dave. "Reminiscences of the Cattle Country for Piano Solo (sheet music)." New York: Associated Music Publishers, 1980.

Burt, Olive W. "The Minstrelsy of Murder." *Western Folklore,* Vol. 17, No. 4, 1958: 263–272.

Bush, Carl. *Indian tribal melodies: four North American legends...v.2.* (orchestral score) New York: C. Fischer, c1918. Accessed February 27, 2021. https://babel.hathitrust.org/cgi/pt?id=ucl.31822016286064&view=1up&seq=3.

Caldbick, John. "1890 Census." Accessed February 27, 2021. https://www.historylink.org/File/9621.

Campbell, Courtney. "Wide Open Country." Accessed February 27, 2021. https://www.wideopencountry.com/dixie-chicks-wide.

Carapella, Aaron. *Native American Nations Map.* Tribal Nations Maps. 2017.

Caves, Will. "Founder of Elks Here In Long Ago: Will Caves Writes of Early-Day Theatrical Attractions of Missoula." *The Missoulian,* March 26, 1922.

Chailley, Jacques. *40,000 years of Music.* New York: Farrar, Straus, and Giroux, 1964.

Chase, Gilbert. "Indianist Movement in American Music," Liner notes, *Anthology of American Music,* New World Records 80542. New York, New York: New World Records, 1998.

Contreras, Felix. NPR Music Interviews, *All Things Considered.* First aired on January 1, 2009. Accessed February 27, 2021. https://www.npr.org/templates/story/story.php?storyId=98884176.

Crawford, Richard. *An Introduction to America's Music.* New York: W.H. Norton, 2001.

Crawford, Tim R. with Dr. Kathleen Joyce-Grendahl, Editor. *Flute Magic An Introduction to the Native American Flute Third Edition.* Suffolk: RainDance Publications, 2008.

Critical Past (video), "U.S. Soldiers watching the performance of Tsianina Redfeather (a.k.a. Tsianina Blackstone), during World War"(Film clip on website*)* Accessed February 26, 2021. https://www.critical-past.com/video/65675023647_US-troops_guitar_American-Indian-Woman.

Crociata, Francis. Liner Notes, "Symphonic Poems by Leo Sowerby (1895–1968)" *CDR 9000 033.* Recorded at the studios of Czech National Radio in Prague: Cedille Records/Cedille Chicago, October 21–24, 1996.

Crum, Beverly, Earl Crum, and Jon P. Dayley. *Newe Hupia: Shoshoni Poetry Songs.* Utah: Utah State

University Press, 2001. Accessed February 27, 2021. https://digitalcommons.usu.edu/cgi/viewcontent. cgi?article=1023&context=usupress_pubs.

Crumm, David. "Complicated life of 'Simple Gifts' Anniversary." *Baltimore Sun,* December 2, 1998. Accessed February 27, 2021. https://www.baltimoresun.com/news/bs-xpm-1998-12-02-1998336046-story.html.

Currie, Heike. "George Quincy: Finding a Native Voice." *The Juilliard Journal.* Accessed February 26, 2021. http://journal.juilliard.edu/journal/george-quincy-finding-native-voice.

Curtis, Natalie. *The Indians' Book, Authentic Native American legends, Lore and Music.* New York: Harper and Brothers Publishers, 1907.

Daniel Little Chief, with descriptive text by Albert Gatschet. "Musical Instruments: NMNH-2016A-O3." Smithsonian (Manuscript 2016-a, National Anthropological Archives, Smithsonian Institution. February 1891. Accessed February 27, 2021. https://learninglab.si.edu/resources/view/193236

Dary, David. *Seeking Pleasure in the Old West.* Lawrence: University Press of Kansas, 1995.

Densmore, Frances. *The American Indian and Their Music.* New York: The Woman's Press, 1926.

Densmore, Frances. *Teton Sioux Music, Bureau of American Ethnology Bulletin 61.* Washington, D.C.: Washington Government Printing Office, 1918.

Dobie, Frank, and John D. Young. *A Vaquero of the Brush Country: The Life and Times of John D. Young.* Austin: University of Texas Press, 1998.

Dobney, Jayson. "The Legacy of Guitar Virtuoso Justin Holland Lives On." *The Met,* February 10, 2014. Accessed February 27, 2021. https://www.metmuseum.org/blogs/of-note/2014/justin-holland.

Don Quijote. "*JARABE TAPATIO.*" Accessed February 27, 2021 https://www.donquijote.org/mexican-culture/traditions/hat-dance-jarabe-tapatio/.

Dunton, Sister Vida Maria. *Music at St. Mary's Academy, Portland Oregon 1859–1905.* Master's Thesis, Seattle: University of Washington, 1959. Retrieved from the Oregon Historical Society Archives.

Erdoes, Richard, and Alfonso Oritz. *American Indian Myths and Legends.* New York: Pantheon Books, 1984.

Ewin, David. *American Composers Today* (Originally found in *Marion and Emilie Frances Bauer* by Susan E. Pickett, Lulu, 2014). New York: H.W. Wilson & Co., 1936.

Farwell, Arthur. *American Indian Melodies harmonized by Arthur Farwell.* Newton Center, MA: Wa-Wan Press, 1901. Notated Music.

Farwell, Arthur. *Impressions of the Wa-Wan Ceremony of the Omahas.* Newton Center, MA: Wa-Wan Press, 1906. Notated Music. Accessed February 27, 2021. https://www.loc.gov/resource/ihas.2001 87362.0/?sp=18MA.

Fazende, H.F. "Texas Cowboy Polka Mazurka." Notated Music. Galveston: Thos. Goggan & Bro, 1886.

Flemons, Dom. "Dom Flemons." Accessed February 27, 2021. https://theamericansongster.com/about/.

Fletcher, Alice C. *Indian Story and Song from North America.* Boston: Small Maynard & Company Publishers, 1900.

Fletcher, Alice C. *A Study of Omaha Indian Music.* Cambridge: Peabody Museum of American Archeology and Ethnology, 1893.

Garland, Hamlin. *A Son of the Middle Border.* New York: The Macmillan Company, 1920.

Geer, Theodore Thurston. *Fifty Years in Oregon.* New York: The Neals Publishing Company, 1912.

Gibson, Susan. "Writing Wide Open Spaces." In an email to Laura Dean. September 28, 2020.

Gibson, Susan. "Writing Wide Open Spaces." In an email to Laura Dean. December 18, 2020.

Goss, Clint. "Anasazi Flutes from the Broken Flute Cave." Accessed February 21, 2021. http://flutopedia. com/brokenflutecave.htm.

Gowdy, Mrs. J.T. "Crossing the Plains Personal Recollections for the Journey to Oregon in 1852." Accessed February 27, 2021. http://www.oregonpioneers.com/KempBook.pdf.

Grinnell, George Bird. *The Cheyenne Indians Volume 1.* Lincoln: University of Nebraska Press, 1972 .

Grinnell, George Bird, and Joseph A. Fitzgerald, editor. *The Cheyenne Indians: Their History and Lifeways.* Indiana: World Wisdom, 2008.

Hafen, Jane. "A Cultural Duet Zitkala Ša and the Sun Dance Opera." *Great Plains Quarterly* 1998. Retrieved from Digital Commons. https://digitalcommons.unl.edu/cgi/viewcontent. cgi?article=3027&context=greatplainsquarterly.

Hafen, Reuben, and Francis Marion Young. *Fort Laramie and the Pageant of the West 1834–1890.* Lincoln: University of Nebraska Press, originally published in 1938, and reprinted in 1984.

Hal Cannon, for NPR Weekend Edition, interview by Mike Searles. "Who Were the Cowboys Behind 'Cowboy Songs'?" December 4, 2010.

Hanson, William. "Sundance Opera, part 1 of 11." William Hanson Papers MSS 299. Provo, Utah: In the L. Tom Perry Special Collection, circa 1908.

Hassebroek, Ashley. "Wise Music Classical (Reviews link*).*" Accessed February 27, 2021. https://www. wisemusicclassical.com/work/14686/Piano-Concerto-No-2-after-Lewis-and-Clark—Philip-Glass/.

Heard Museum Guild. "Princess Tsianina Red Feather." Accessed February 27, 2021. https://www.heard-guild.org/princess-tsianina-red-feather/.

Henneberry, Miss E.T., and Miss M.M. "Butte's Fatal Explosion (printed sheet music)." *Murray Family Collection, MC0732, Box 4 Accession 2012.164. Butte-Silver Bow Public Archives,*. Butte, Montana: No Publisher, 1895.

Hensley, Betty Austin. "Thurlow Lieurance Indian Flutes (report)." Presented to the Wichita State University Music Library on the occasion of the dedication of the Thurow Lieurance Indian Flutes May 17, 1990.

Holmes, Kenneth L. *Best of Covered Wagon Women.* Norman: University of Oklahoma Press, 2008.

Holmes, Kenneth L. *Covered Wagon Women: Diaries and Letters From the Western Trails, 1840–1849, Volume 1.* Lincoln: University of Nebraska Press, 1996.

Horowitz, Joseph. "Dvorak in America, UNLV Symphony Orchestra." Program notes, University of Nevada Las Vegas, Artemus W. Ham Concert Hall Performing Arts Center, April 7, 2019. Accessed February 27, 2021. https://www.unlv.edu/system/files/file_attachments_private/UNLV%20Symphony%20Orchestra%20Program.pdf.

Houghton, Eric. *Pioneer Songs.* 2018. Accessed February 27, 2021. https://pioneersongs.com/composition/.

Hull, Myra. "Cowboy Ballads." *Kansas Historical Quarterly,* February (Vol.8, No. 1) 1938.

Hunter, J. Marvin, editor. *The Trail Drivers of Texas: Interesting Sketches of the early Cowboys and Their Experiences on the Range.* San Antonio: Jackson Printing Company, c1920.

Hymnary. Accessed February 27, 2021. https://hymnary.org.

Irving, Washington. *The Works of Washington Irving, Vol. VIII, Astoria Tour of the Prairies.* New York: G.P. Putnam, 1859.

Jackson, Royal G. *Oral Histories of Northern Cheyenne Descendants of the Battle of the Little Bighorn.* Transcript of the Oral Histories in three volumes, Corvallis, Oregon: Special Collections and Archives Research Center, Oregon State University Library and Press, 1985–1987.

Johnson, Jean and Leroy. "The Journal of a Young Gold Seeker, Illinois to Los Angeles." *Overland Journal,* Summer 2020.

Lavender, David. *The Way to the Western Sea, Lewis and Clark Across the Continent,* Chapter 20. 2001. Chapter on Website. Accessed February 27, 2021. https://lewisandclarkjournals.unl.edu/item/lc.sup.lavender.01.20.

Lewis, M.G. "Crazy Jane. Sung by Mrs. Hodgkinson." Notated Music, no publisher, c. 1800. Retrieved from the Library of Congress. Accessed February 27, 2021. https://www.loc.gov/resource/musm1a1.10101.0/?sp=1&r=-0.948,-0.106,2.896,1.444,0

Lewis and Clark Trail-Tail Legacy Project (website). Accessed February 27, 2021. http://lc-triballegacy.org/video.php?vid=530&era=1&subcat=.

Library of Congress. "Biography of Arthur Farwell (1872–1952)." Accessed February 27, 2021. https://www.loc.gov/item/ihas.200035729/.

Lomax, John. *Cowboy Songs and Other Frontier Ballads.* New York: Macmillan, 1986.

Lomax, John, and Duncan Emrich, editor. *Cowboy Songs, Ballads, and Cattle Calls from Texas.* Washington: Library of Congress, 1952. Accessed February 27, 2021. https://www.loc.gov/folklife/LP/CowboySongs_opt.pdf .

Love, Nat. *The Life and Adventures of Nat Love, Better Known in the Cattle Country as Deadwood Dick.* Los Angeles: Wayside Press, 1907.

Mader, Jerry. *The Road to Lame Deer.* Lincoln: University of Nebraska Press, 2002.

Mardones, José. "El arriero, My love is a muleteer," Comp. Francisco di Nogero, 1918. Audio recording, Columbia Label. Accessed February 27, 2021. https://www.loc.gov/item/jukebox-817098/.

Marzell, Terry Lee. *Chalkboard Heroes: Twelve Courageous Teachers and Their Deeds of Valor.* Tucson: Wheatmark, Inc., 2015.

McCoy, Joseph G. *Historic Sketches of the Cattle Trade of the West and Southwest.* Kansas City, MO: Ramsey, Millett, and Hudson, 1874.

Minnesota Public Radio. *Aaron Copland: Writing the Soundtrack of the American West.* November 14, 2005. Accessed February 24, 2021. https://www.classicalmpr.org/story/2005/11/14/aaron-copland-writing-the-soundtrack-of-the-american-west.

Monaghan, Leila. "Cheyenne and Lakota Women and the Battle of the Little Bighorn." *Montana the Magazine of Western History,* Autumn 2017.

Morin, Marvin Fatty. "Marvin Fatty Morin on cassette tape," from Al Wiseman's Personal Collection. n.d.

Mussulman, Joseph. "Medicine Songs Interview." Interview with Pelah Hoyt and Pat Williams. Accessed February 27, 2021. http://www.lewis-clark.org/article/1395.

Mussulman, Joseph. "Music on the Trail." Accessed February 27, 2021. http://www.lewis-clark.org/article/1229#toc-2.

Nakai, R. Carlos. "Nakai Biography." Accessed, February 27, 2021. http://rcarlosnakai.com/r-carlos-nakai-biography/.

Nakai, R. Carlos. "Nakai Reviews." Accessed February 27, 2021. http://rcarlosnakai.com/reviews/.

National Park Service. "The Fort Laramie Treaty Council, 1851." Accessed February 21, 2021. https://www.nps.gov/parkhistory/online_books/hh/20/hh20h.htm.

New York Philharmonic Society. "Archives New York Philharmonic Society." Accessed February 23,

2021. https://archives.nyphil.org/index.php/artifact/1118e84e-eb59-46cc-9119-d903375e65e6-0.1/fullview#page/1/mode/2up.

Newman, Marshall. "Martin." *The Journal of Acoustic Guitars,* January 20, 2019.

Old Mouse, Jay. "Jay Old Mouse." Interviewed in person by Laura Dean. August 13, 2017.

Old Mouse, Jay. "Jay Old Mouse FaceTime Interview." Interviewed by Laura Dean. June 25, 2020.

Olsen, Dale A., and Daniel E. Sheehy. *The Garland Handbook of Latin American Music, Second Edition.* New York: Garland, 2000.

Oregon Pioneer Association. *Transactions of the Oregon Pioneer Association.* Salem, Oregon: E.M. Waite, 1875.

Page, Jack. *In the Hands of the Great Spirit.* New York: Free Press, 2003.

Parkman, Francis, Jr. *The Oregon Trail: Sketches of Prairie and Rocky Mountain Life.* Boston: Little, Brown and Company, 1912.

Parrett, Aaron. *Montana Americana Music.* Charleston: History Press, 2016.

PBS. "The West Episode Four *(1856–1868),* Death Runs Riot, Preachers and Jack Ass Rabbits." Website. Accessed February 27, 2021. https://www.pbs.org/weta/thewest/program/episodes/four/preachers.htm.

PBS. "The West, Program Five, Cowboys, The Grandest Enterprise Under God." Website. Accessed February 27, 2021. https://www.pbs.org/weta/thewest/program/episodes/five/cowboys.htm.

Pelissier, Victor. *Pelissier's Columbian Melodies: Music for the New York and Philadelphia Theaters.* Madison: A-R Editions, 1984.

Penrose, S.B.L. President Emeritus of Whitman College. *At Waiilatpu: Impressions and Recollections of Visitors to the Whitman Mission 1836–1847.* Whitman Centennial Souvenir. Walla Walla, Washington: Whitman Publishing, 1937.

Perison, Harry D. "The "Indian" Operas of Charles Wakefield Cadman." *College Music Symposium, Vol. 22, No. 2,* 1982.

Peters, De Witt Clinton. *The Life and Adventure of Kit Carson, the Nestor of the Rocky Mountains, From Facts and Narratives by Himself.* New York: W. R. C. Clark and Co., 1858.

Pickett, Susan E. *Marion and Emilie Frances Bauer: From the Wild West to American Musical Modernism.* Lulu Publishing Service, 2014.

Pickett, Susan. "Portland Youth Philharmonic Preview: Marion Bauer shines again." Oregon Arts Watch Archive (website), March 1, 2016. Accessed February 27, 2021. https://archive.orartswatch.org/portland-youth-philharmonic-preview-marion-bauer-shines-again/.

Pike, Zebulon Montgomery. *The Expeditions of Zebulon Montgomery Pike, to headwaters of the Mississippi River, through Louisiana in New Spain, during the years 1805–6–7.* New York: F.P. Harper, 1895.

Ralph, Talia. "World's oldest-known musical instruments discovered in Germany." May 25, 2012. *PRI, The World.* Accessed February 27, 2021. https://www.pri.org/stories/2012-05-25/worlds-oldest-known-musical-instruments-discovered-germany.

Schlissel, Lilian. *Women's Diaries of the Westward Journey.* New York: Schocken Books, 1982.

Searles, Mike, and Franklin Willis. "Who Were the Cowboys Behind 'Cowboy Songs.'" Interview by Hal Cannon, December 4, 2010.

Siringo, Charles. *A Texas Cowboy: Or, Fifteen Years on the Hurricane Deck of a Spanish Pony.* Chicago: Penguin Books, 2000.

Slim Chance Music. "Early Idaho Songs of the Month," September 2008. Accessed February 21, 2010. http://www.bonafidaho.com/September2008SongsOfMonth.html.

Smith, Catherine Parsons. "An Operatic Skeleton on the Western Frontier: Zitkala-Sa, William F. Hanson, and the Sun Dance Opera." From *Women in Music. Kansas: University Press,* 2001. Retrieved at Gale Academic OneFile. Accessed February 27, 2021. https://link.gale.com/apps/doc/A82092548/AONE?u=spl_main&sid=AONE&xid=36e013af.

Smithsonian Folk Ways Recordings. *Dom Flemons Black Cowboys.* Smithsonian Folkways Recordings, 2018. Accessed February 27, 2021. https://folkways.si.edu/dom-flemons/black-cowboys.

Smithsonian Folkways Recordings. Liner Notes for *Dom Flemons Black Cowboys.* Smithsonian Folkways Recordings, 2018. Accessed February 27, 2021. https://folkways-media.si.edu/liner_notes/smithsonian_folkways/SFW40224.pdf.

Stands in Timber, John, and Margot Liberty. *Cheyenne Memories (Second Edition).* New Haven: Yale University Press, 1998.

Stevens Funeral Home. "Jay Old Mouse, age 53, of Busby (October 9, 1966–September 25, 2020)." Accessed February 27, 2021. https://stevensonfuneralhomes.com/obituaries/j-d-oldmouse.

Sutton, Rebecca. "Art Talk with Composer Jerod Impichchaachaaha' Tate." November 19, 2019. Accessed February 27, 2021. https://www.arts.gov/stories/blog/2019/art-talk-composer-jerod-impichchaachaaha-tate.

Tate, Jarod. "Jarod Tate, Composer." Accessed February 27, 2021. http://jerodtate.com/recordings/.

Texas Historical Commission: "A Guide for Heritage Travelers. The Chisholm Trail." Accessed February 27, 2021. https://www.thc.texas.gov/public/upload/publications/chisholm-trail.pdf.

Texas History Notebook. "The Cowgirl Who Passed Herself Off as a Cowboy." 2017. Accessed February 27, 2021. https://texoso66.com/2017/03/09/the-cowgirl-who-passed-herself-off-as-a-cowboy/.

Thorp, Nathan Howard. "Jack," *Songs of the Cowboys*. Boston and New York: Houghton Mifflin Company, 1921.

Thorp, Nathan Howard. "Jack." *Songs of the Cowboys Compiled by N. Howard Thorp*. Cambridge: The Riverside Press 1908.

Tompkins, Jim. "In Their Own Words, Camp Life." Accessed February 27, 2021. http://www.oregonpioneers.com/CampQuotes.htm.

Trimble, Marshall. "Bandit Queen Belle Starr." March 23, 2017. Accessed February 27, 2021. https://truewestmagazine.com/bandit-queen-belle-starr/.

Troyer, Carlos. *Traditional Songs of the Zunis Transcribed and Harmonized*. Newton Center: Wa-Wan Press, 1904.

Upham, Warren. *The Life and Military Service of Zebulon M. Pike*. St. Paul: The Society, 1908. Accessed February 27, 2021. https://www.loc.gov/item/2007498066/.

Vodges, Ada. "The Journal of Ada Vodges 1868–1870." Oregon Trails Association/Merrill J. Mates Collection. Accessed February 27, 2021. https://www.octa-journals.org/merrill-mattes-collection/the-journal-of-ada-vodges-1868–1870.

Wagner, Tricia. "Charley Willis (1847–1930)." August 25, 2012. Accessed February 27, 2021. https://www.blackpast.org/african-american-history/charley-willis-1847–1930/.

Wapp, Ed Jr. "Smithsonian Folklife Festival Past Programs." Smithsonian Folklife Festival, Native Americans (1973). Accessed February 27, 2021. https://festival.si.edu/articles/1973/the-courting-flute-in-native-american-tradition.

Webb, Jaci. "Northern Cheyenne Flute Maker to Be Honored Friday in Helena." *Billings Gazette*. April 25, 2014. Accessed February 27, 2021. https://billingsgazette.com/news/local/northern-cheyenne-flute-maker-to-be-honored-friday-in-helena/article_15be8b7b-e67d-542c-8cf9-42d644998180.html.

Wein, Gail. "'Iholba': Haunting Wind Music." *The Washington Post*, September 23, 2005. Online article accessed February 27, 2021. https://www.washingtonpost.com/archive/lifestyle/2005/09/23/iholba-haunting-wind-music-in-chickasaw/0ce055b1-f047-468b-898a-b5ac1b52f184/.

Westermeier, Clifford P. "The Dodge City Cowboy Band." *The Kansas Historical Quarterly, Volume 19, No. 1 (accessed online:* https://www.kshs.org/p/the-dodge-city-cowboy-band/13097, 1951, Volume 19, No. 1.

Western Resources, *Butte, Montana at the Dawn of the Twentieth Century, Number 134*. Denver: Western Resources, 1901. Copy of Magazine held at the Butte-Silver Bow Public Library.

Whitman, Narcissa. *"PBS: The Letters and Journals of Narcissa Whitman 1836–1847."* Accessed February 27, 2021. https://www.pbs.org/weta/thewest/resources/archives/two/whitman1.htm.

Whitman, Narcissa Prentiss. "Marcus and Narcissa Whitman Collection, 1834–1936." Whitman College Penrose Library Arminda Collections. Accessed February 27, 2021. https://archiveswest.orbiscascade.org/ark:/80444/xv25842.

Wiseman, Alfred. "Métis Fiddle Memories." Phone interview by Laura Dean, March 13, 2020.

Wrenn, Sara B., and Sarah L. Byrd. *Pioneer Life*. Oregon, 1939. Manuscript/Mixed Material. Accessed February 28, 2021. https://www.loc.gov/item/wpalh001998/.

Wyeth, S. Douglas. *The Public School Singing Book: A Collection of Original and Other Songs, Odes, Hymns, Anthems, and Chants*. 1848. Lancaster, PA: Murray, Young, and Co. Accessed on Hathi Trust February 27, 2021. https://hdl.handle.net/2027/nc01.ark:/13960/t93801q18.

Zotigh, Dennis. "Native Perspectives on the 40th Anniversary of the American Indian Religious Freedom Act." *Smithsonian Magazine*. November 2018, 2018. Accessed February 27, 2021. https://www.smithsonianmag.com/blogs/national-museum-american-indian/2018/11/30/native-perspectives-american-indian-religious-freedom-act/.

Index

Numbers in **bold italics** indicate pages with illustrations